FOR ORGANS, PIANOS & ELECTRONIC KEYBOARDS

E-Z PLAY TODAY 203

THE Best **BROADWAY** SONGS Ever

P9-CBY-011

Contents

HAL•LEONARD®
CORPORATION

7777 W. BLUEMOUND RD. P.O. BOX 13819 MILWAUKEE, WI 53213

E-Z Play ® TODAY Music Notation © 1975 HAL LEONARD PUBLISHING CORPORATION
Copyright © 1991 HAL LEONARD PUBLISHING CORPORATION
International Copyright Secured   All Rights Reserved

ISBN 0-7935-0625-5

All I Ask Of You

Registration 8
Rhythm: 8 Beat or Rock

Music by Andrew Lloyd Webber
Lyrics by Charles Hart
Additional Lyrics by Richard Stilgoe

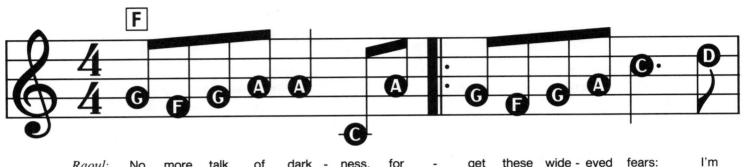

Raoul: No more talk of dark - ness, for - get these wide - eyed fears: I'm
let me be your light; you're

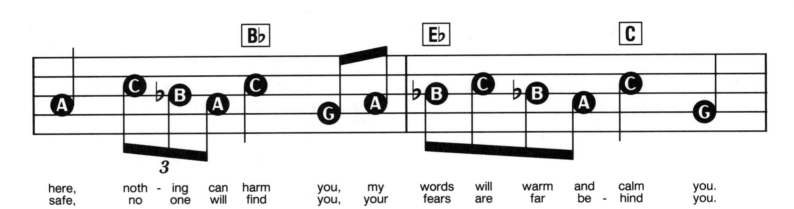

here, noth - ing can harm you, my words will warm and calm you.
safe, no one will harm find you, your fears are far be - hind you.

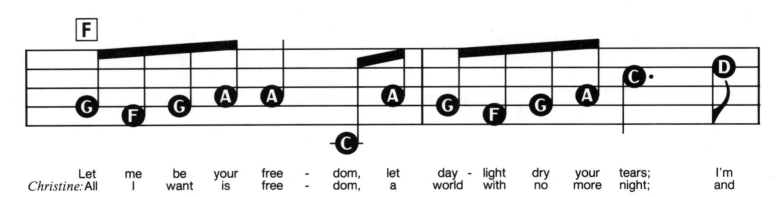

Let me be your free - dom, let day - light dry your tears; I'm
Christine: All I want is free - dom, a world with no more night; and

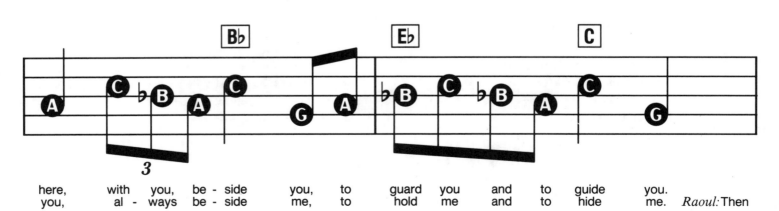

here, with you, be - side you, to guard you and to guide you.
you, al - ways be - side me, to hold me and to hide me. *Raoul:* Then

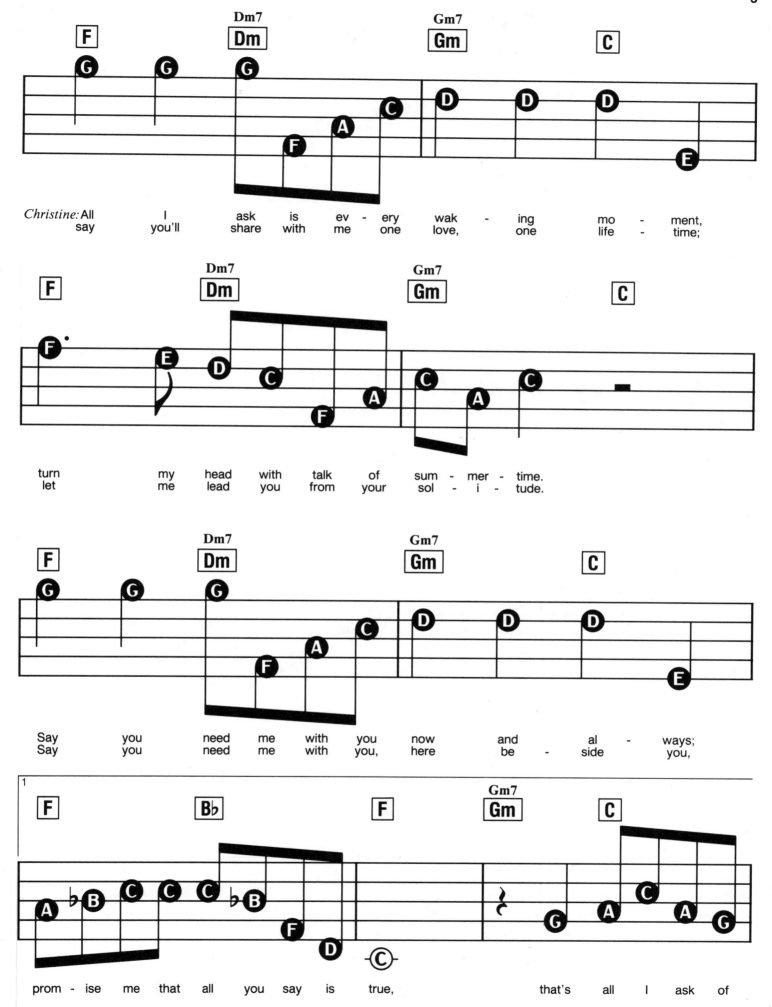

Raoul: Let me be your shel - ter, an - y - where you go, let me go,

too, Chris - tine, that's all I ask of you. *Christine:* All I ask for is one

love, one life - time; say the word and I will fol - low you.

Both: Share each day with me, each night, each morn - ing.

All The Things You Are

(From "VERY WARM FOR MAY")

Registration 2
Rhythm: Ballad or Fox Trot

Lyrics by Oscar Hammerstein II
Music by Jerome Kern

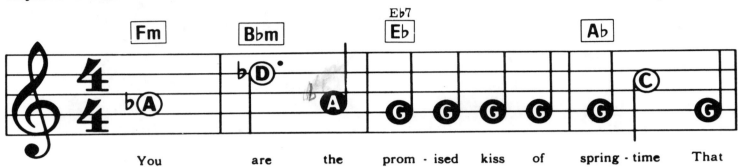

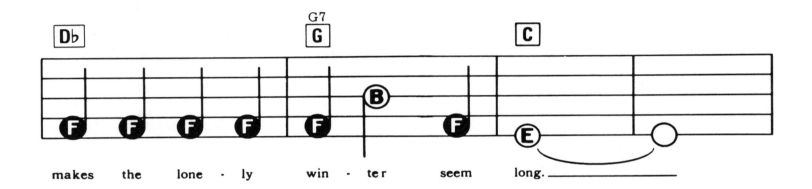

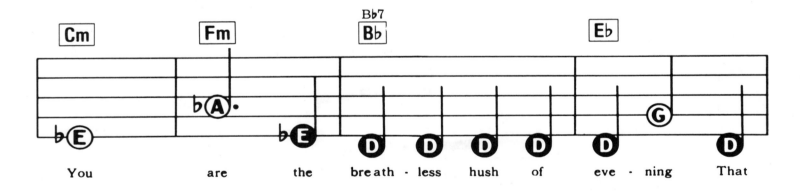

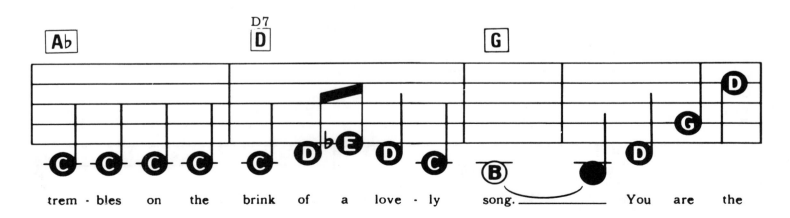

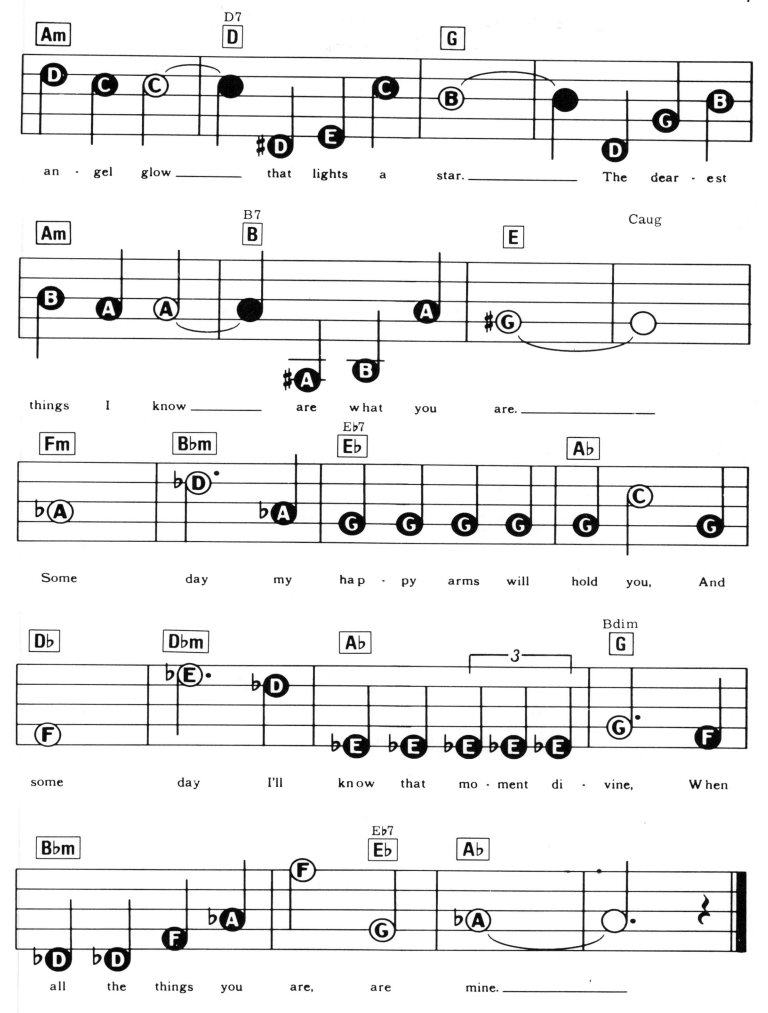

And All That Jazz

(From "CHICAGO")

Registration 5
Rhythm: Swing or Jazz

Words by Fred Ebb
Music by John Kander

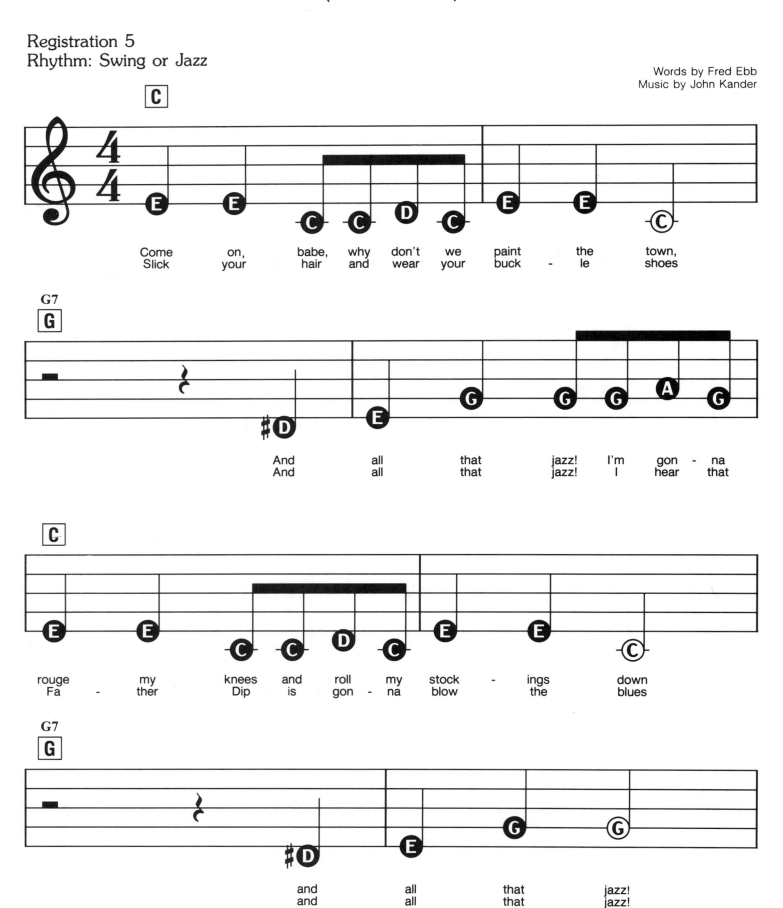

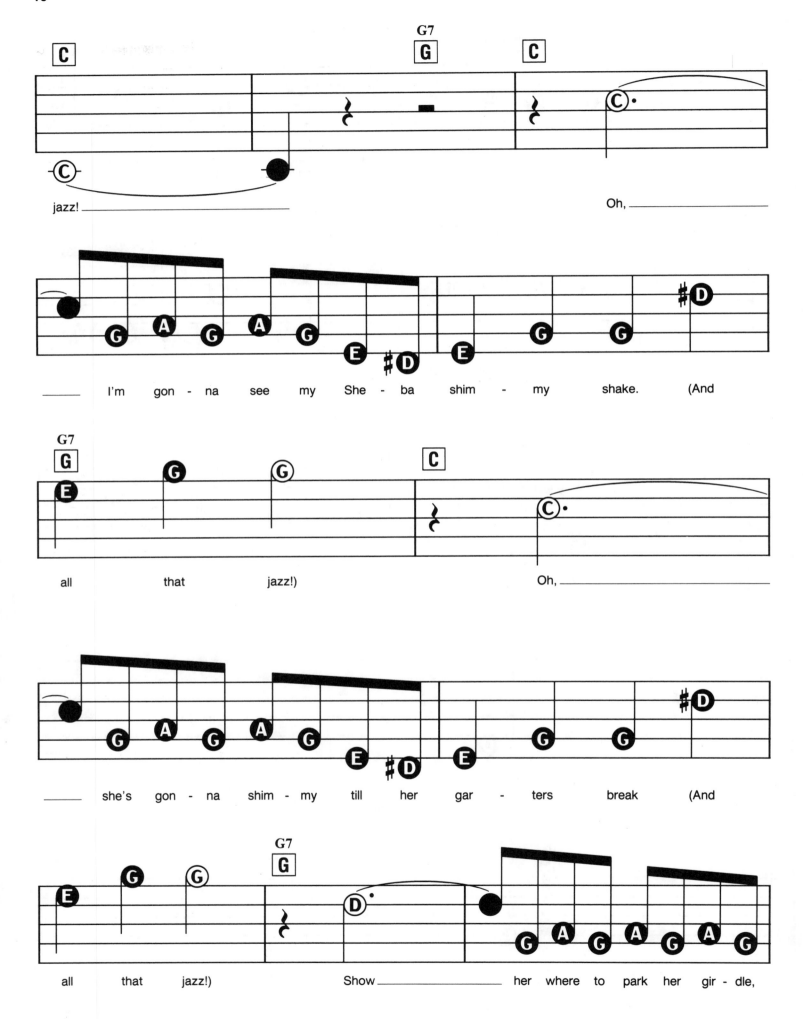

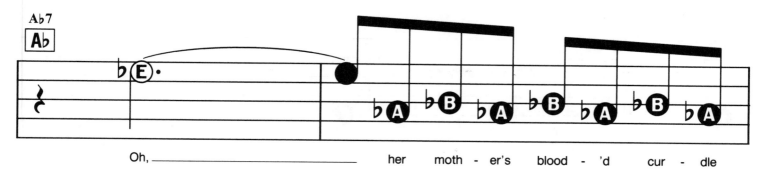

Oh, _____ her moth - er's blood - 'd cur - dle

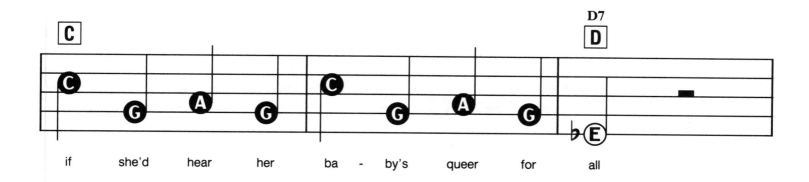

if she'd hear her ba - by's queer for all

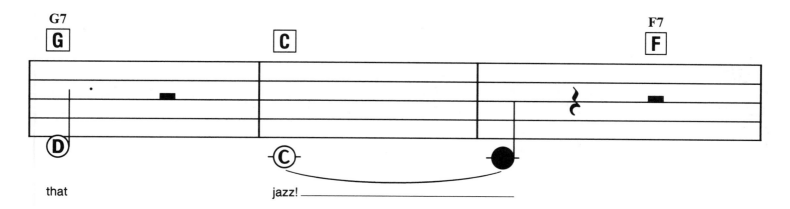

that jazz! _____

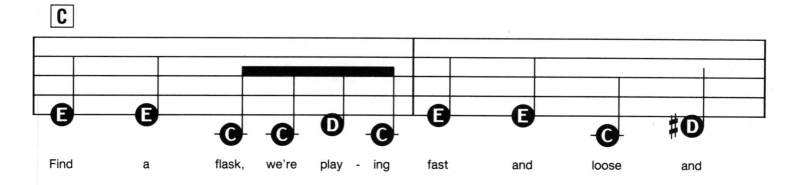

Find a flask, we're play - ing fast and loose and

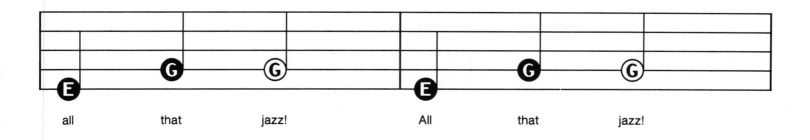

all that jazz! All that jazz!

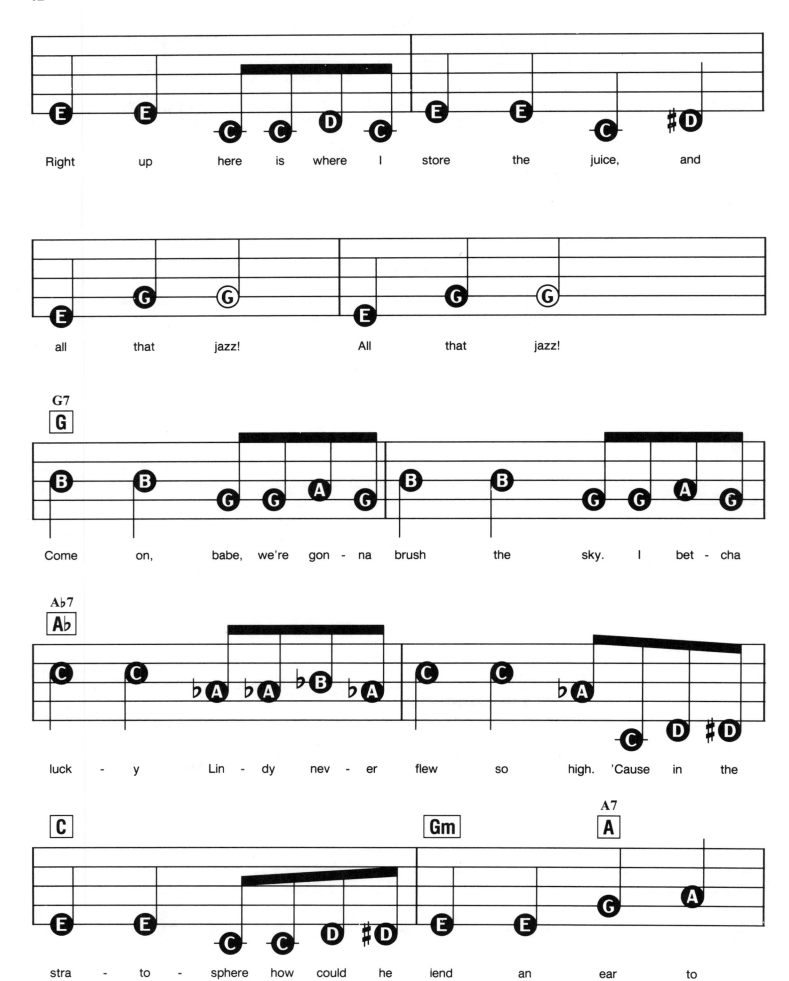

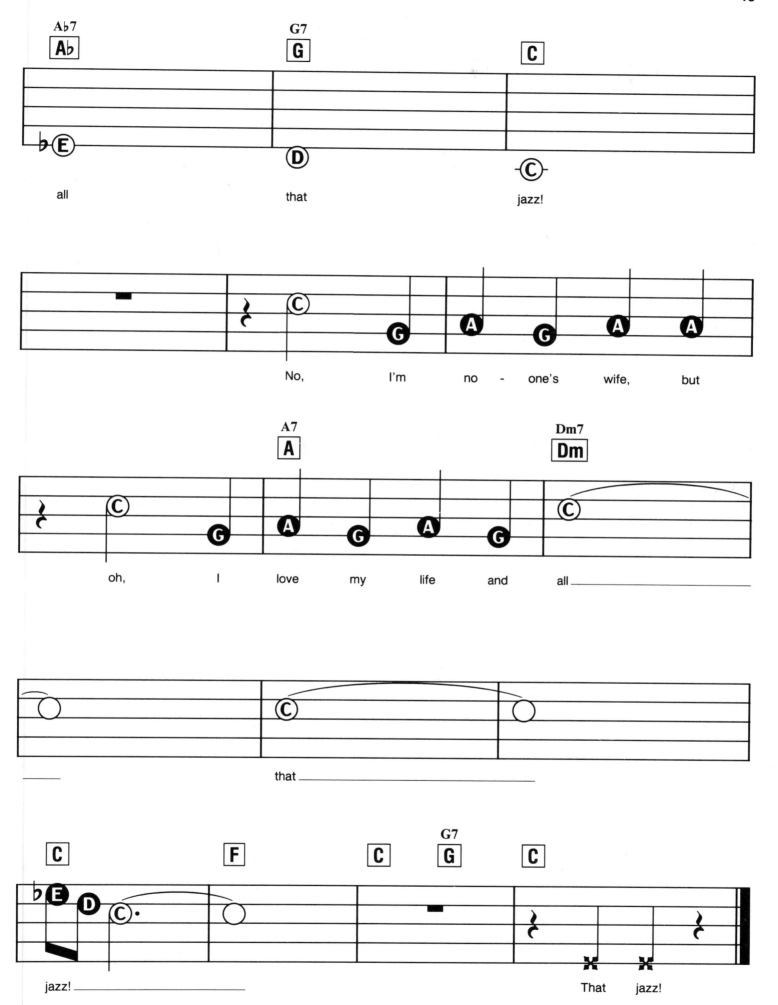

Another Op'nin', Another Show

(From "KISS ME, KATE")

Registration 4
Rhythm: Disco

Words and Music by Cole Porter

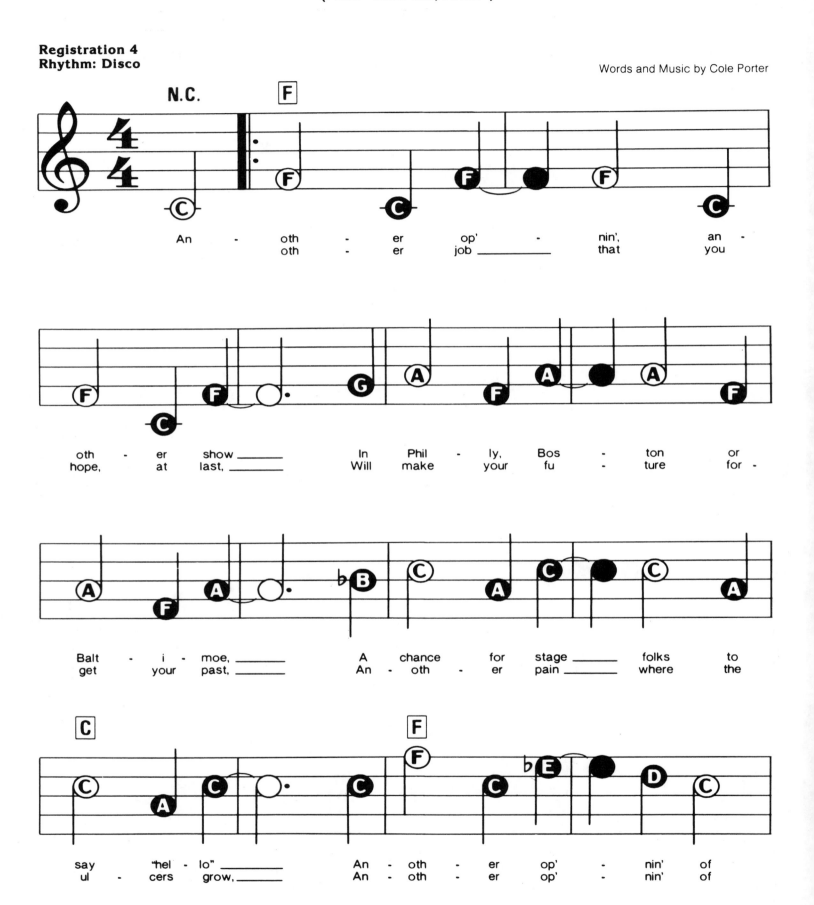

An - oth - er op' - nin', an -
oth - er job _____ that you

oth - er show _____ In Phil - ly, Bos - ton or
hope, at last, _____ Will make your fu - ture for -

Balt - i - moe, _____ A chance for stage _____ folks to
get your past, _____ An - oth - er pain _____ where the

say "hel - lo" _____ An - oth - er op' - nin' of
ul - cers grow, _____ An - oth - er op' - nin' of

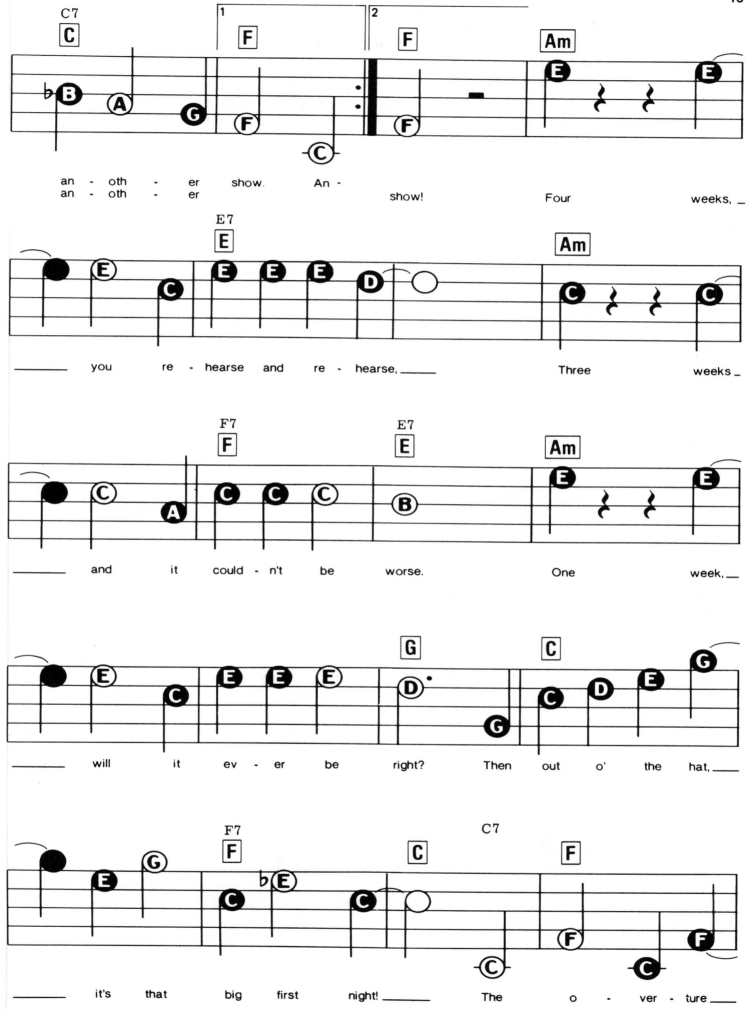

an - oth - er show.   An -
an - oth - er   show!   Four   weeks, _

_____ you   re - hearse   and   re - hearse, _____   Three   weeks _

_____ and   it   could - n't   be   worse.   One   week, _

_____ will   it   ev - er   be   right?   Then   out   o'   the   hat, _____

_____ it's   that   big   first   night! _____   The   o - ver - ture _____

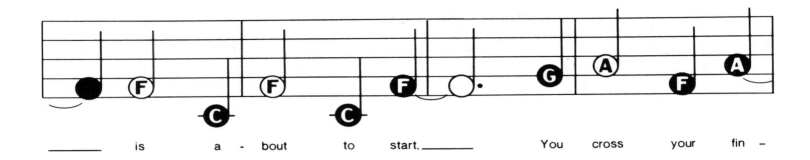

_____ is a - bout to start, _____ You cross your fin -

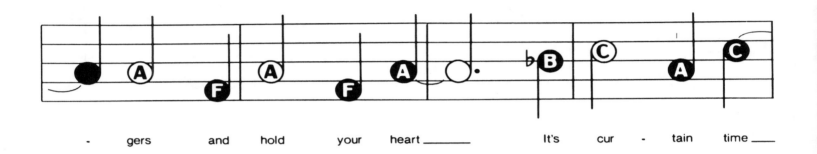

- gers and hold your heart _____ It's cur - tain time ___

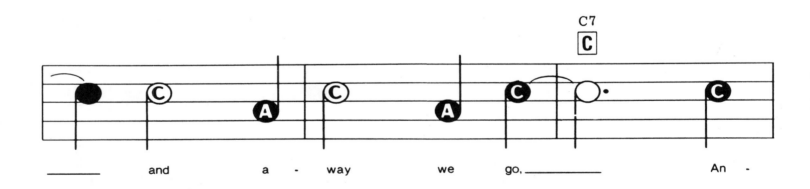

_____ and a - way we go, _____ An -

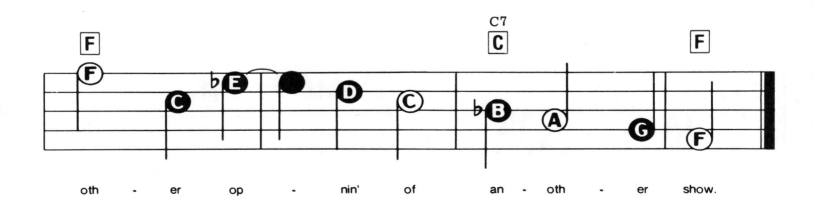

oth - er op - nin' of an - oth - er show.

Anyone Can Whistle

(From "ANYONE CAN WHISTLE")

Registration 5
Rhythm: Swing or Jazz

Words and Music by
Stephen Sondheim

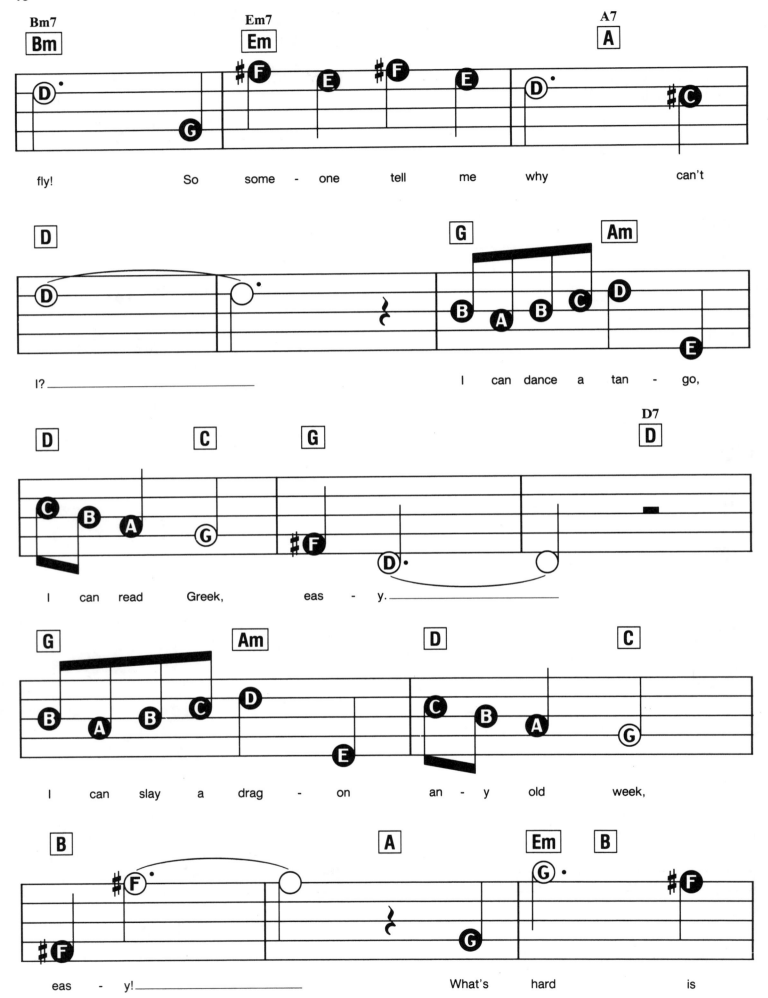

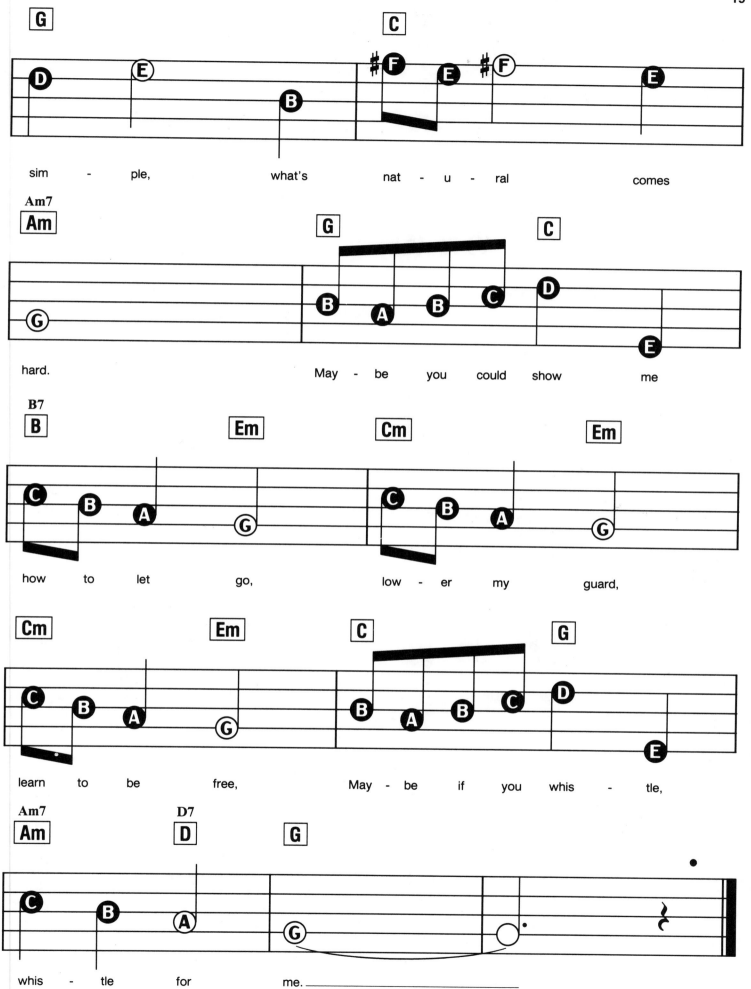

As Long As He Needs Me

(From the Columbia Pictures-Romulus film "OLIVER!")

Registration 1
Rhythm: Fox Trot or Swing

Words and Music by
Lionel Bart

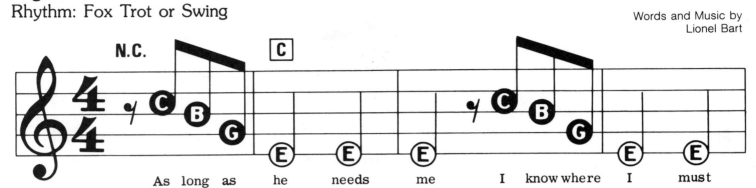

As long as he needs me I know where I must

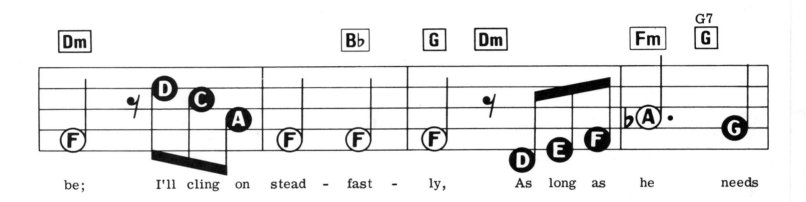

be; I'll cling on stead - fast - ly, As long as he needs

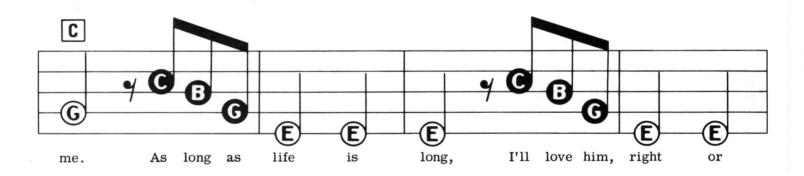

me. As long as life is long, I'll love him, right or

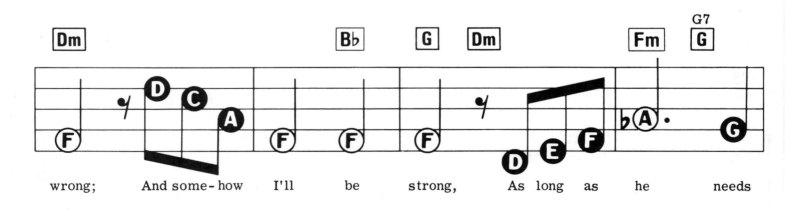

wrong; And some-how I'll be strong, As long as he needs

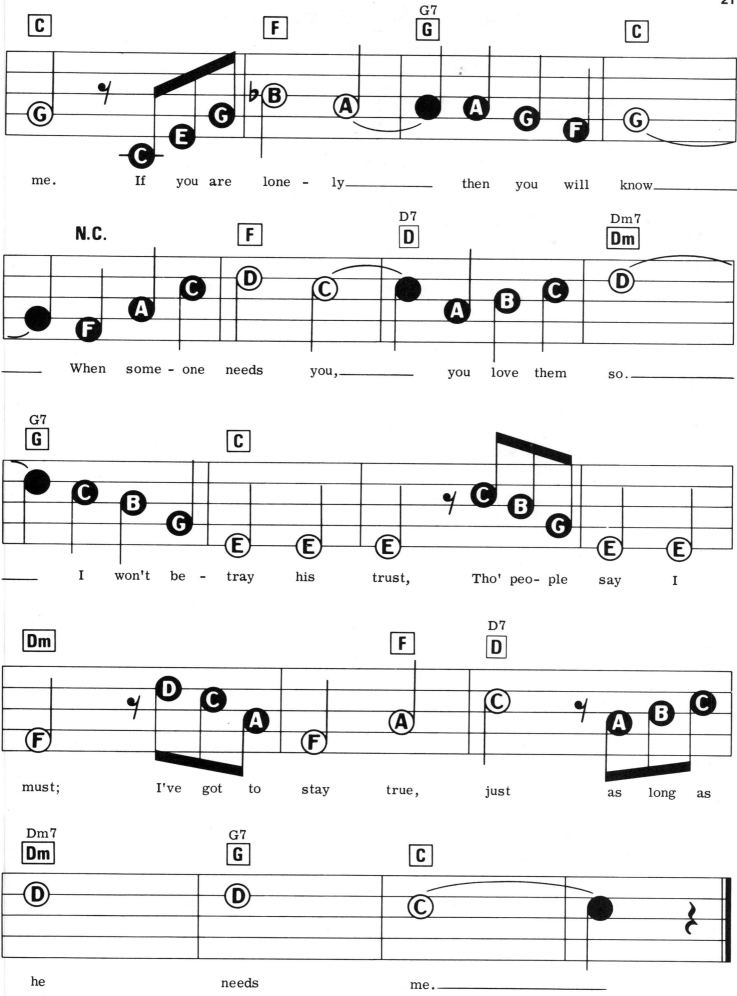

Being Alive

(From "COMPANY")

Registration 4
Rhythm: Fox Trot or Swing

Words and Music by
Stephen Sondheim

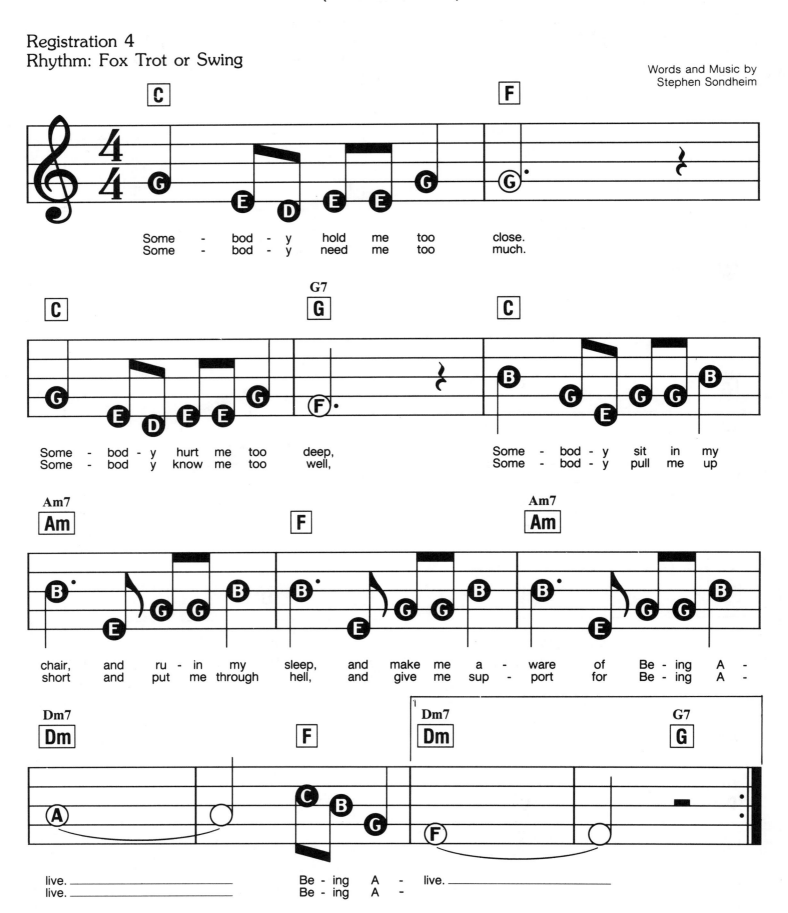

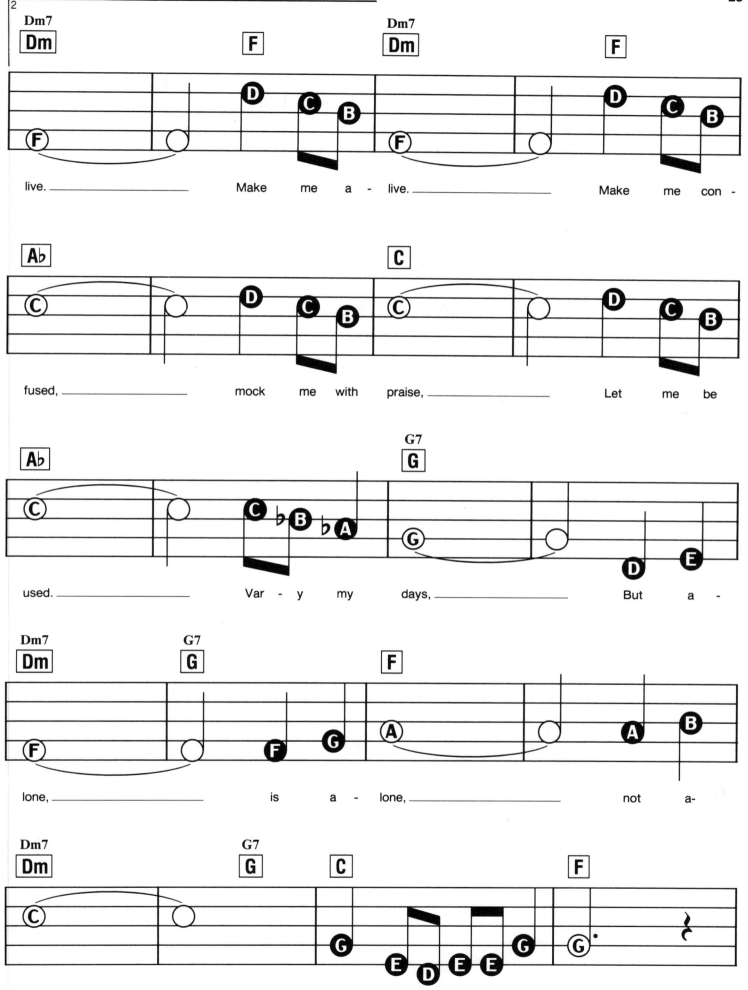

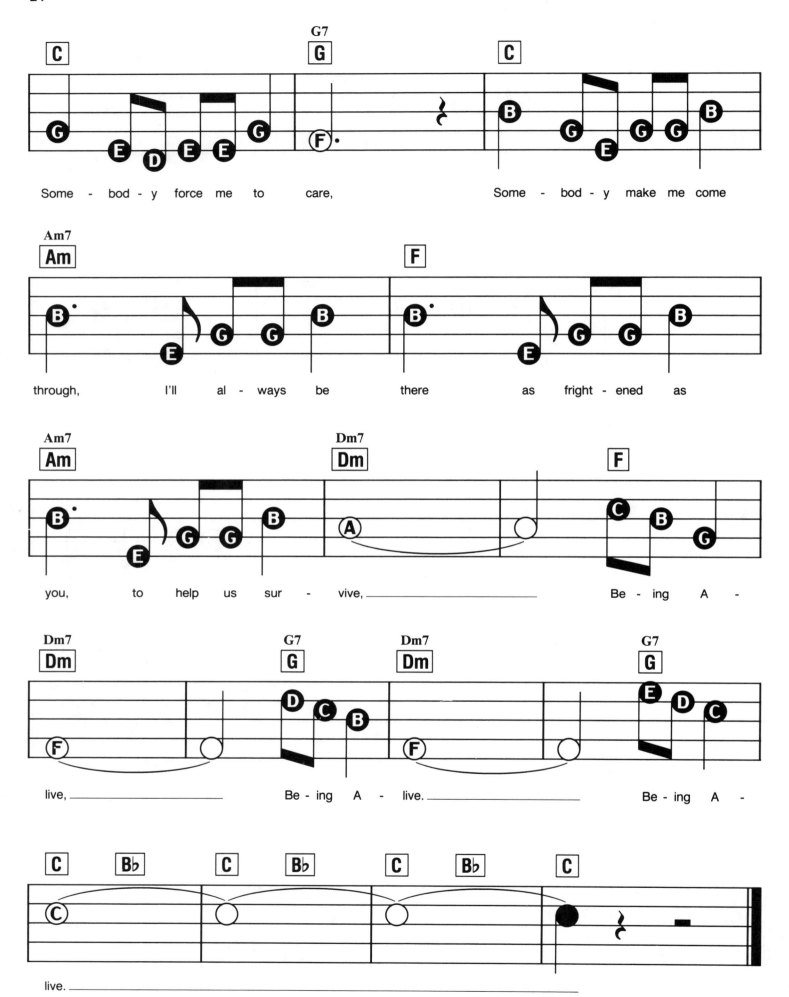

Some - bod - y force me to care, Some - bod - y make me come

through, I'll al - ways be there as fright - ened as

you, to help us sur - vive, _____ Be - ing A -

live, _____ Be - ing A - live. _____ Be - ing A -

live. _____

Bess, You Is My Woman

(From "PORGY AND BESS")

Words by Dubose Heyward and Ira Gershwin
Music by George Gershwin

Registration 2
Rhythm: Ballad or Fox Trot

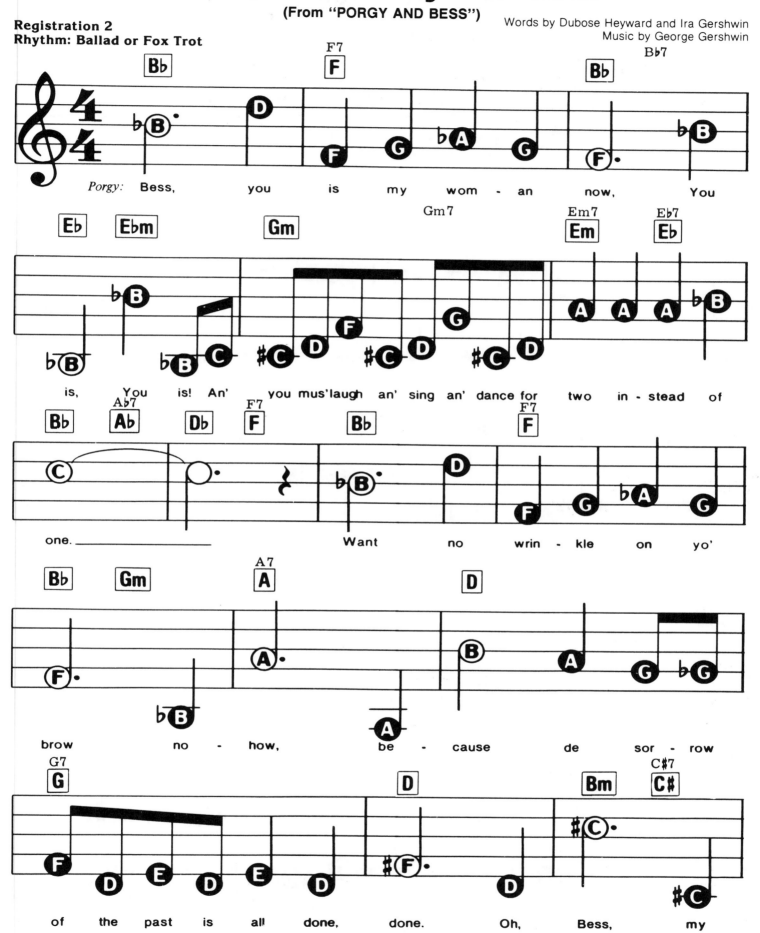

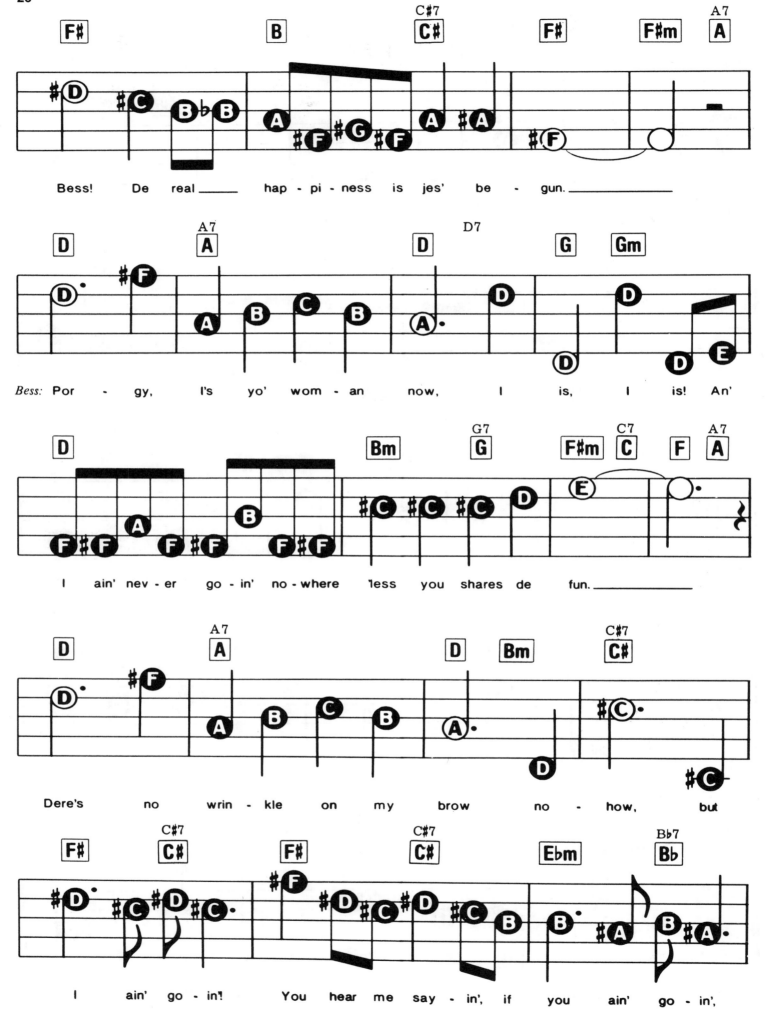

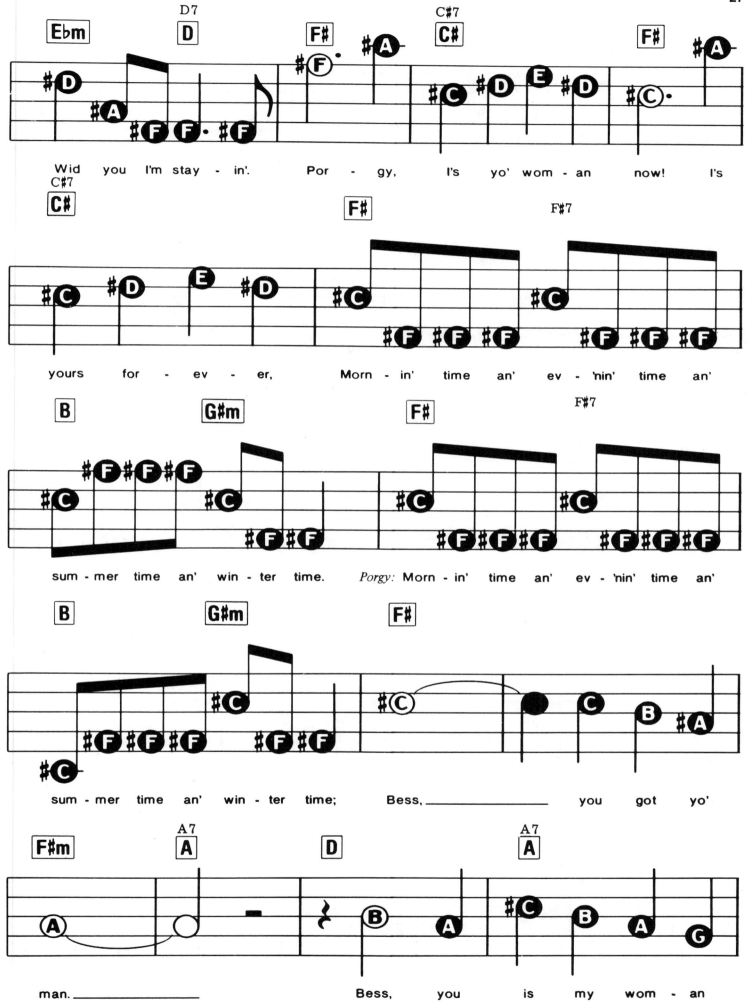

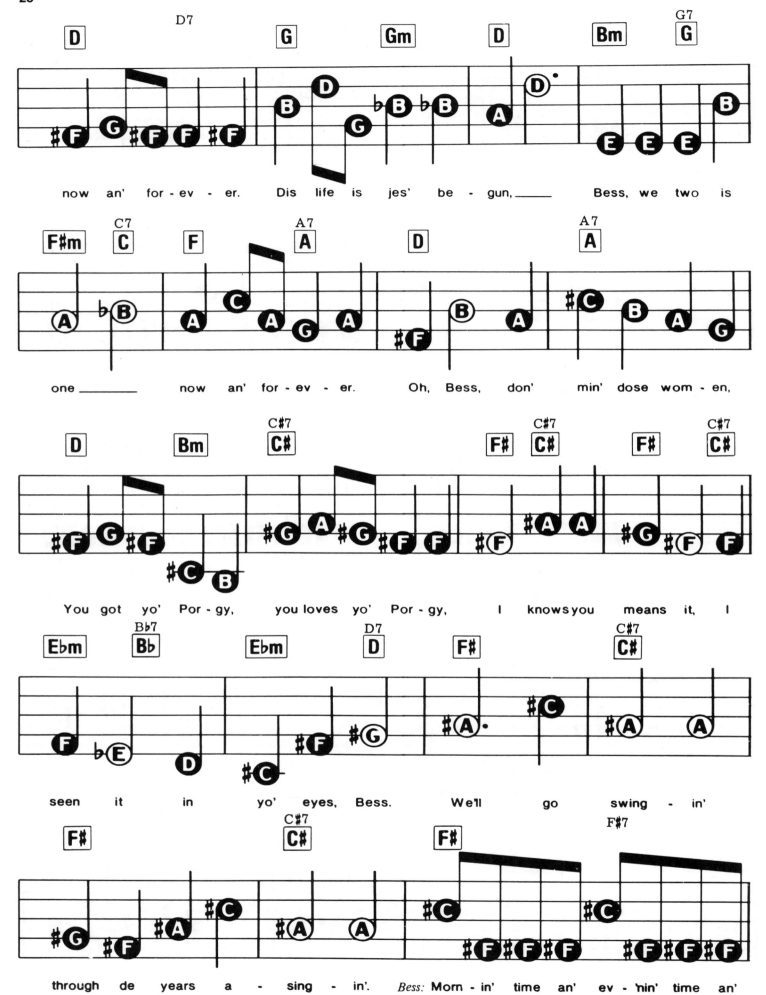

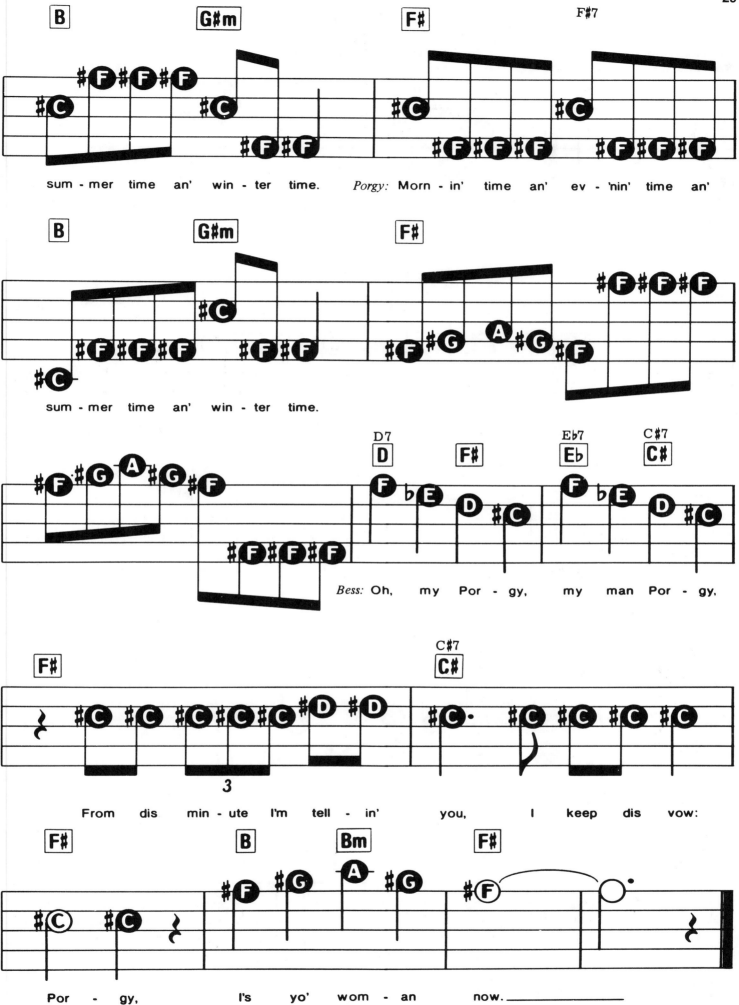

Bewitched

(From "PAL JOEY")

Words by Lorenz Hart
Music by Richard Rodgers

Registration 10
Rhythm: Ballad or Fox Trot

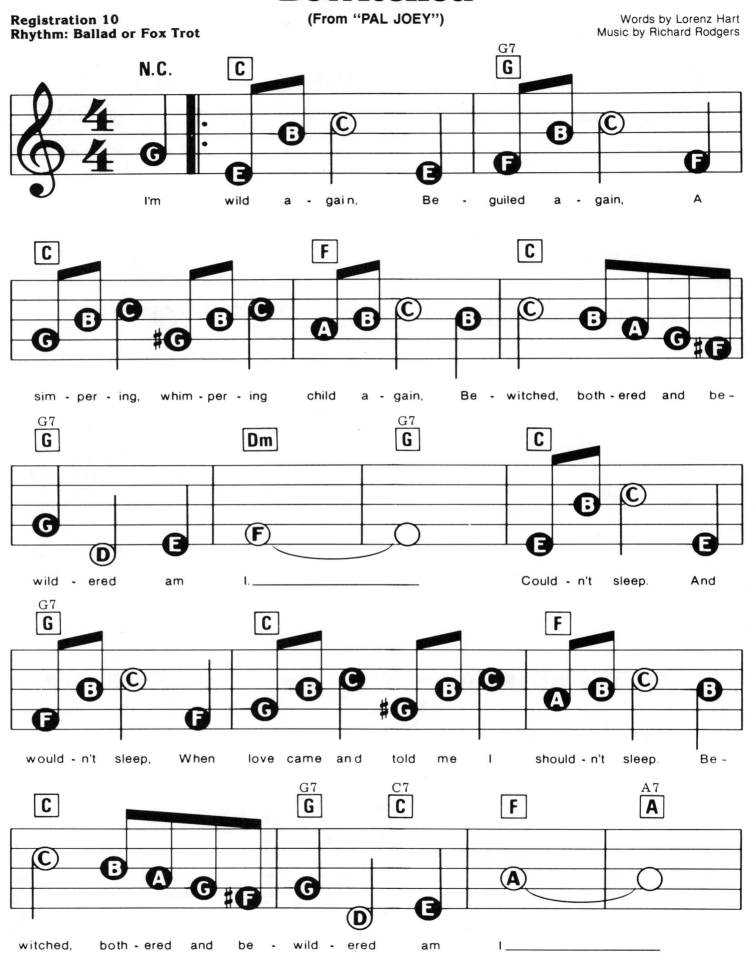

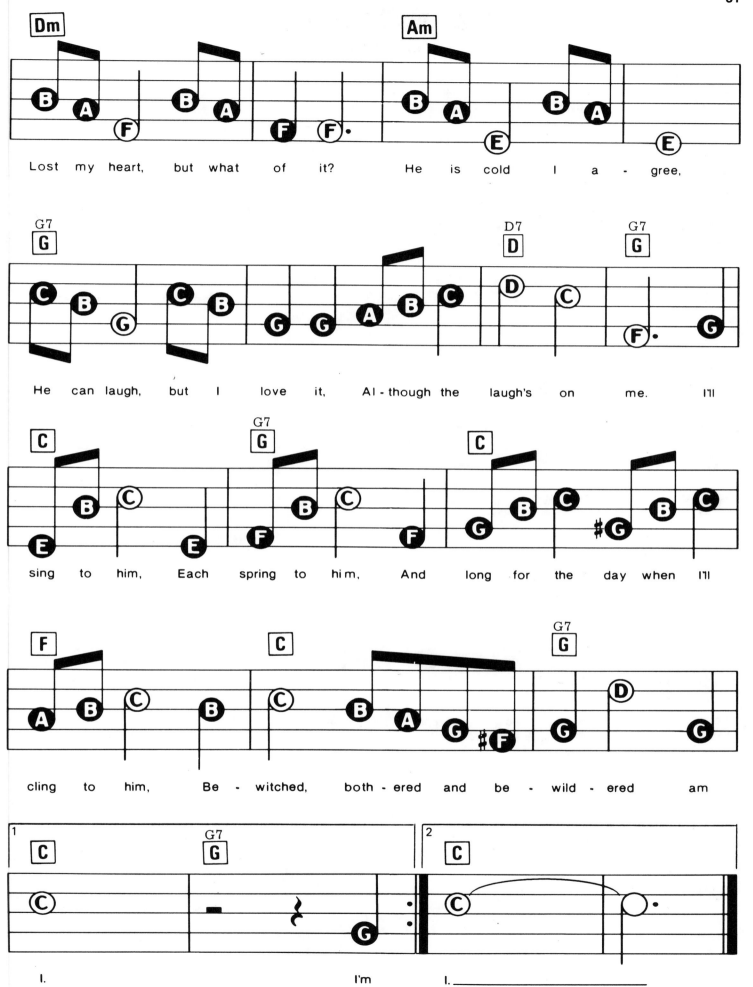

Lost my heart, but what of it? He is cold I a - gree,

He can laugh, but I love it, Al - though the laugh's on me. I'll

sing to him, Each spring to him, And long for the day when I'll

cling to him, Be - witched, both - ered and be - wild - ered am

I. I'm

I. _____

Broadway Baby

(From "FOLLIES")

Registration 5
Rhythm: Swing or Jazz

Words and Music by
Stephen Sondheim

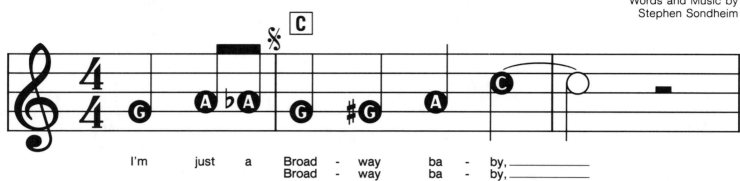

I'm just a Broad - way ba - by, _____
Broad - way ba - by, _____

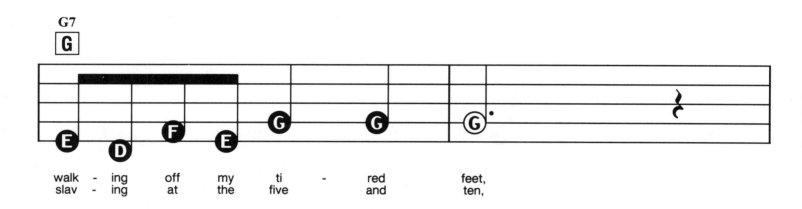

walk - ing off my ti - red feet,
slav - ing at the five and ten,

Pound - ing For - ty Sec - ond Street to be in a
Dream - ing of the great day when I'll be in a

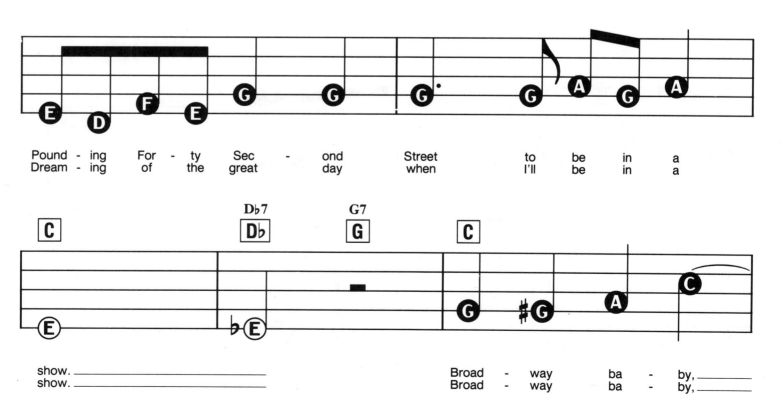

show. _____
show. _____

Broad - way ba - by, _____
Broad - way ba - by, _____

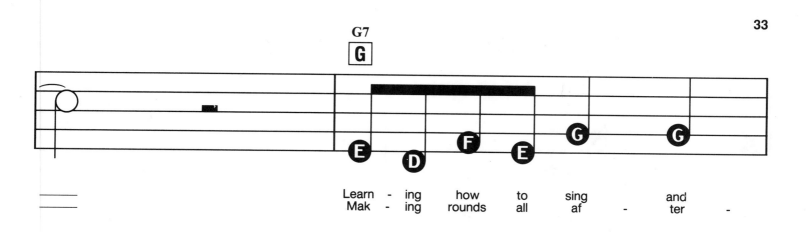

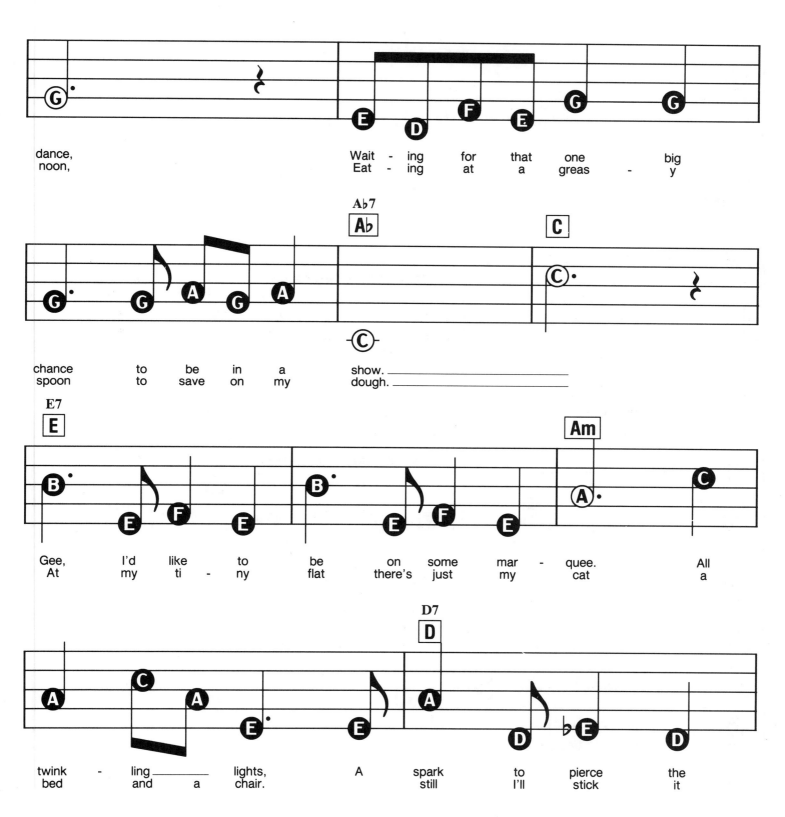

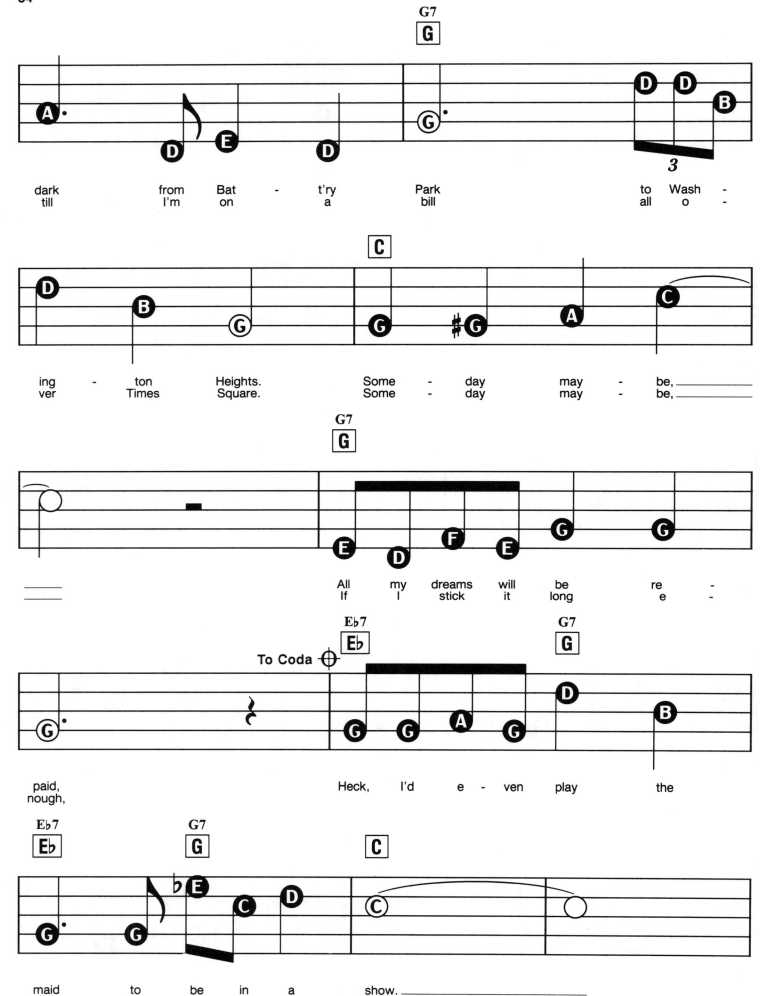

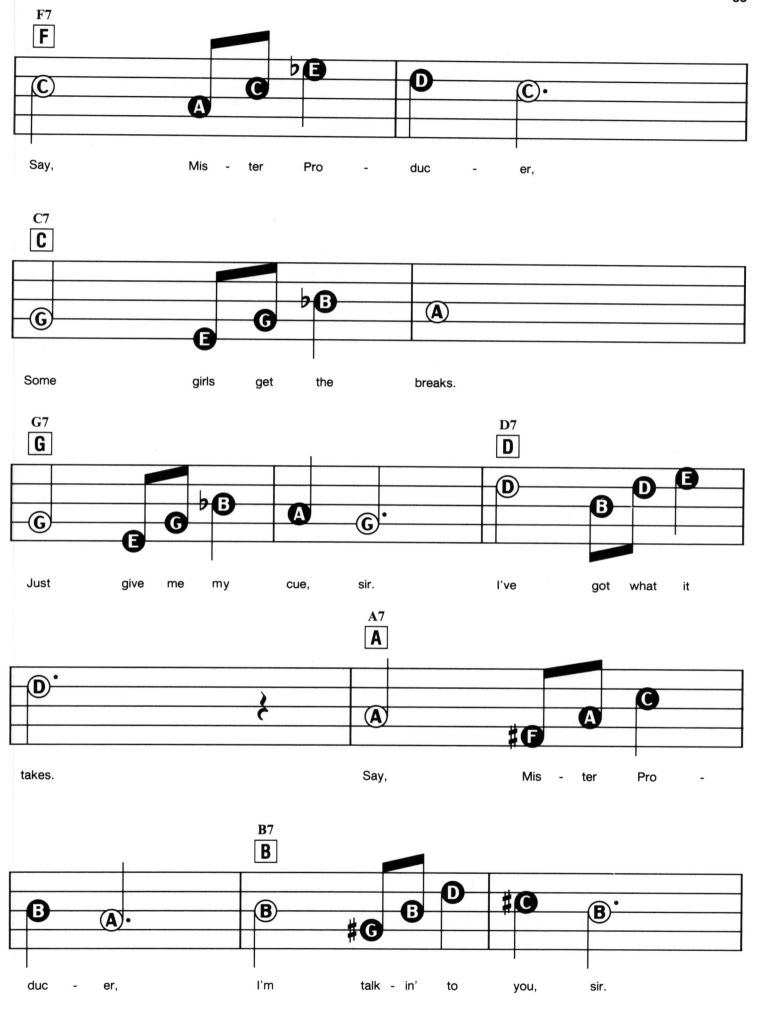

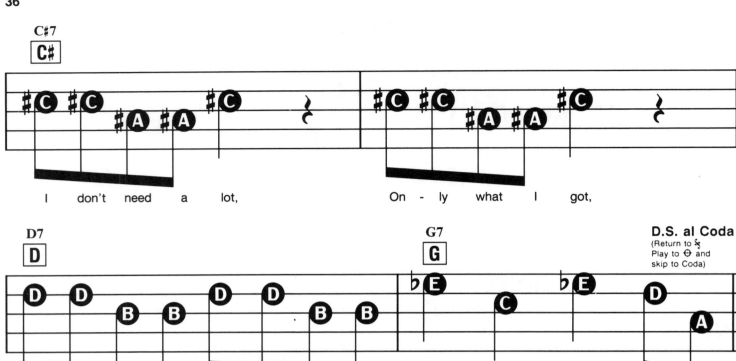

I don't need a lot, On - ly what I got,

Plus a tube of grease - paint and a fol - low spot! I'm a

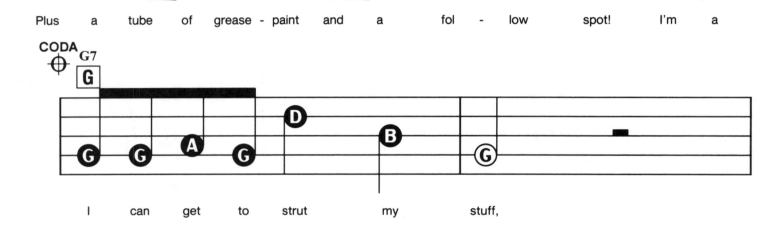

I can get to strut my stuff,

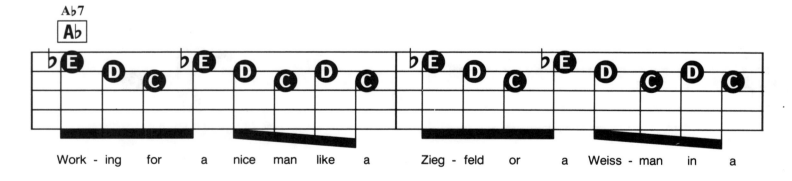

Work - ing for a nice man like a Zieg - feld or a Weiss - man in a

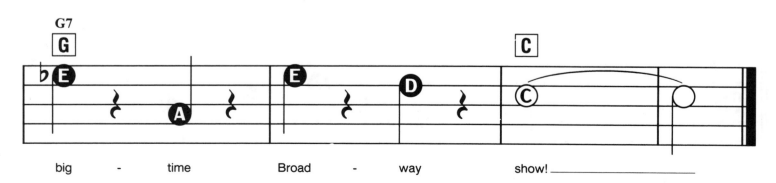

big - time Broad - way show! _____

Cabaret
(From the Musical "CABARET")

Registration 7
Rhythm: Swing

Music by John Kander
Words by Fred Ebb

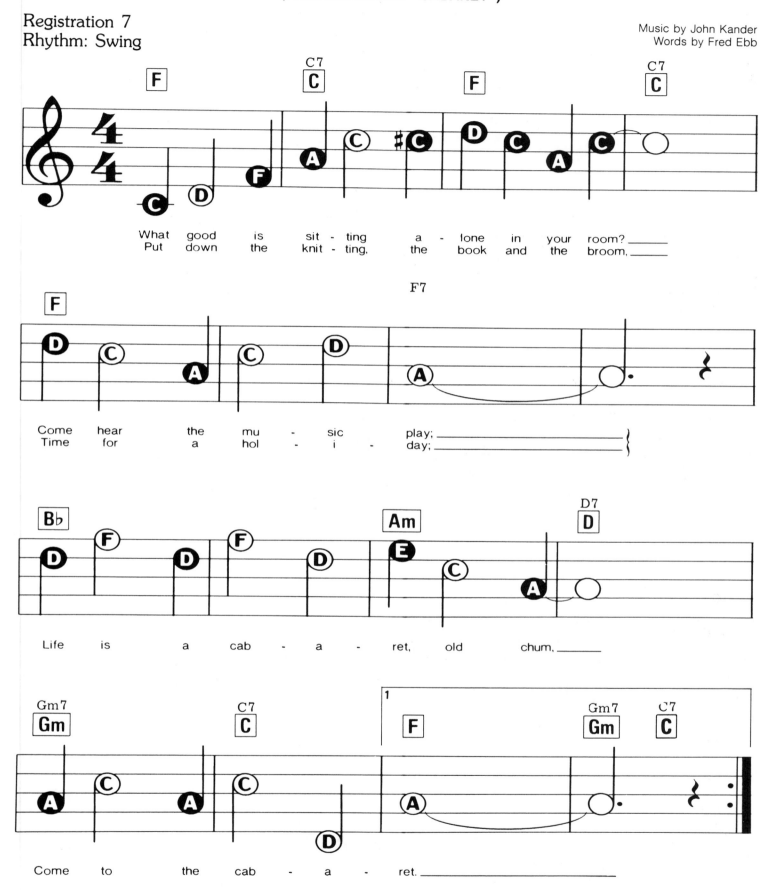

What good is sit-ting a-lone in your room? _____
Put down the knit-ting, the book and the broom, _____

Come hear the mu-sic play; _____
Time for a hol-i-day; _____

Life is a cab-a-ret, old chum, _____

Come to the cab-a-ret. _____

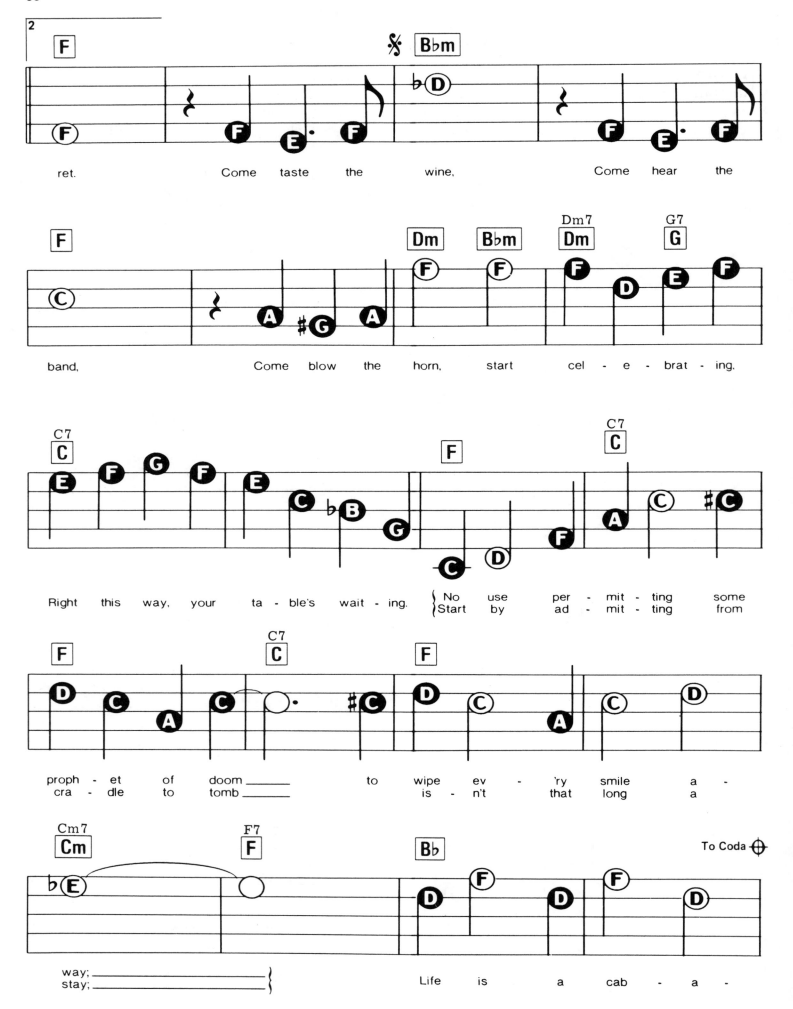

ret. Come taste the wine, Come hear the

band, Come blow the horn, start cel - e - brat - ing,

Right this way, your ta - ble's wait - ing. No use per - mit - ting some
Start by ad - mit - ting some from

proph - et of doom _____ to wipe ev - 'ry smile a -
cra - dle to tomb _____ is - n't that long a

To Coda

way; _____
stay; _____ Life is a cab - a -

Camelot

(From "CAMELOT")

Words by Alan Jay Lerner
Music by Frederick Loewe

Registration 4
Rhythm: Fox Trot or Ballad

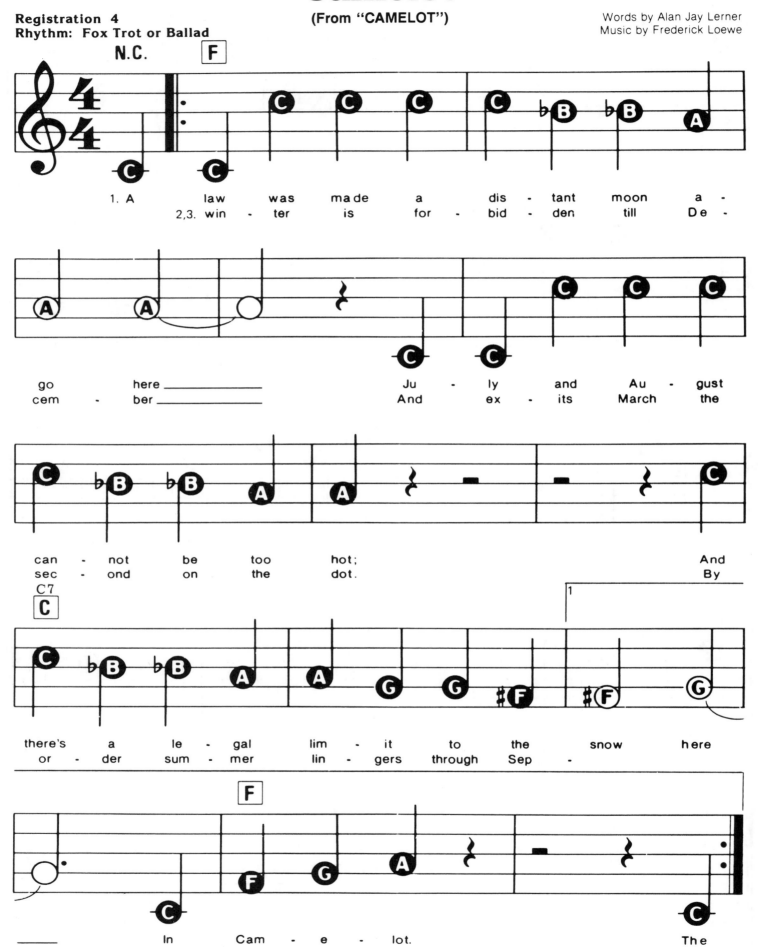

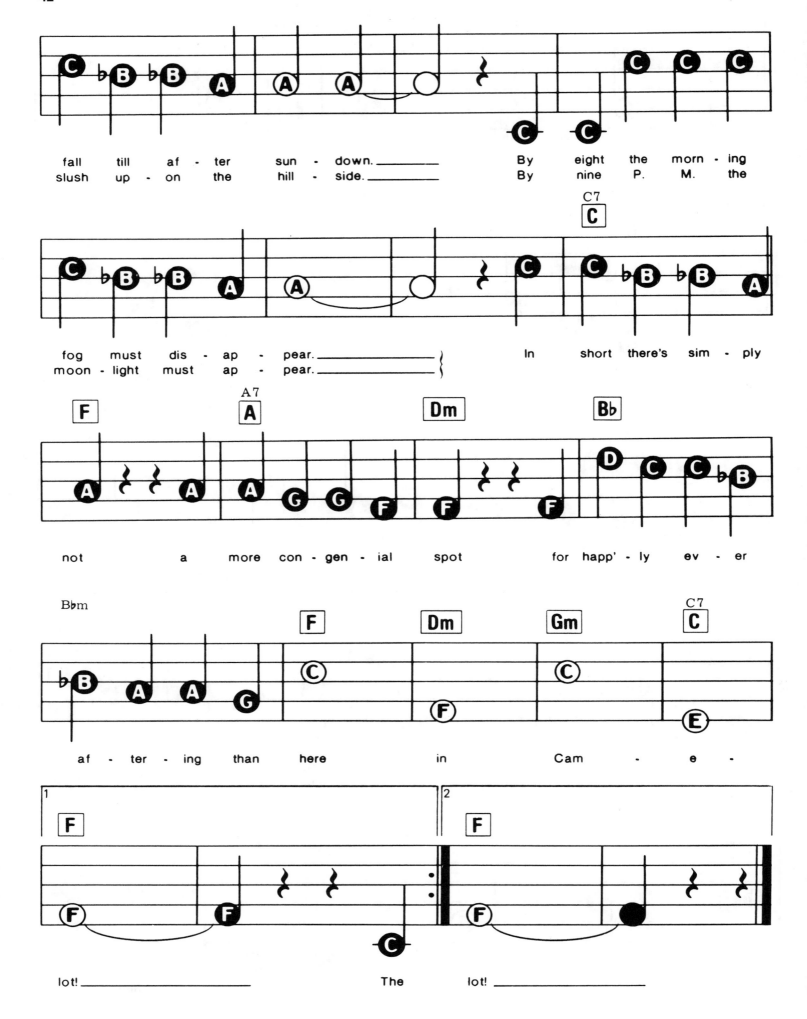

Comedy Tonight

(From "A FUNNY THING HAPPENED ON THE WAY TO THE FORUM")

Registration 2
Rhythm: March or Polka

Words and Music by
Stephen Sondheim

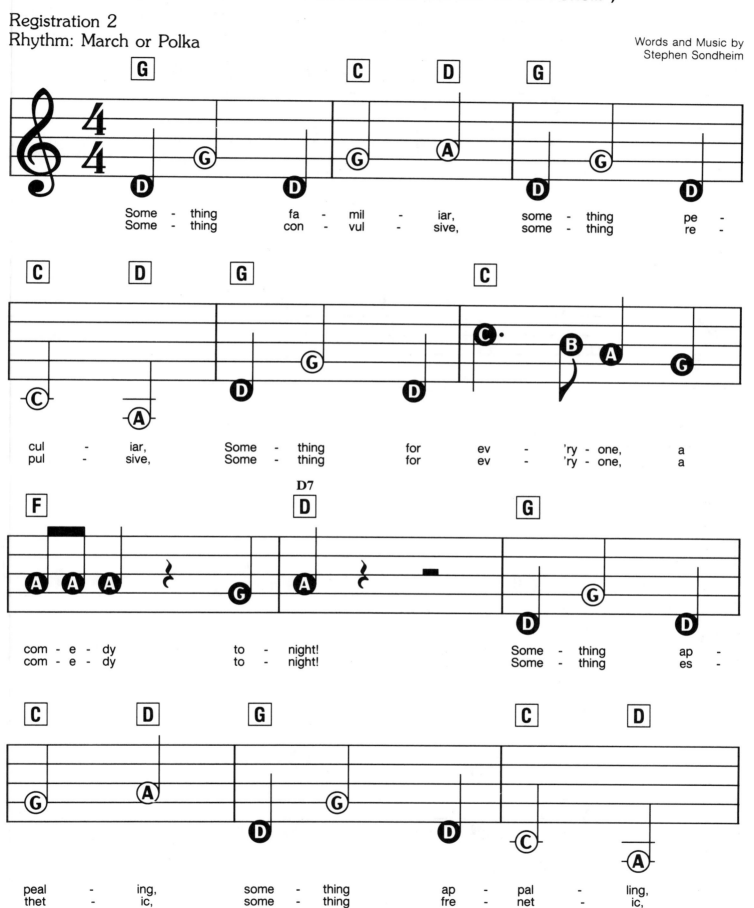

44

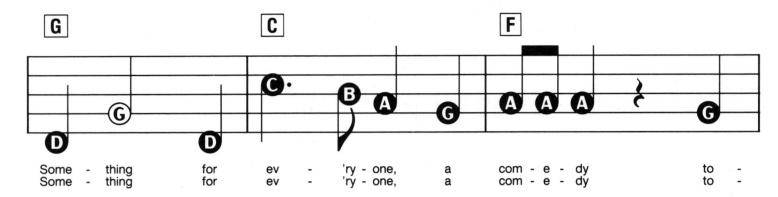

Some - thing   for   ev - 'ry - one,   a   com - e - dy   to -
Some - thing   for   ev - 'ry - one,   a   com - e - dy   to -

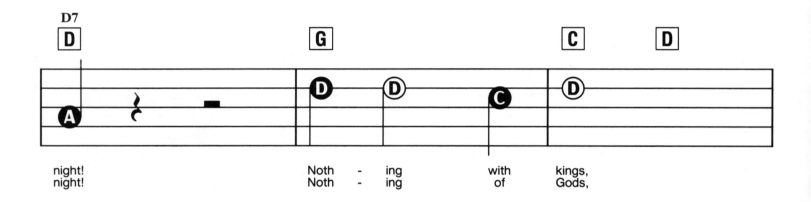

night!   Noth - ing   with   kings,
night!   Noth - ing   of   Gods,

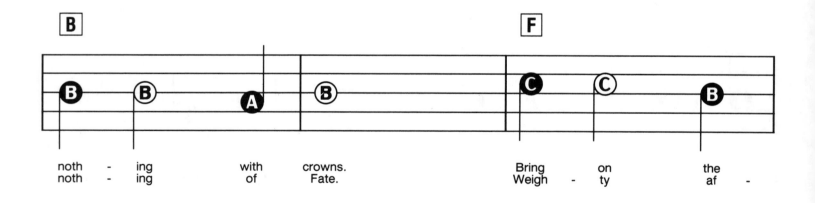

noth - ing   with   crowns.   Bring   on   the
noth - ing   of   Fate.   Weigh - ty   af -

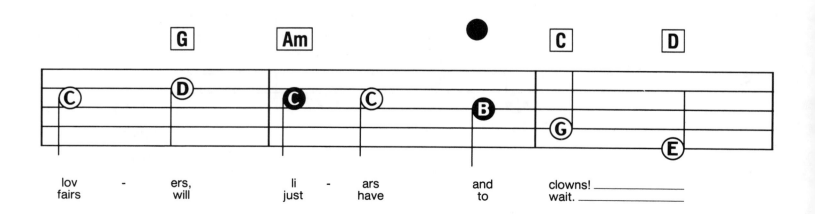

lov - ers,   li - ars   and   clowns! _____
fairs   will   just   have   to   wait. _____

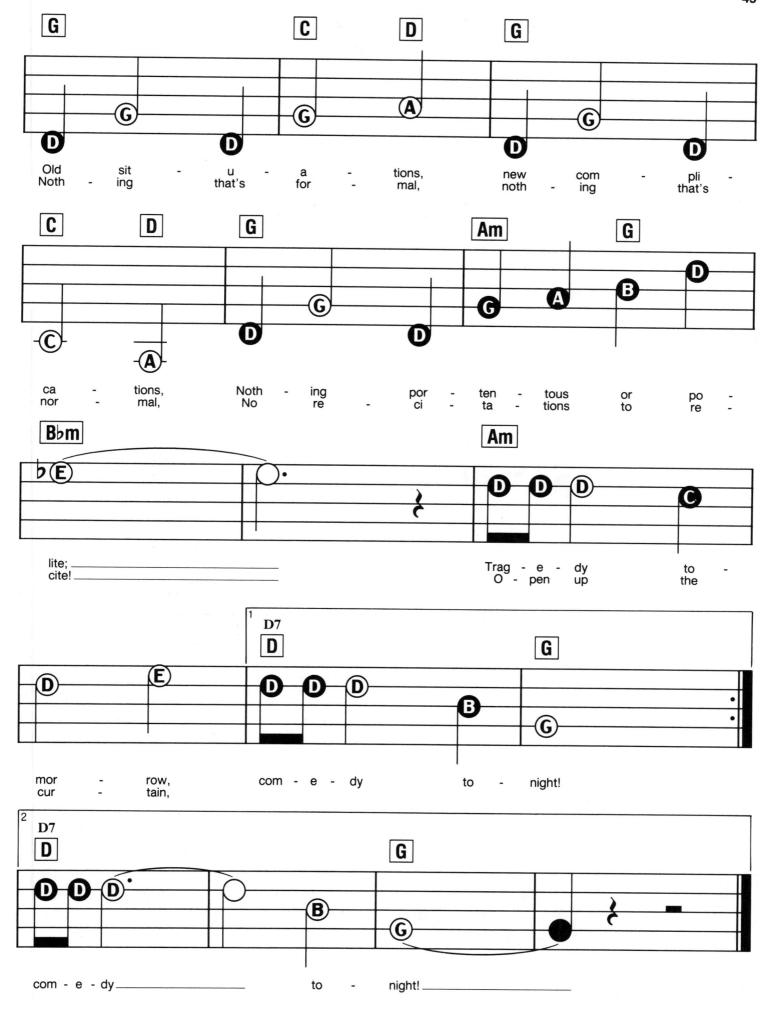

Climb Ev'ry Mountain

(From "THE SOUND OF MUSIC")

Registration 5
Rhythm: Fox Trot

Lyrics by Oscar Hammerstein II
Music by Richard Rodgers

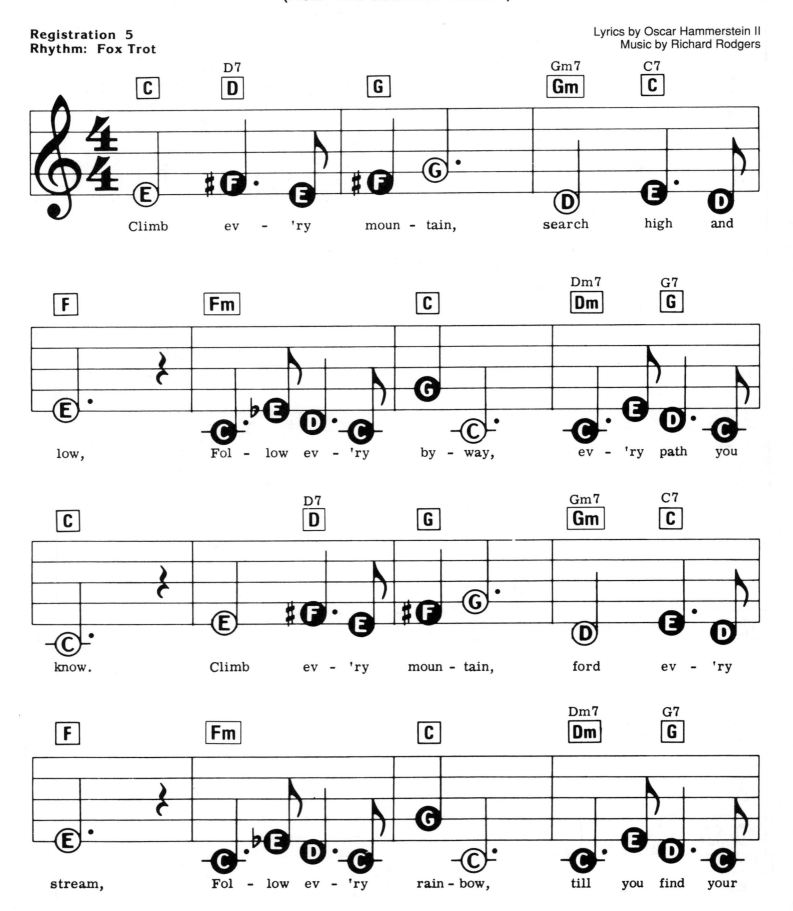

47

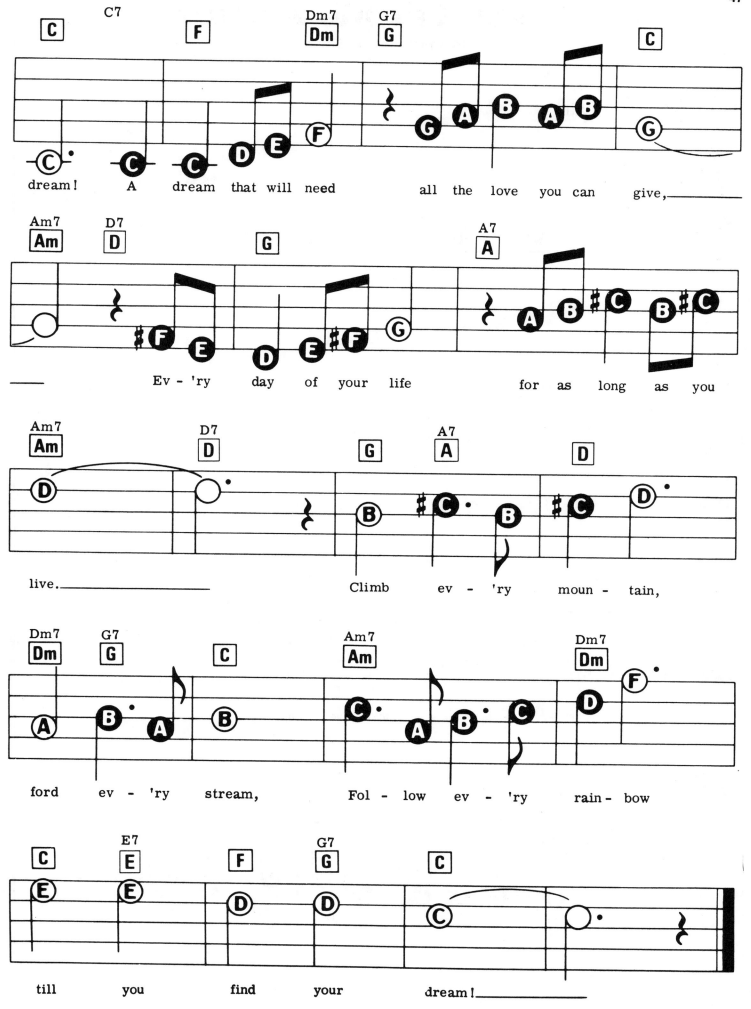

Don't Cry For Me Argentina

(From the opera "EVITA")

Registration 9
Rhythm: Tango or Latin

Lryic by Tim Rice
Music by Andrew Lloyd Webber

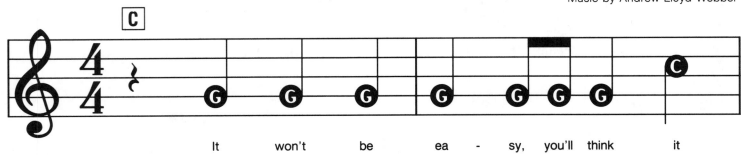

It won't be ea - sy, you'll think it

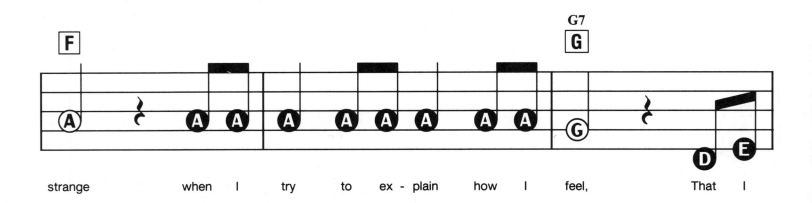

strange when I try to ex - plain how I feel, That I

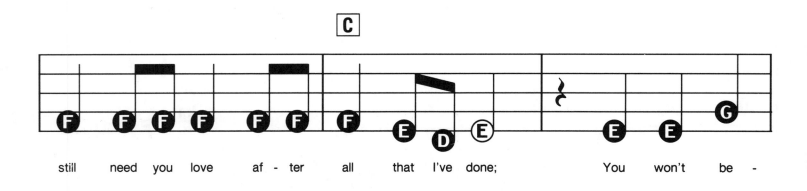

still need you love af - ter all that I've done; You won't be -

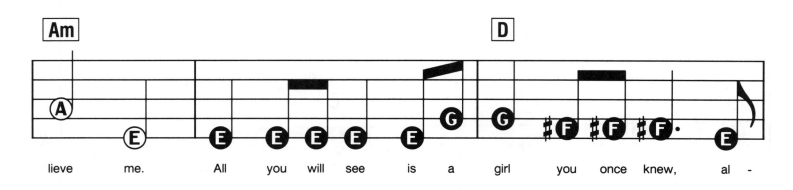

lieve me. All you will see is a girl you once knew, al -

MCA MUSIC

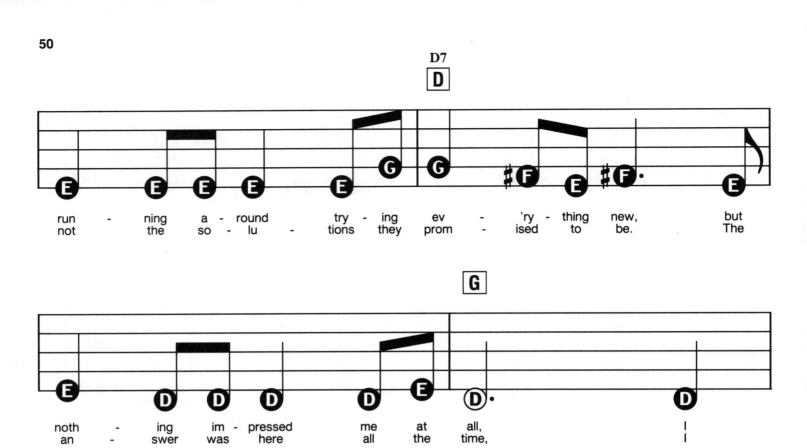

run - ning a - round try - ing ev - 'ry - thing new, but
not the so - lu - tions they prom - ised to be. The

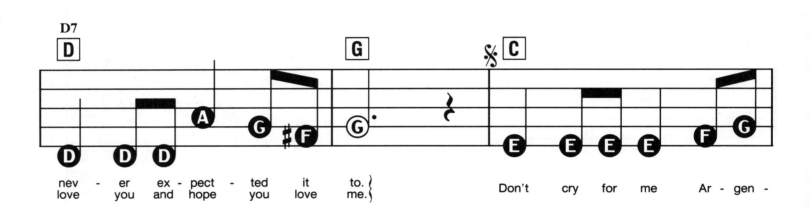

noth - ing im - pressed me at all, I
an - swer was here all the time, I

nev - er ex - pect - ted it to.
love you and hope you love me.

Don't cry for me Ar - gen -

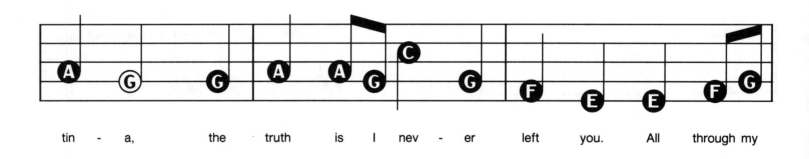

tin - a, the truth is I nev - er left you. All through my

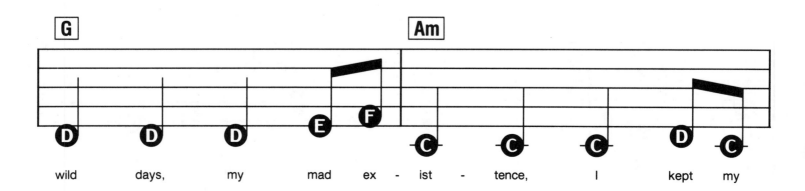

wild days, my mad ex - ist - tence, I kept my

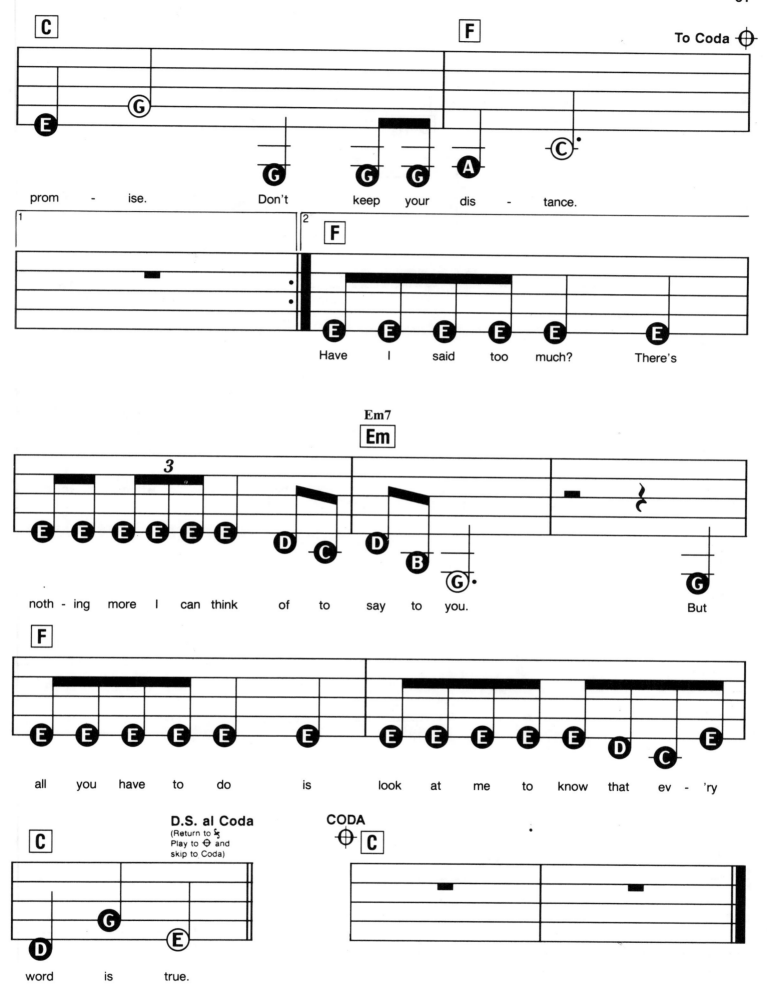

Everything's Coming Up Roses

(From "GYPSY")

Registration 1
Rhythm: Fox Trot or Polka

Words by Stephen Sondheim
Music by Jule Styne

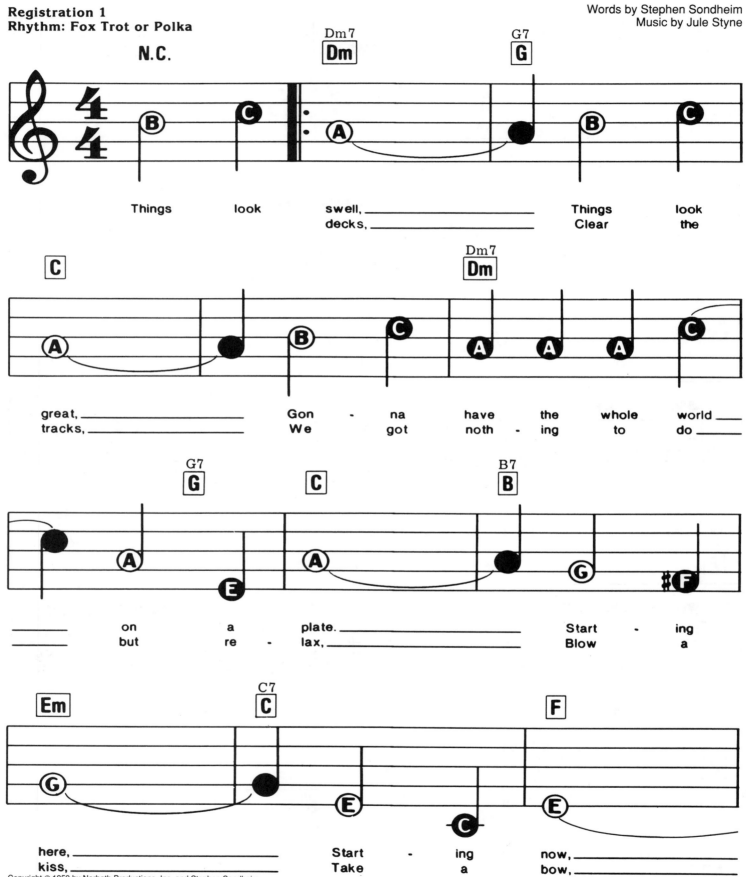

Things   look   swell, _____   Things   look
decks, _____   Clear   the

great, _____   Gon - na   have   the   whole   world _____
tracks, _____   We   got   noth - ing   to   do _____

_____   on   a   plate. _____   Start - ing
_____   but   are   re - lax, _____   Blow   a

here, _____   Start - ing   now, _____
kiss,   Take   a   bow, _____

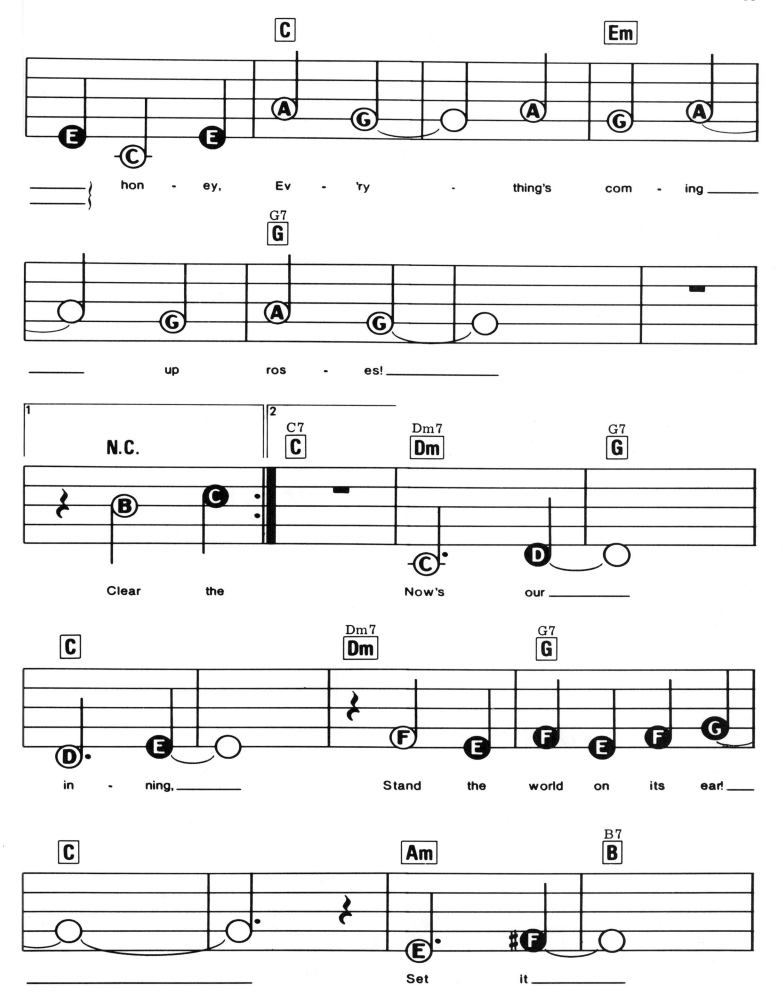

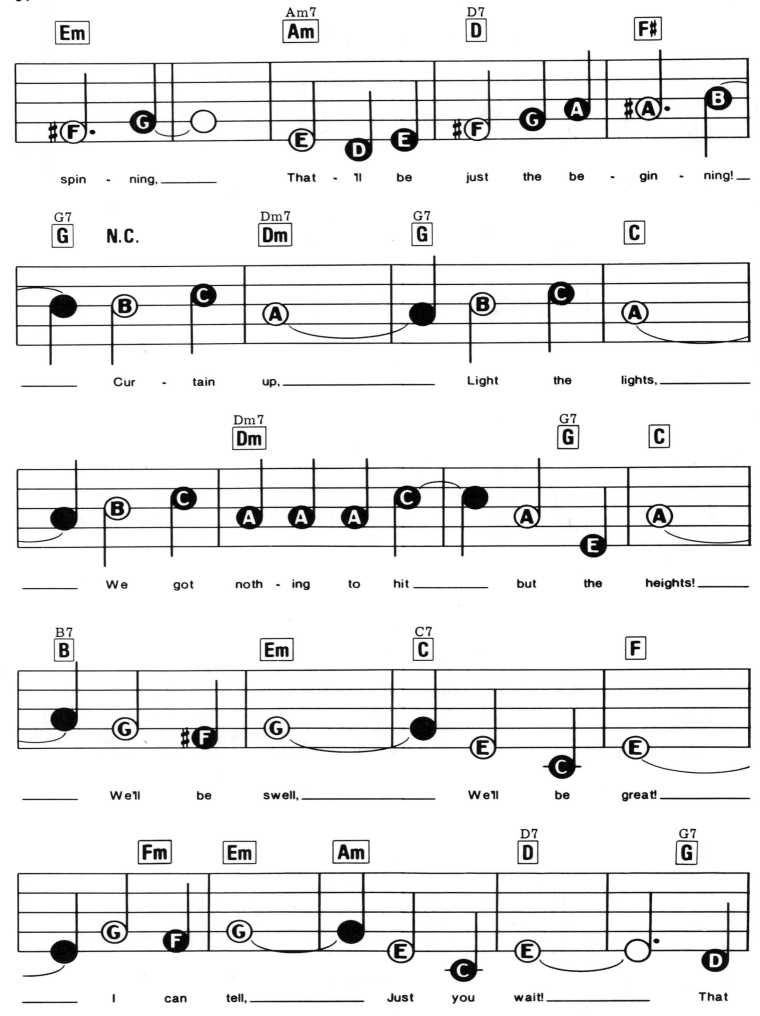

Falling In Love With Love

(From "THE BOYS FROM SYRACUSE")

Registration: 5
Rhythm: Waltz

Words by Lorenz Hart
Music by Richard Rodgers

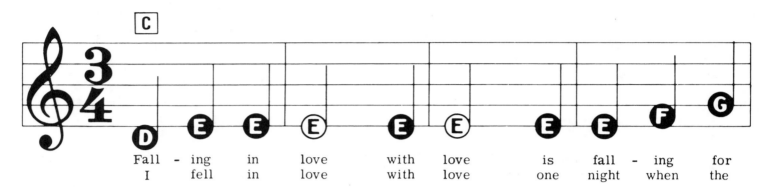

Fall - ing in love with love is fall - ing for
I fell in love love with with love is one night when for the

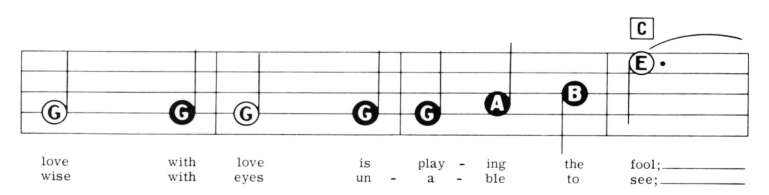

make be - lieve, _____ Fall - ing in
moon was full, _____ I was un -

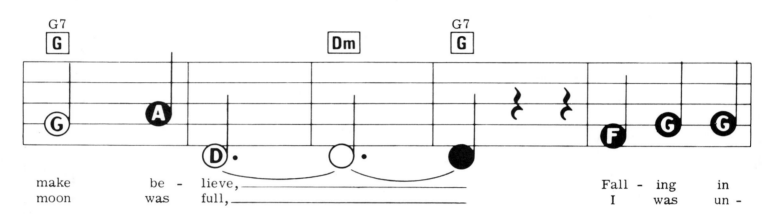

love with love is play - ing the fool; _____
wise with eyes un - a - ble to see; _____

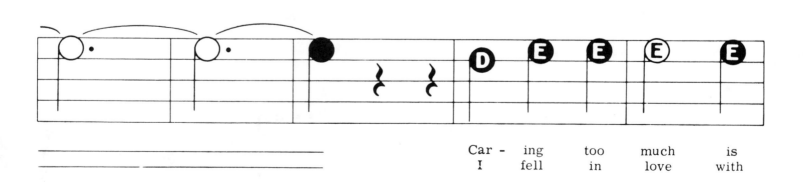

_____
_____ Car - ing too much is
I fell in love with

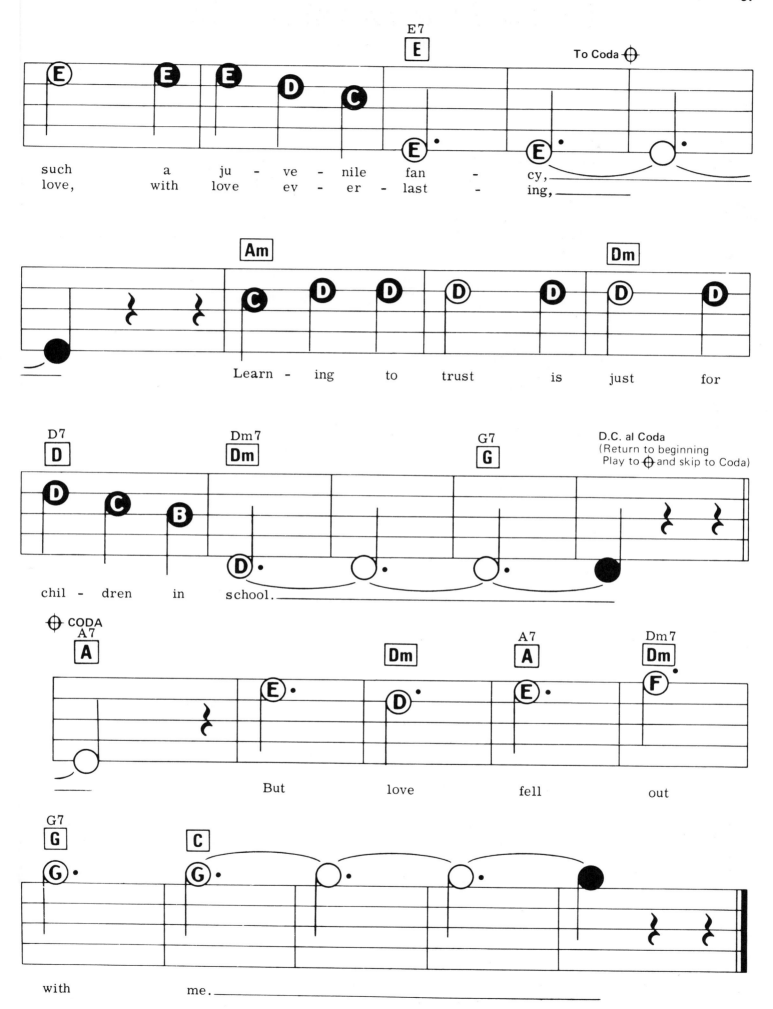

From This Moment On

(From "OUT OF THIS WORLD")

Registration 5
Rhythm: Swing

Words and Music by Cole Porter

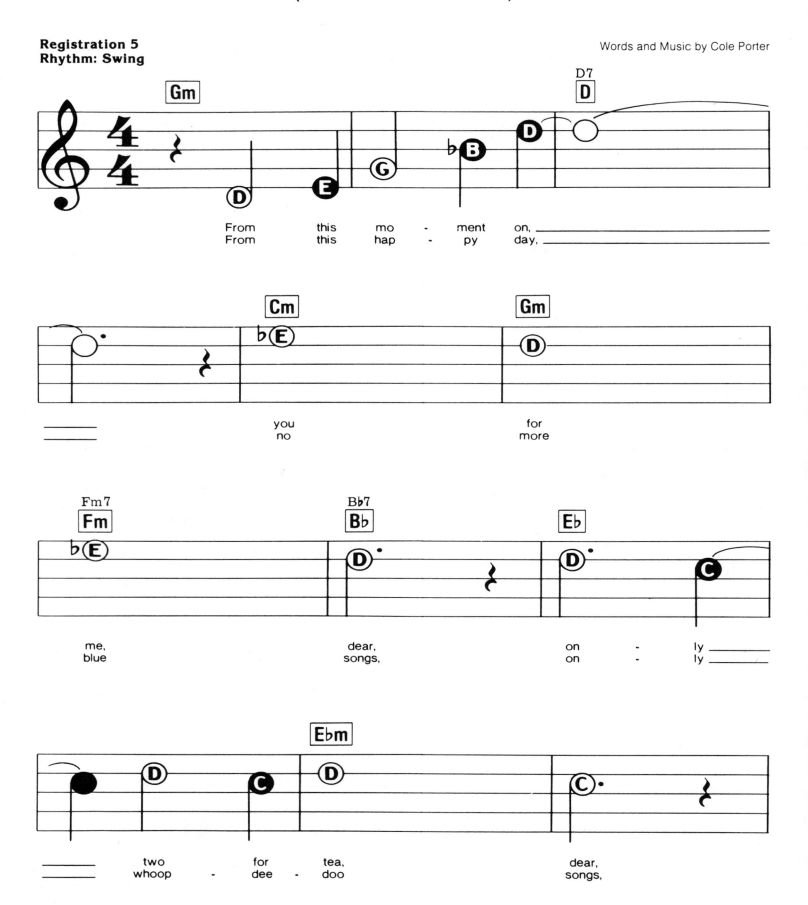

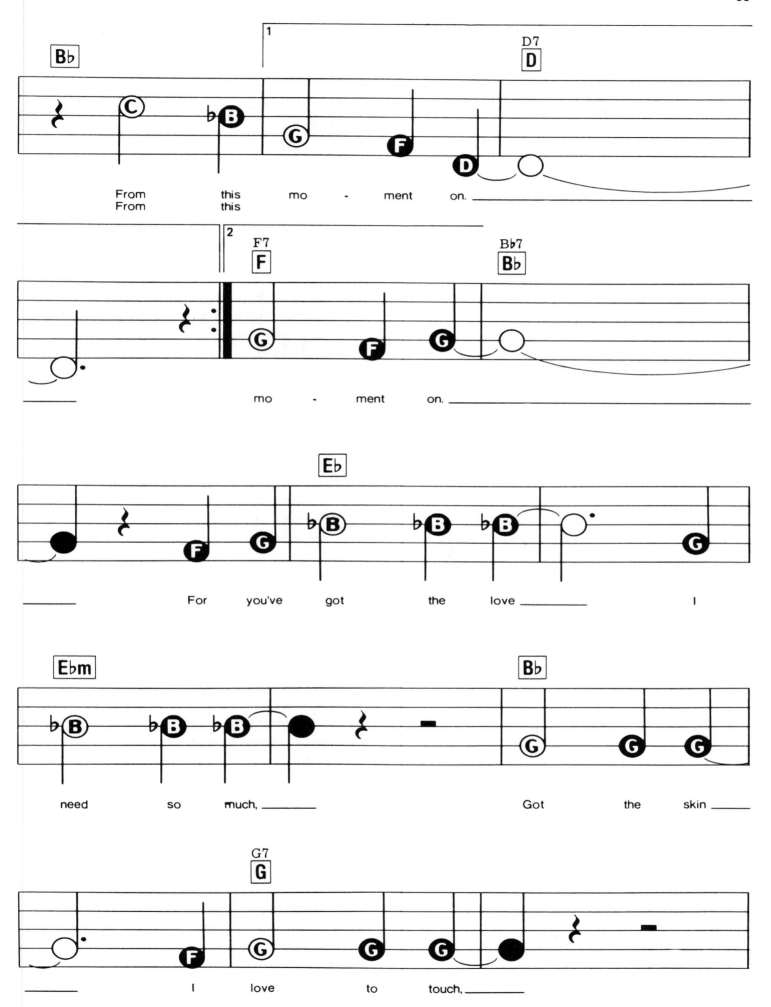

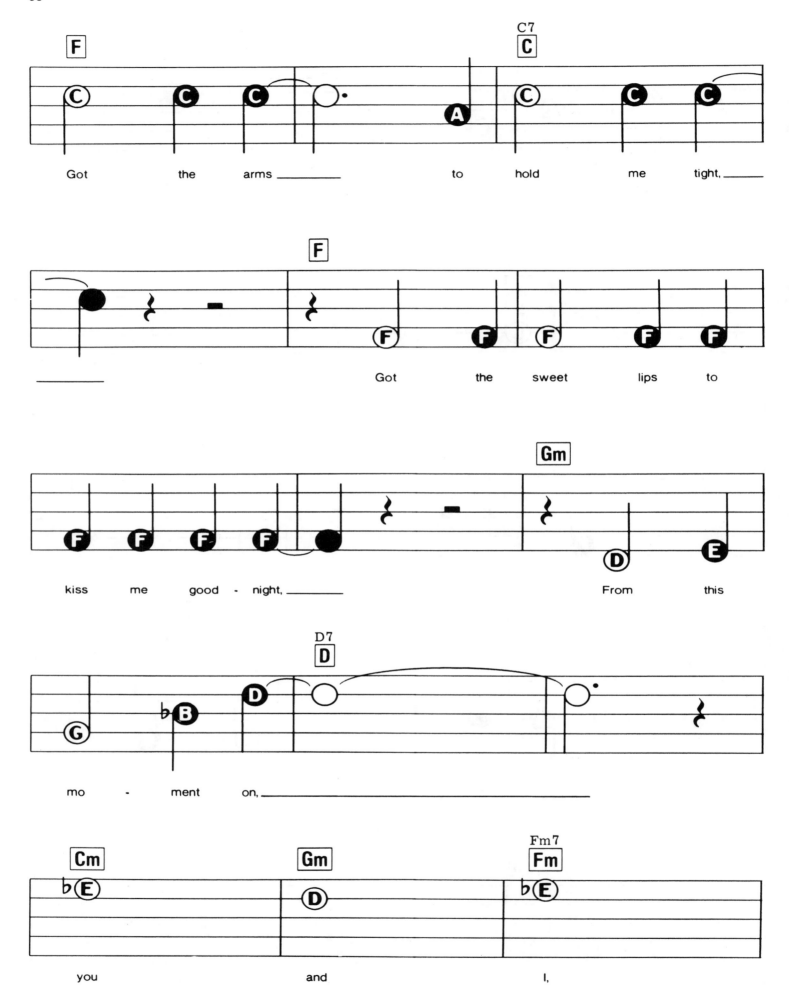

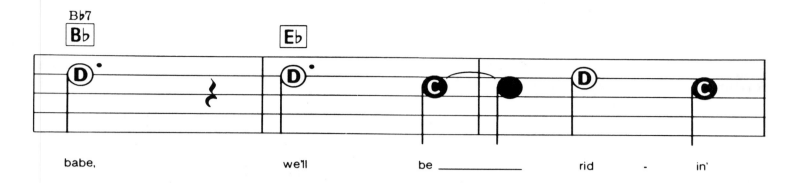

babe,   we'll   be _____ rid - in'

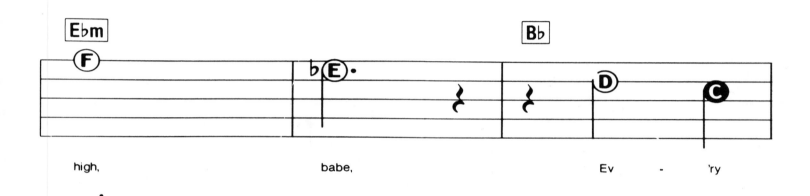

high,   babe,   Ev - 'ry

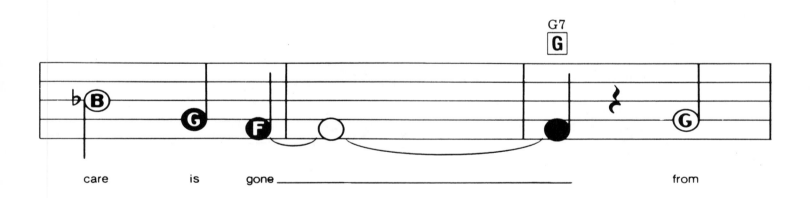

care   is   gone _____ from

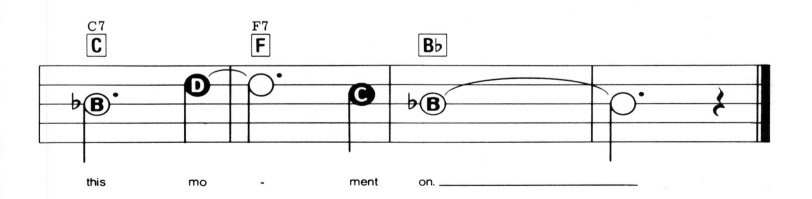

this   mo - ment   on. _____

Getting To Know You

(From "THE KING AND I")

Lyrics by Oscar Hammerstein II
Music by Richard Rodgers

Registration 8
Rhythm: Fox Trot or Swing

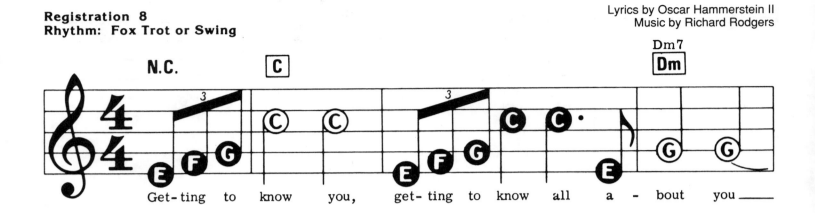

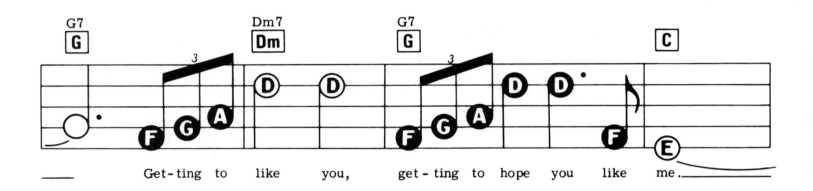

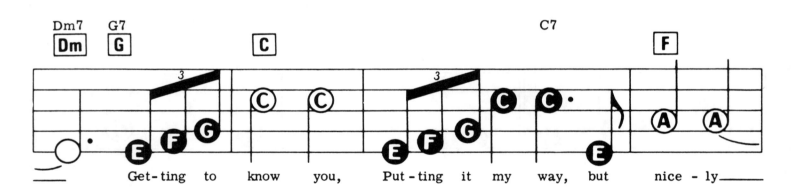

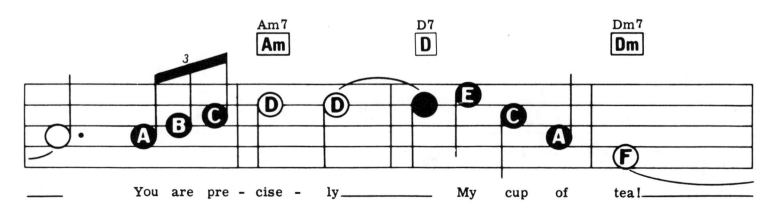

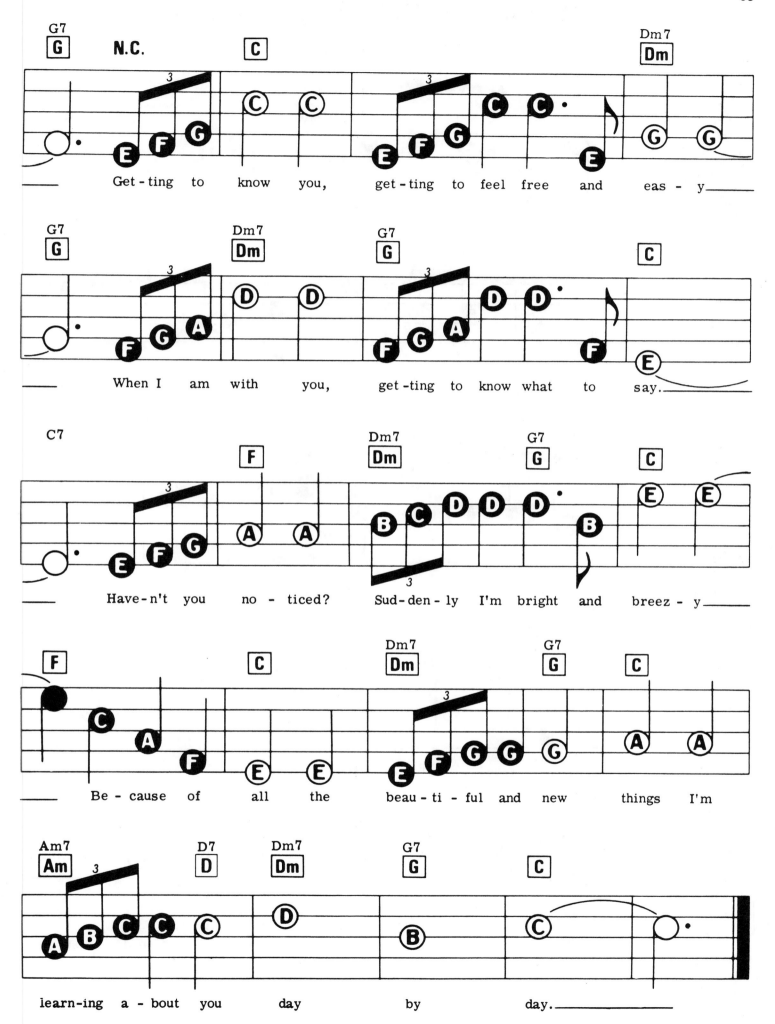

Don't Rain On My Parade

(From "FUNNY GIRL")

Registration 4
Rhythm: Samba or Latin

Words by Bob Merrill
Music by Jule Styne

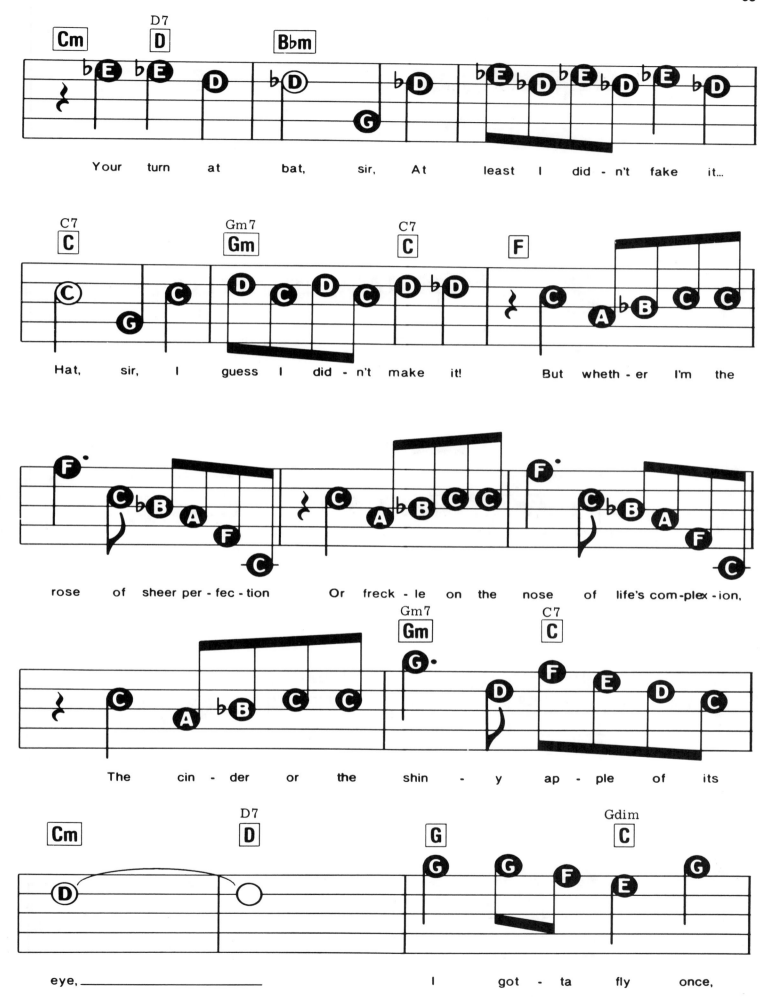

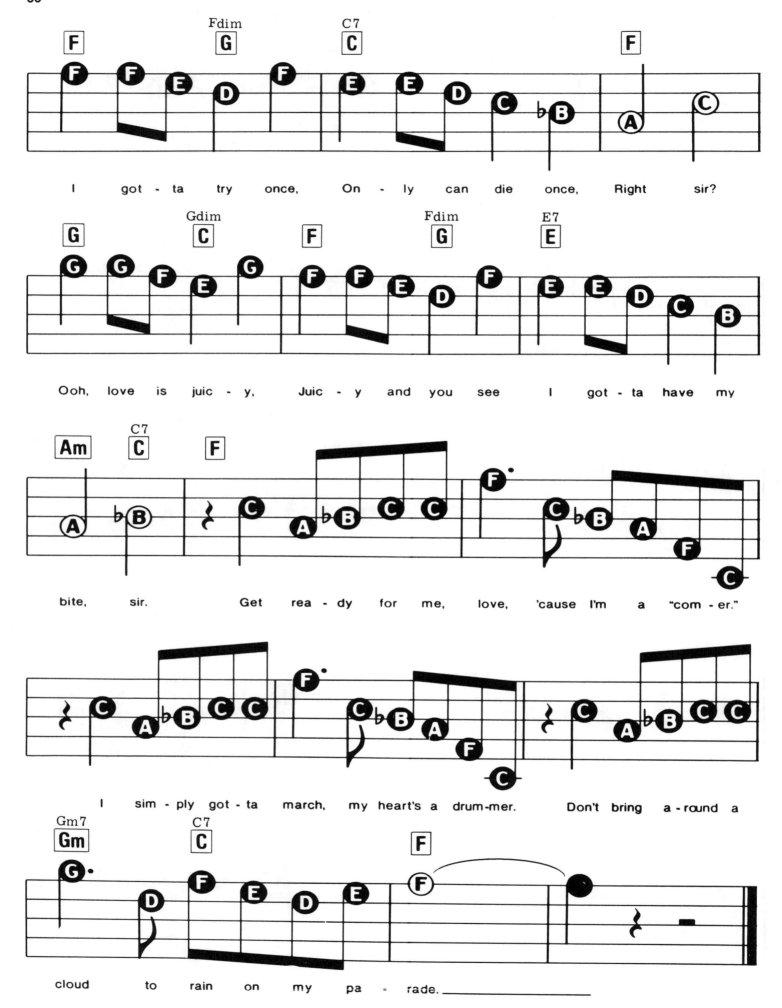

Hello, Young Lovers

(From "THE KING AND I")

Registration 1
Rhythm: Waltz

Lyrics by Oscar Hammerstein II
Music by Richard Rodgers

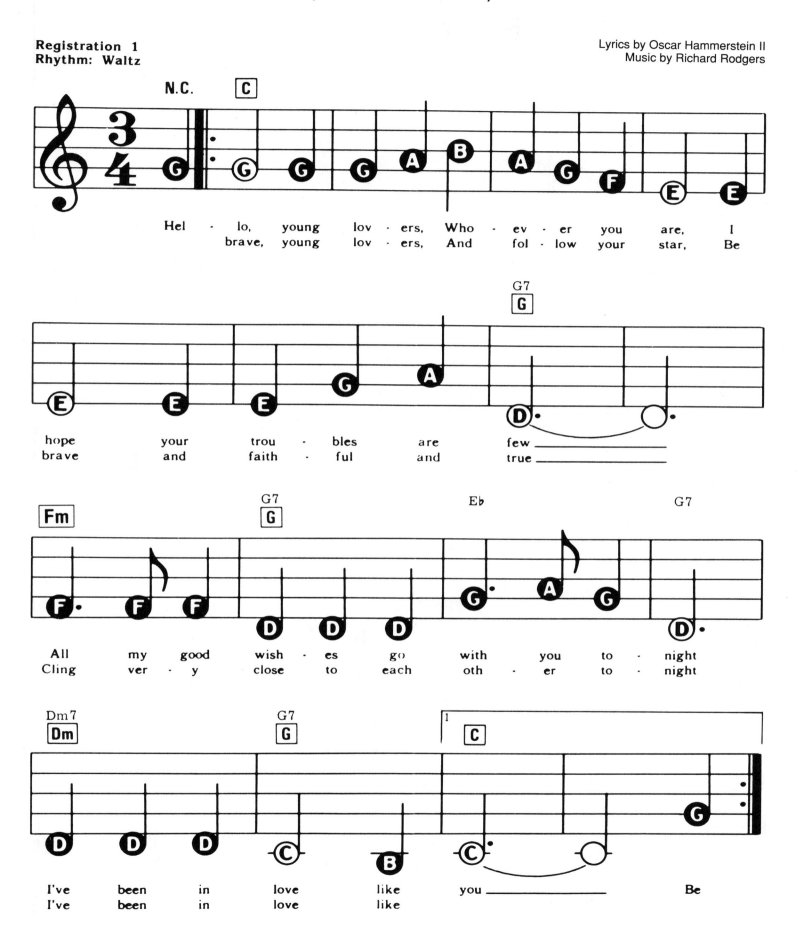

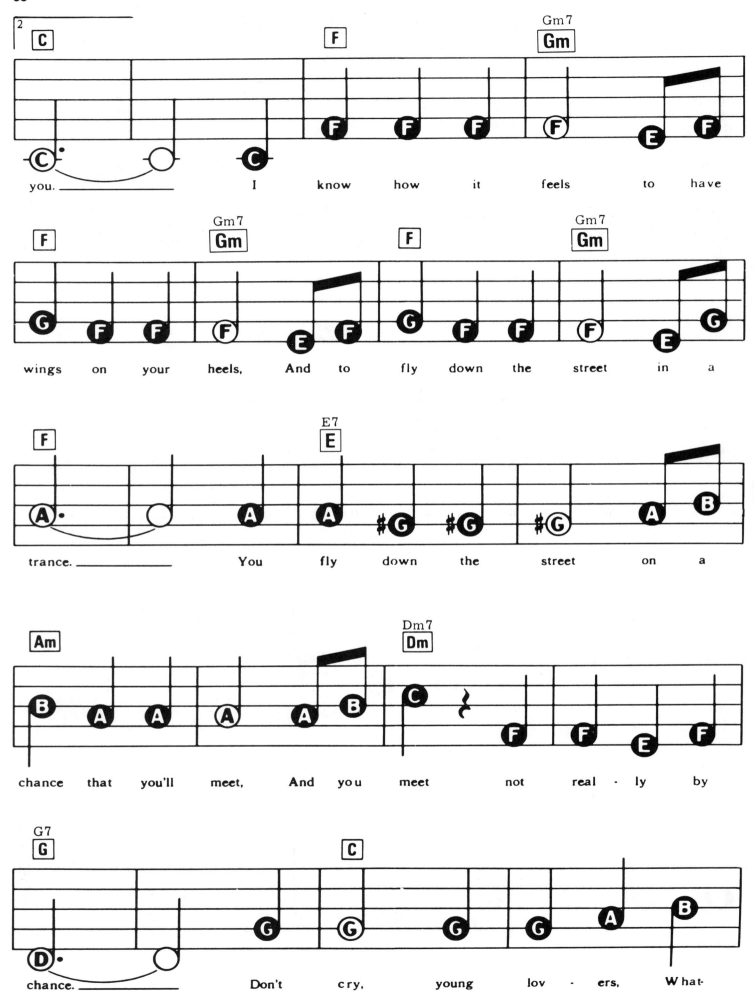

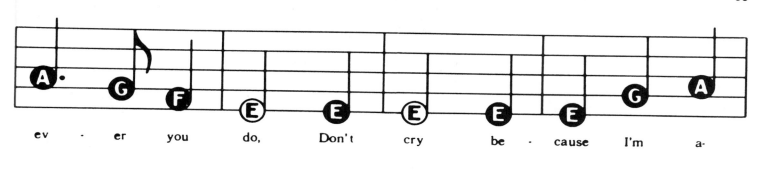

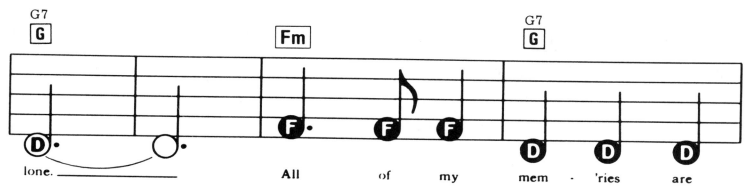

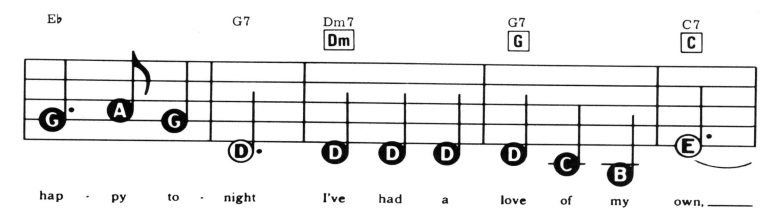

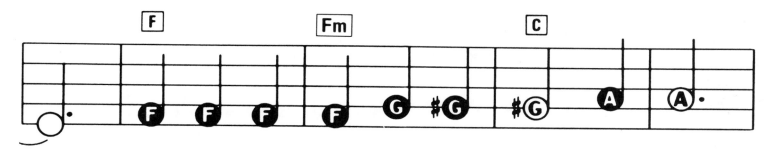

How Are Things In Glocca Morra

(From "FINIAN'S RAINBOW")

Registration 10
Rhythm: Fox Trot or Ballad

Words by E. Y. Harburg
Music by Burton Lane

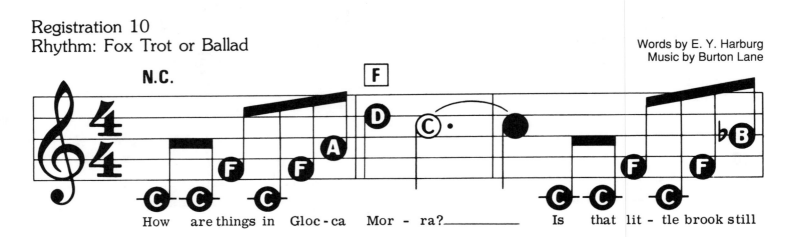

How are things in Gloc-ca Mor-ra?_____ Is that lit-tle brook still

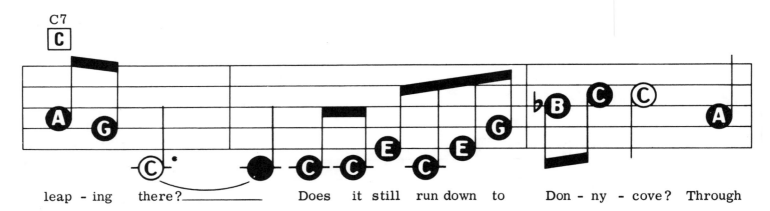

leap-ing there?_____ Does it still run down to Don-ny-cove? Through

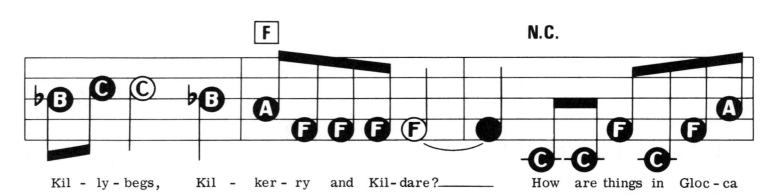

Kil-ly-begs, Kil-ker-ry and Kil-dare?_____ How are things in Gloc-ca

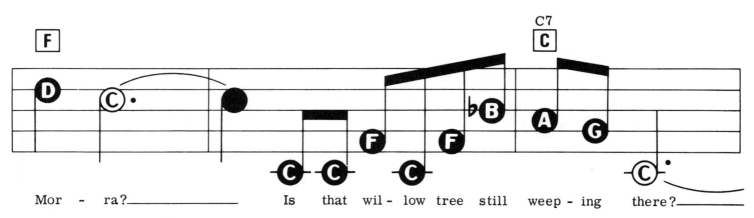

Mor-ra?_____ Is that wil-low tree still weep-ing there?_____

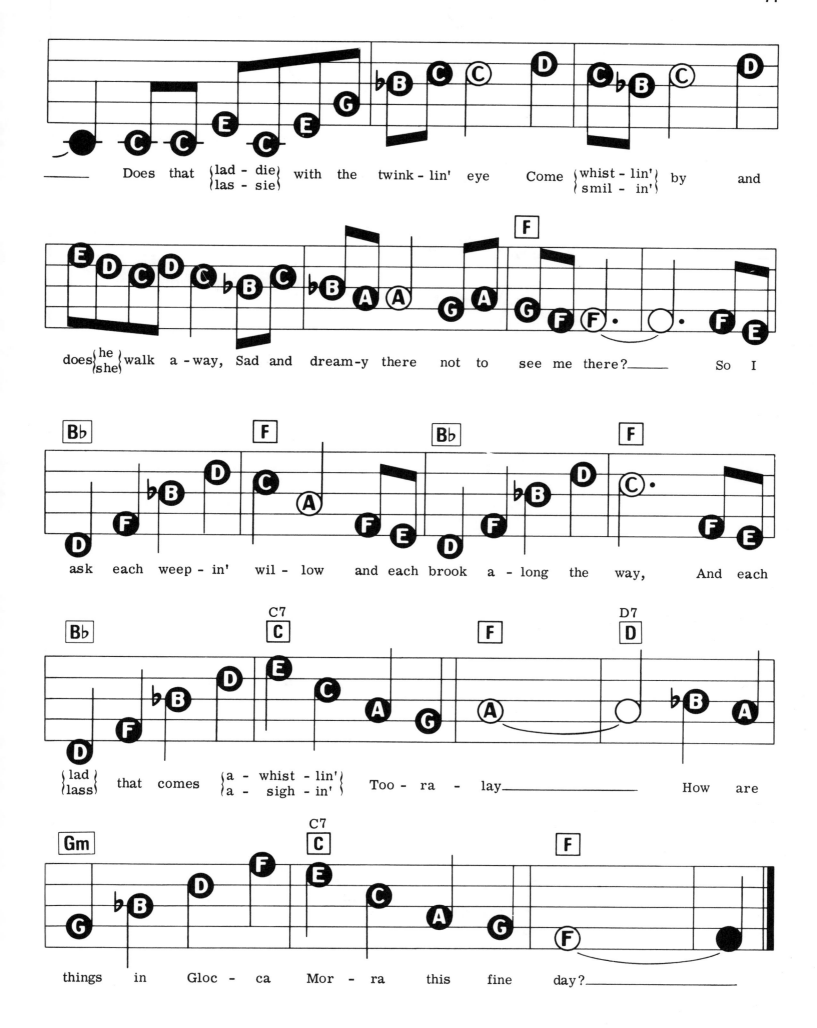

I Believe In You

(From "HOW TO SUCCEED IN BUSINESS WITHOUT REALLY TRYING")

Registration 1
Rhythm: Fox Trot or Swing

Words and Music by
Frank Loesser

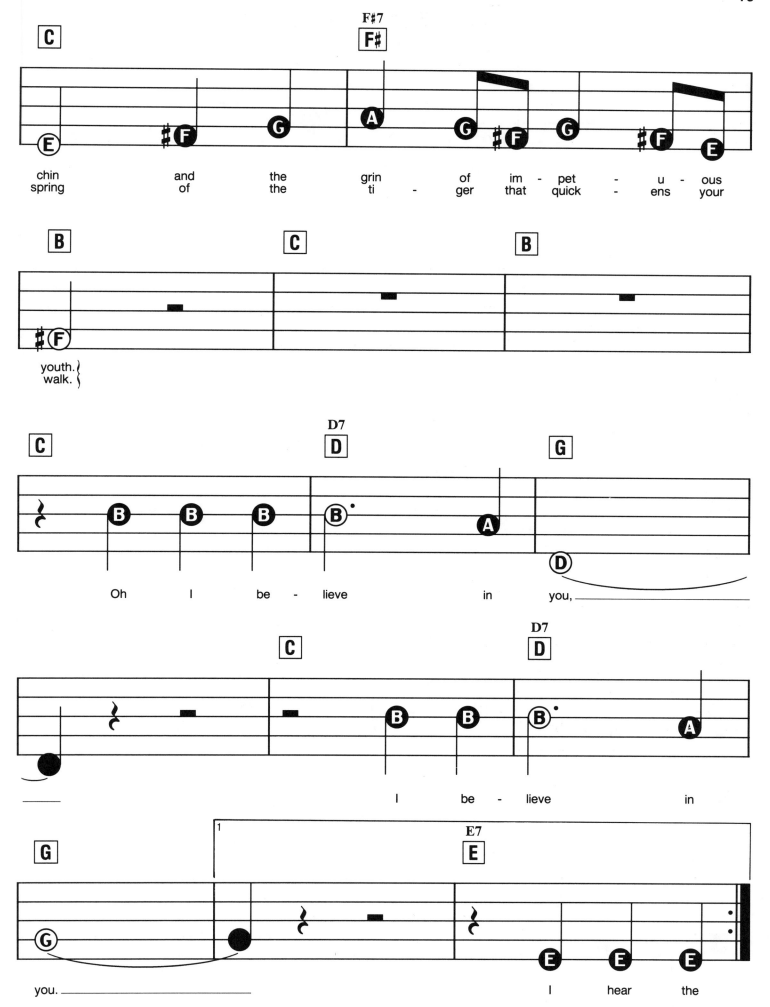

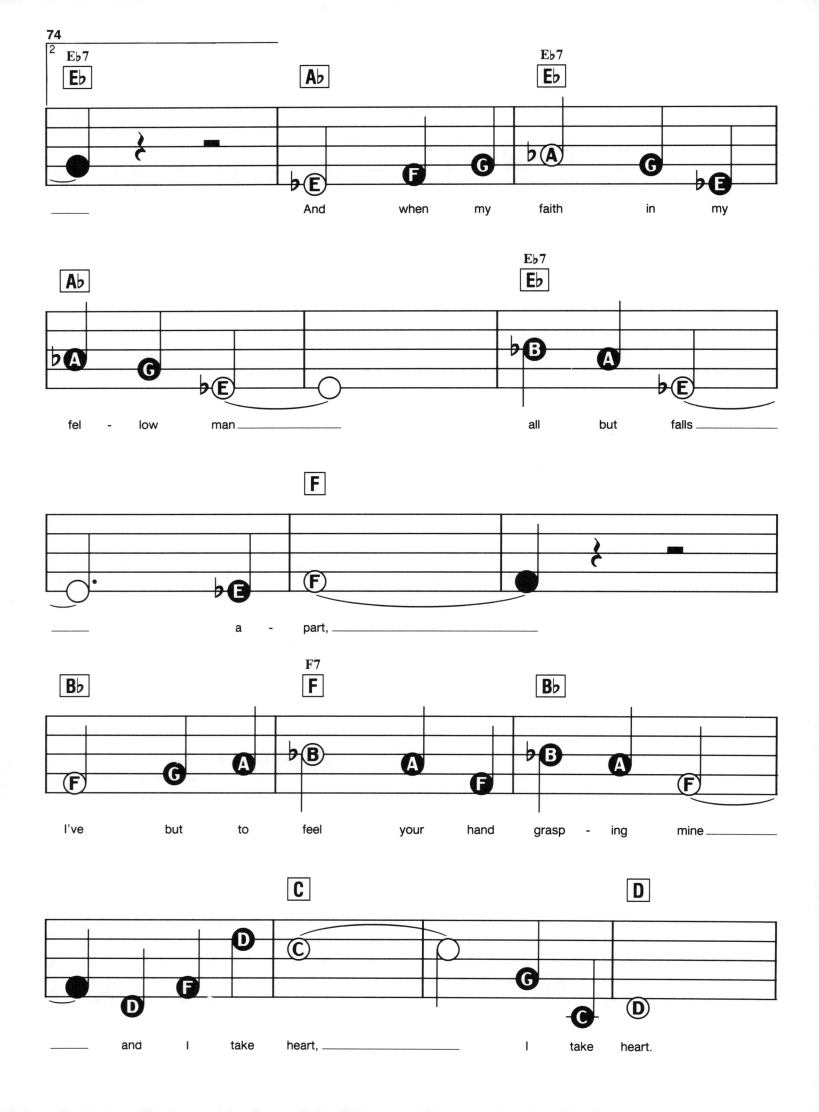

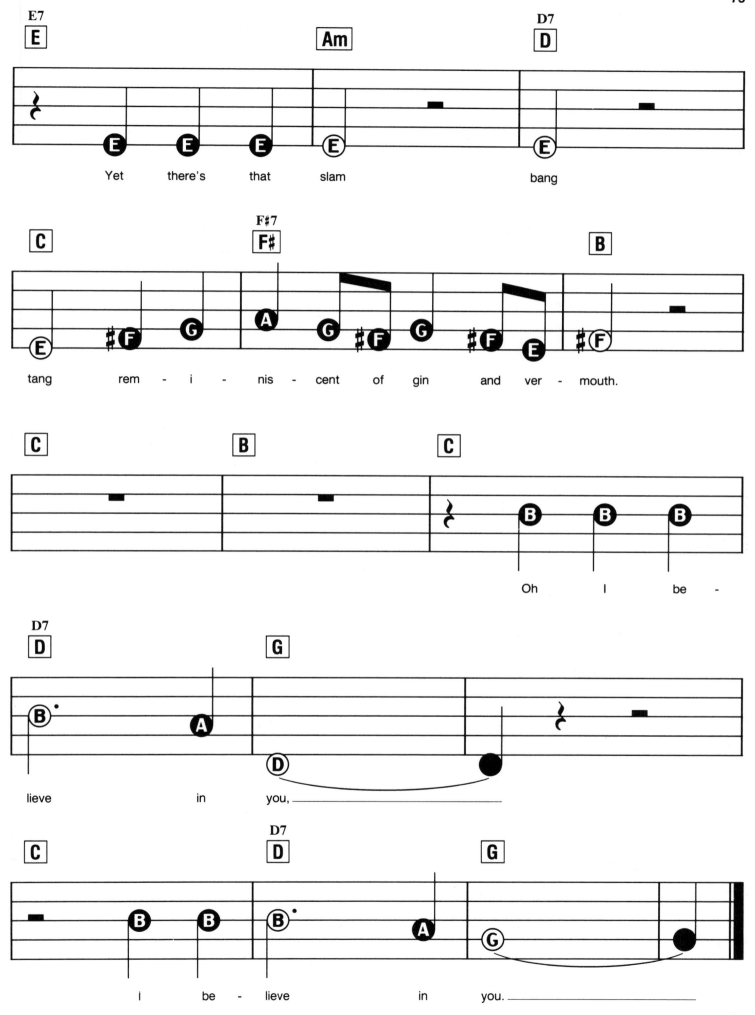

I Could Have Danced All Night

(From "MY FAIR LADY")

Registration 4
Rhythm: Beguine

Words by Alan Jay Lerner
Music by Frederick Loewe

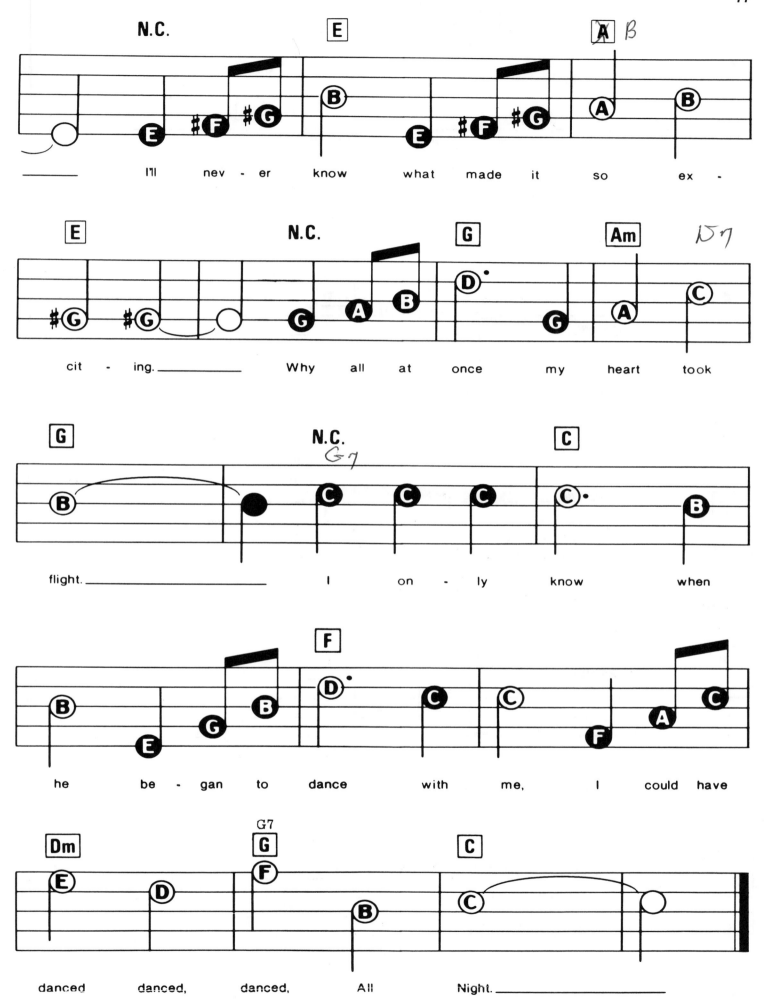

I Dreamed A Dream

Lyrics by Herbert Kretzmer
Original Text by Alain Boublil & Jean-Marc Natel
Music by Claude Michel Schonberg

Registration 1
Rhythm: Fox Trot or Ballad

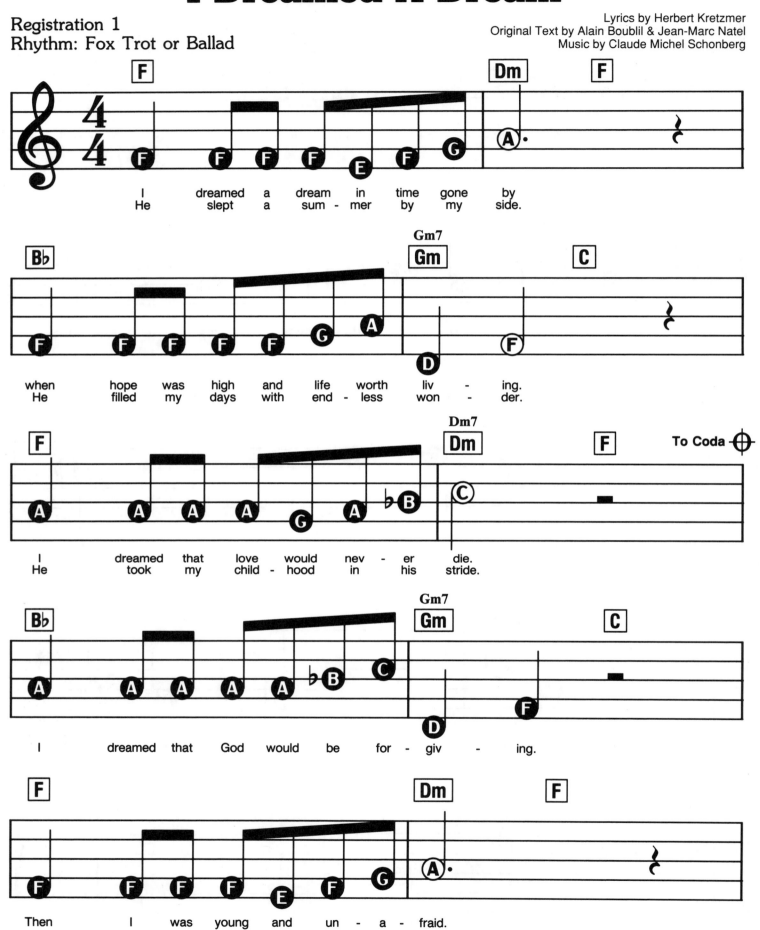

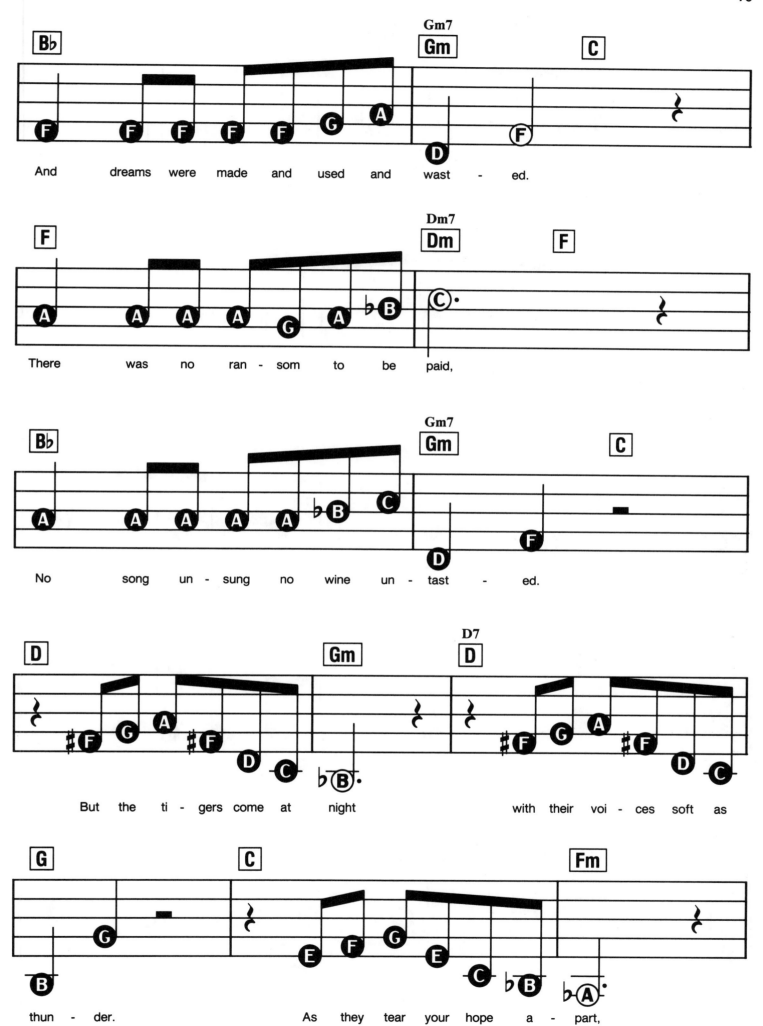

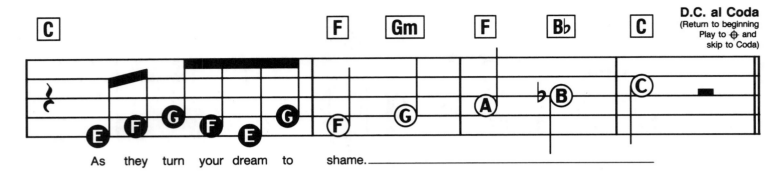

As they turn your dream to shame._____

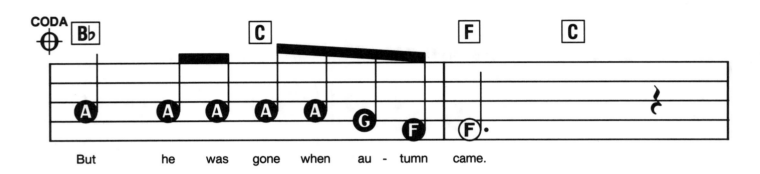

But he was gone when au - tumn came.

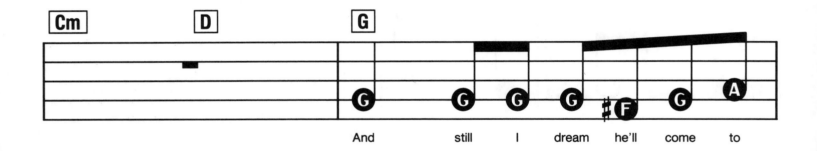

And still I dream he'll come to

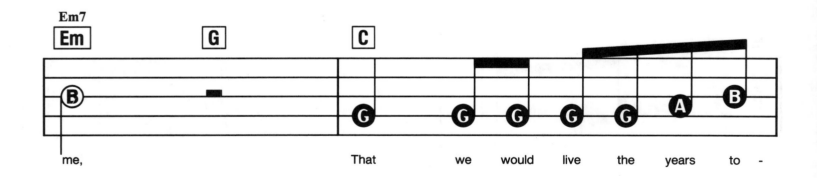

me, That we would live the years to -

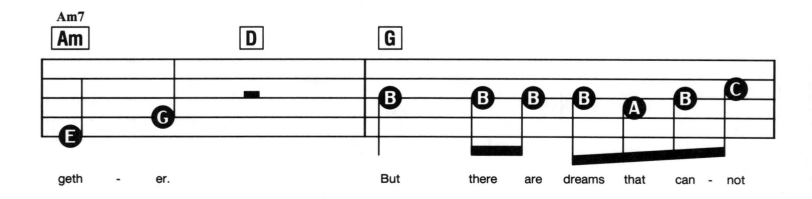

geth - er. But there are dreams that can - not

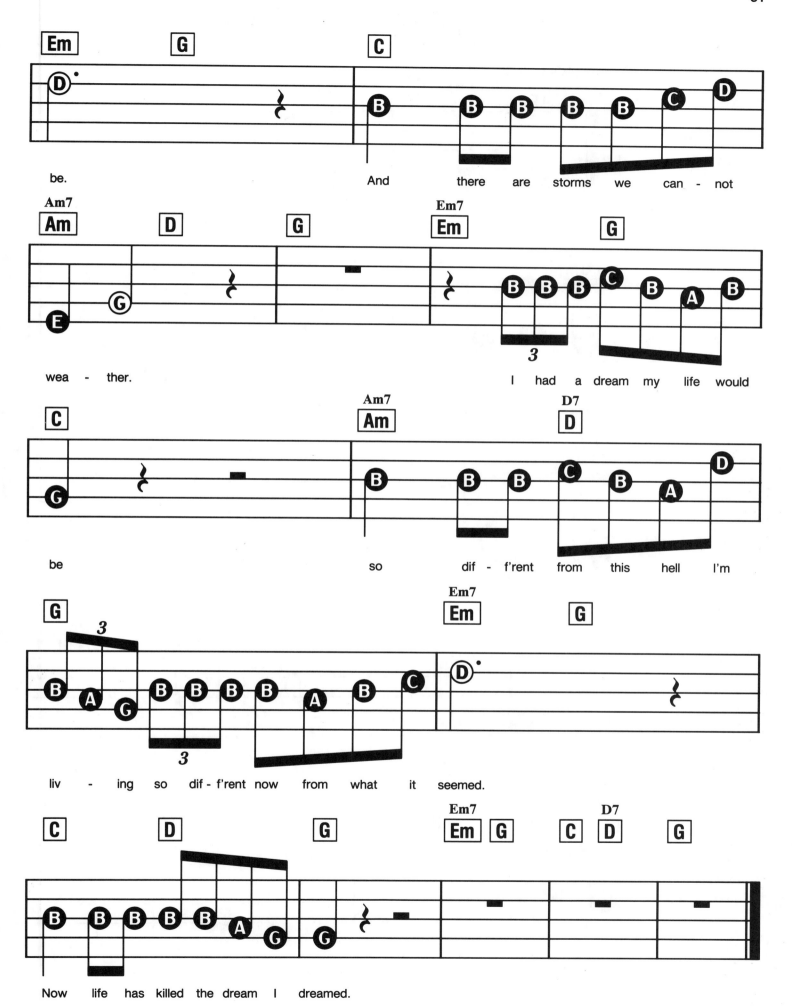

be.

And there are storms we can-not

wea - ther.

I had a dream my life would

be

so dif - f'rent from this hell I'm

liv - ing so dif - f'rent now from what it seemed.

Now life has killed the dream I dreamed.

I Got Plenty O' Nuttin'

(From "PORGY AND BESS")

Words by Ira Gershwin and DuBose Heyward
Music by George Gershwin

Registration 7
Rhythm: Fox Trot or Country Western

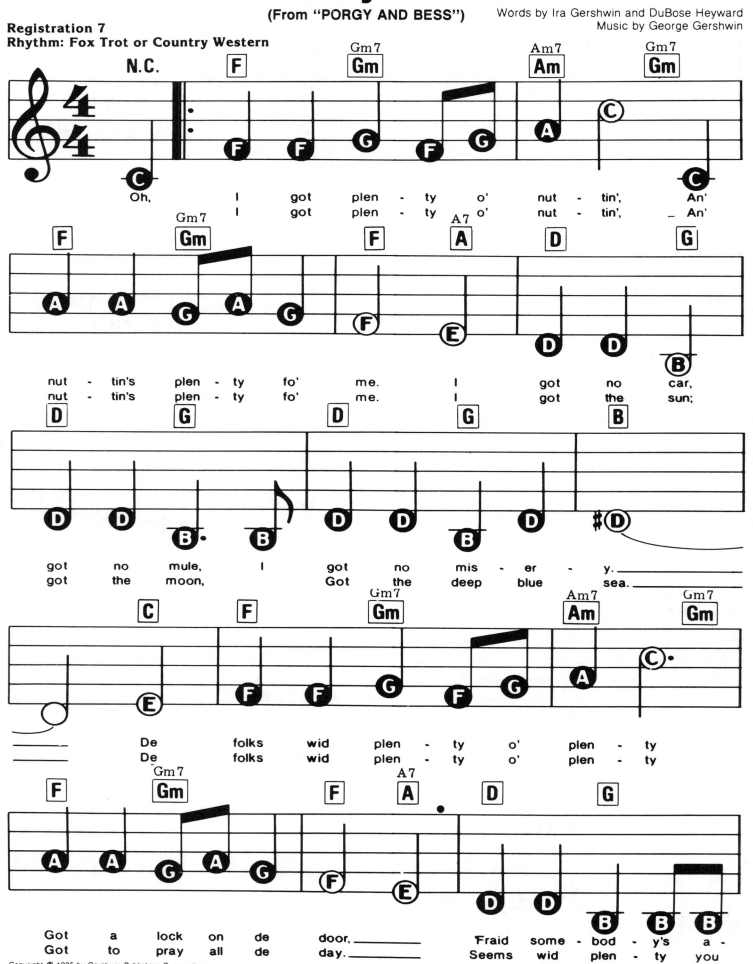

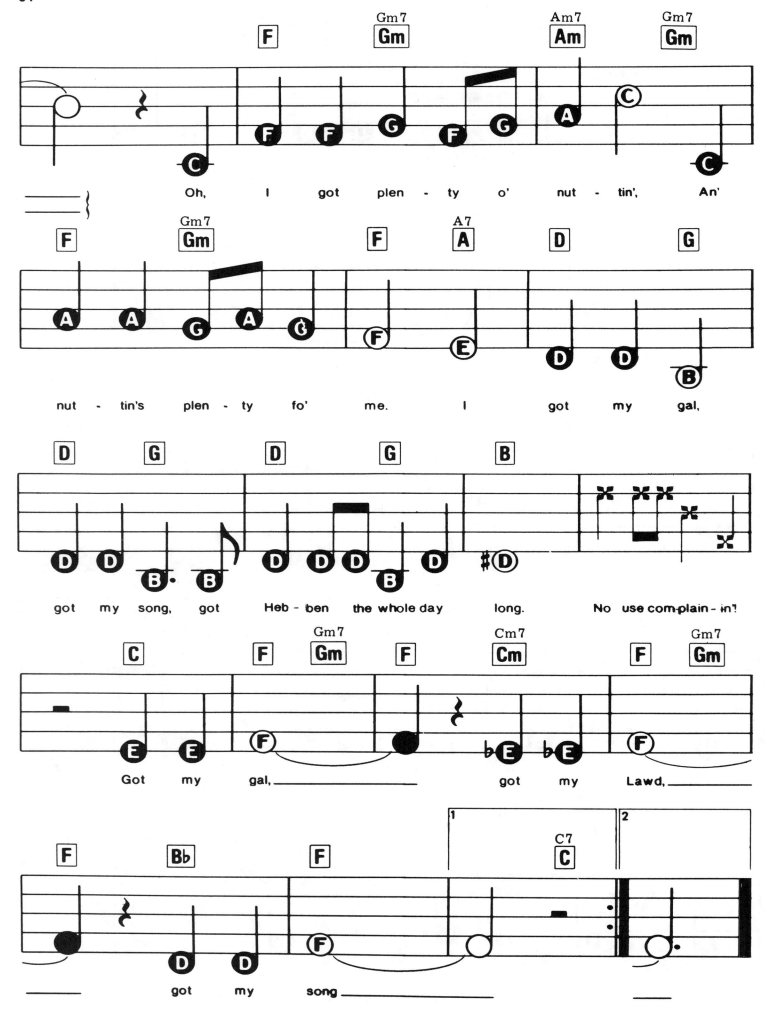

It's All Right With Me

(From "CAN CAN")

Registration 3
Rhythm: Swing or Fox Trot

Words and Music by
Cole Porter

It's the wrong time _____ and the
wrong song _____ in the
wrong game _____ with the

wrong place _____ tho' your face is charm -
wrong style _____ tho' your smile is love -
wrong chips, _____ tho' your lips are tempt -

- ing, it's the wrong face, _____ it's not
- ly, it's the wrong smile, _____ it's not
- ing, they're the wrong lips, _____ They're not

her face _____ but such a charm - ing face _____
her smile _____ but such a love - ly smile _____
her lips, _____ but they're such tempt - ing lips _____

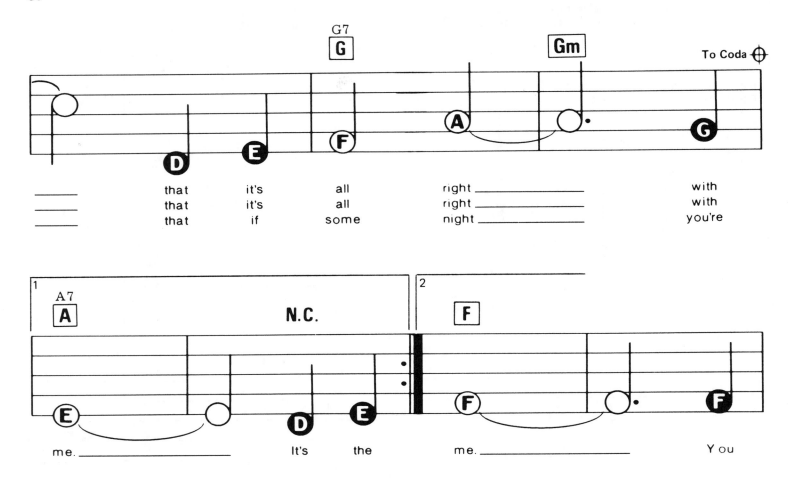

that   it's   all   right _____ with
that   it's   all   right _____ with
that   if   some   night _____ you're

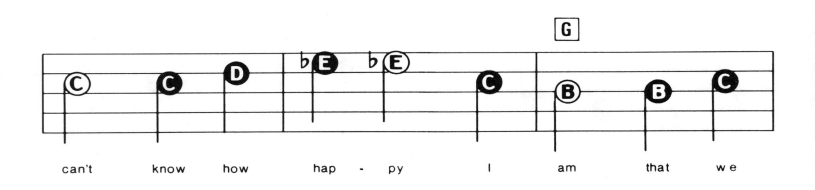

me. _____   It's   the   me. _____   You

can't   know   how   hap - py   I   am   that   we

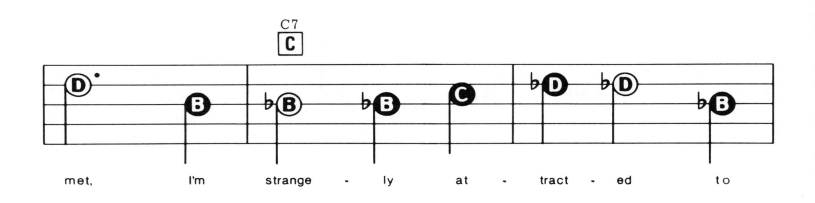

met,   I'm   strange - ly   at - tract - ed   to

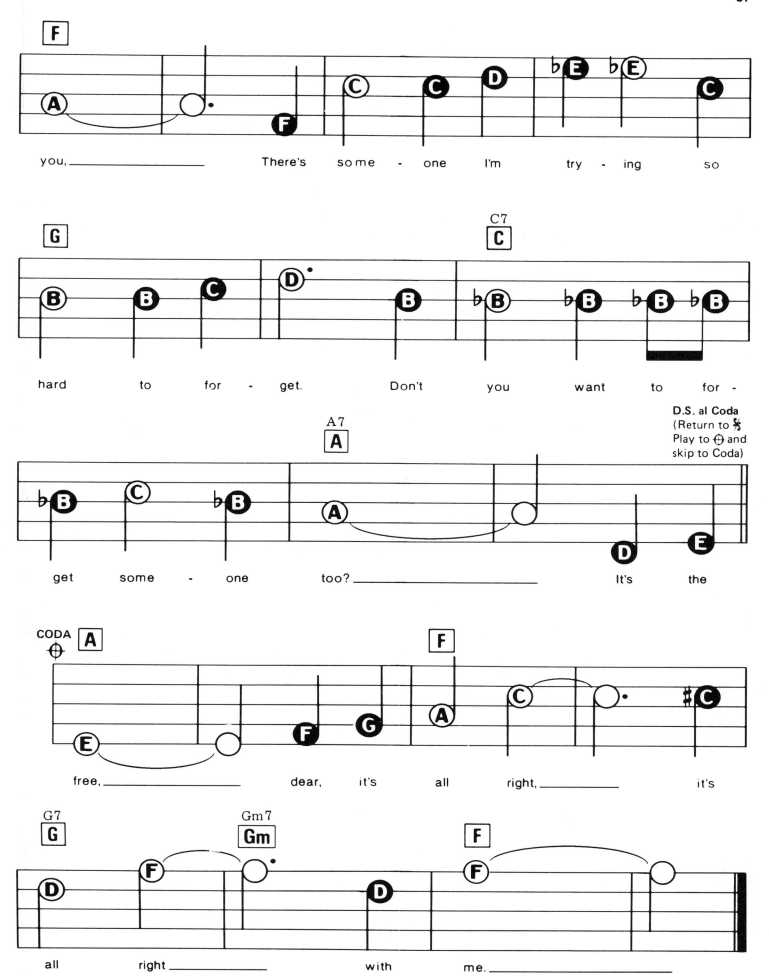

I Remember It Well

(From "GIGI")

Words by Alan Jay Lerner
Music by Frederick Loewe

Registration 1
Rhythm: Waltz

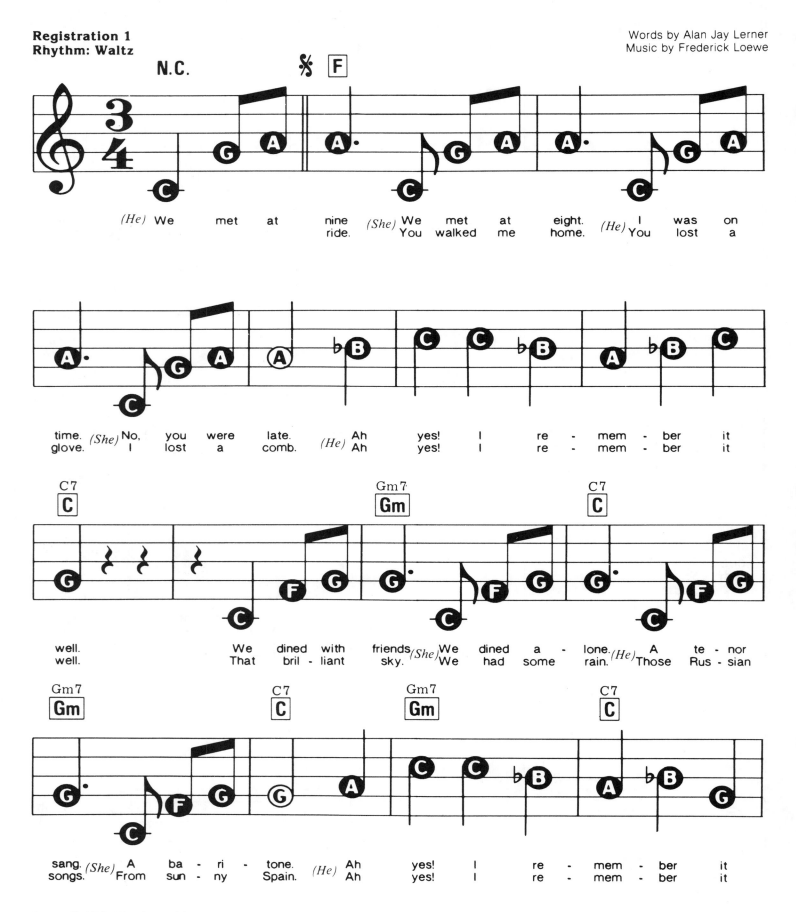

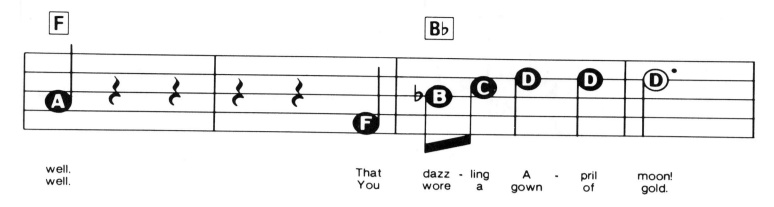

well.
well.

That dazz - ling A - pril moon!
You wore a gown of gold.

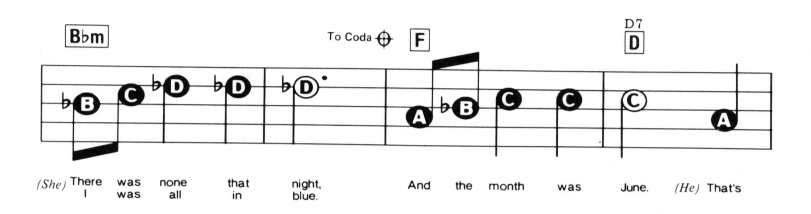

(She) There was none that night,
I was all in blue.

And the month was June. (He) That's

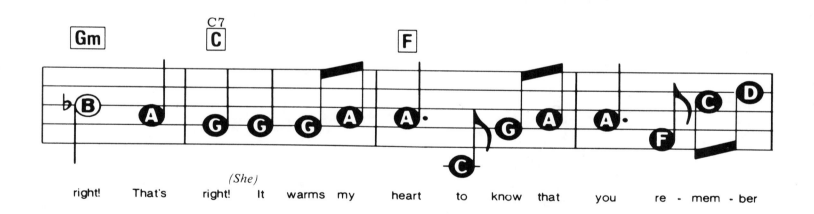

right! That's right! It warms my heart to know that you re - mem - ber

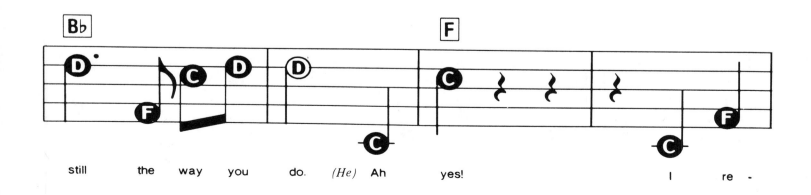

still the way you do. (He) Ah yes! I re -

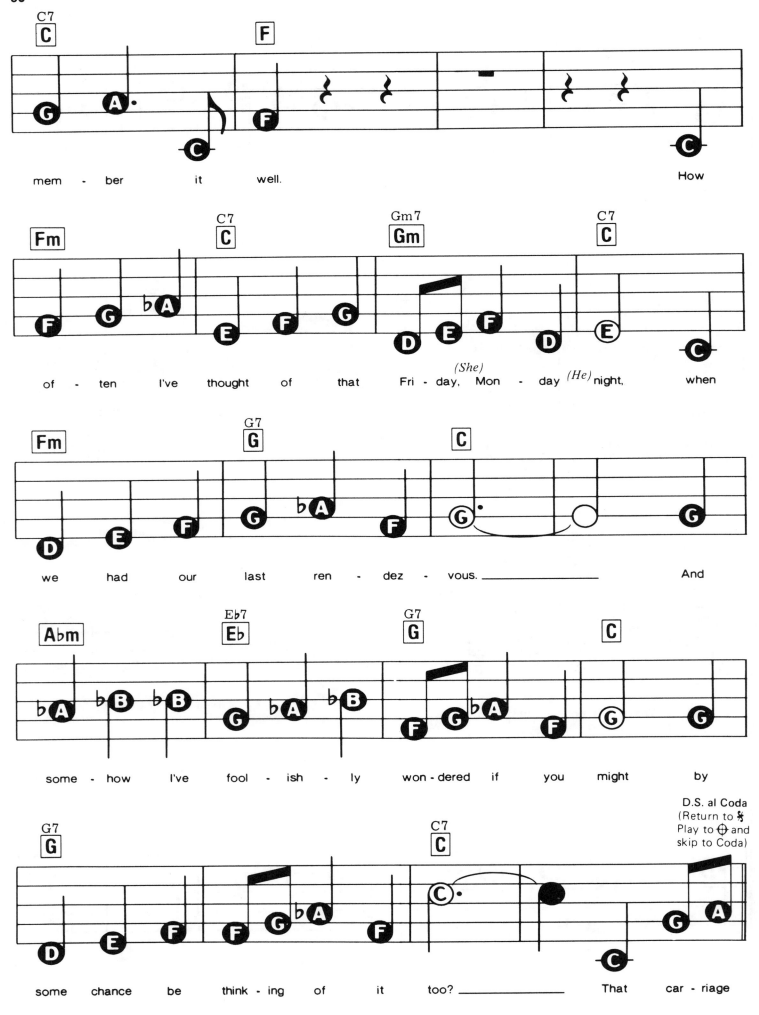

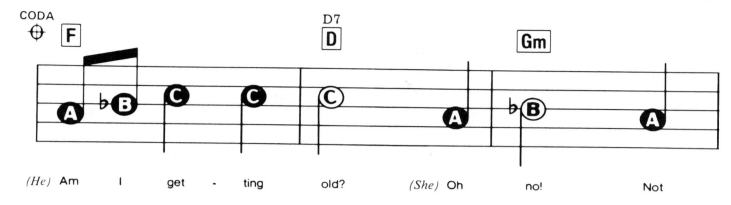

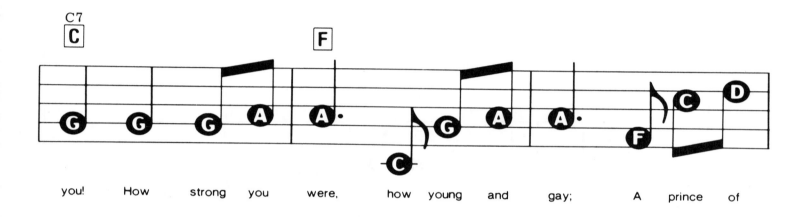

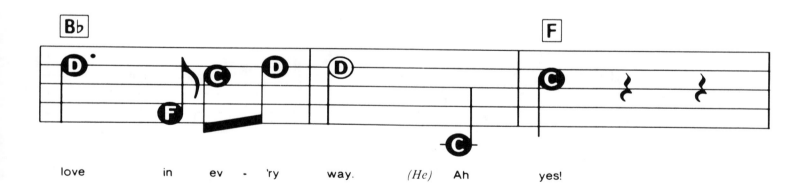

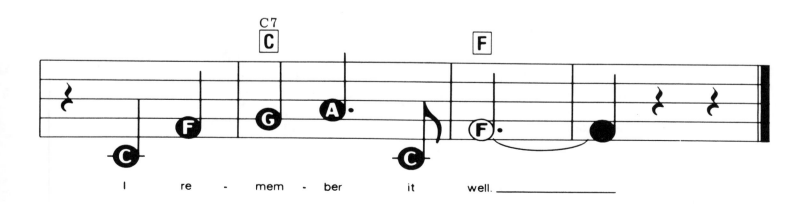

I'll Be Seeing You

(From "RIGHT THIS WAY")

Words and Music by Irving Kahal
and Sammy Fain

Registration 5
Rhythm: Ballad

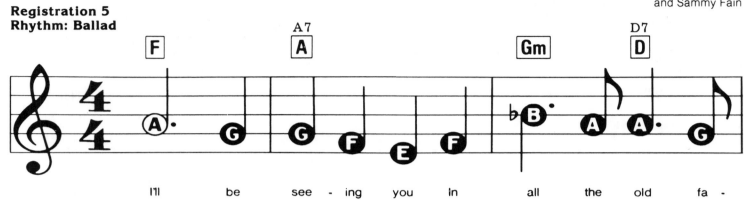

I'll be see - ing you in all the old fa -

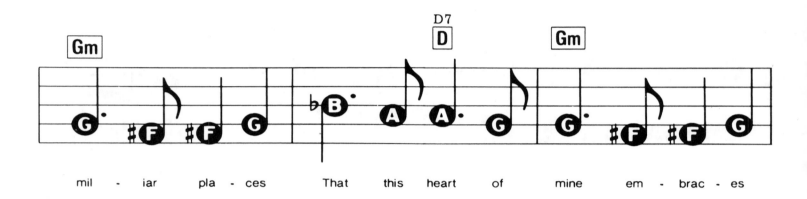

mil - iar pla - ces That this heart of mine em - brac - es

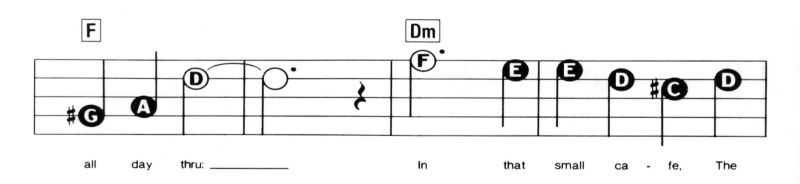

all day thru: _____ In that small ca - fe, The

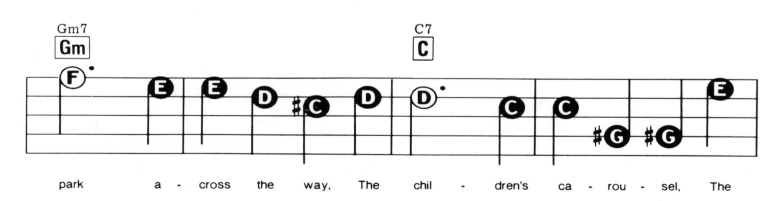

park a - cross the way, The chil - dren's ca - rou - sel, The

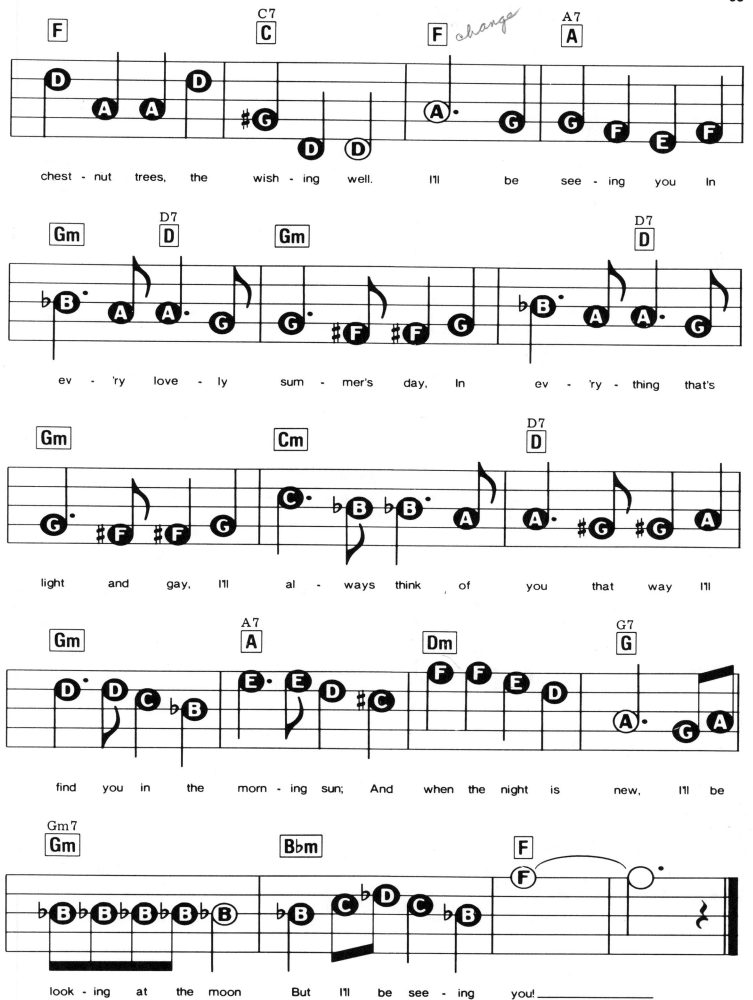

I've Grown Accustomed To Her Face

(From "MY FAIR LADY")

Registration 10
Rhythm: Fox Trot

Words by Alan Jay Lerner
Music by Frederick Loewe

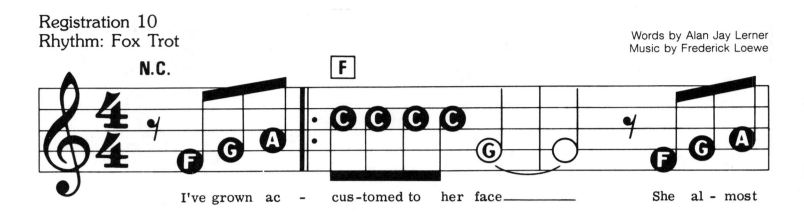

I've grown ac - cus-tomed to her face____ She al - most

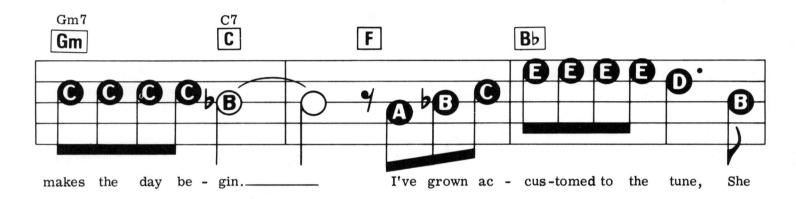

makes the day be - gin._____ I've grown ac - cus-tomed to the tune, She

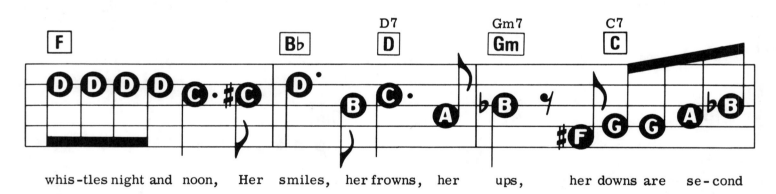

whis-tles night and noon, Her smiles, her frowns, her ups, her downs are se - cond

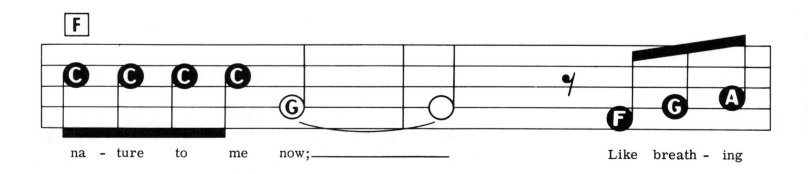

na - ture to me now;_____ Like breath - ing

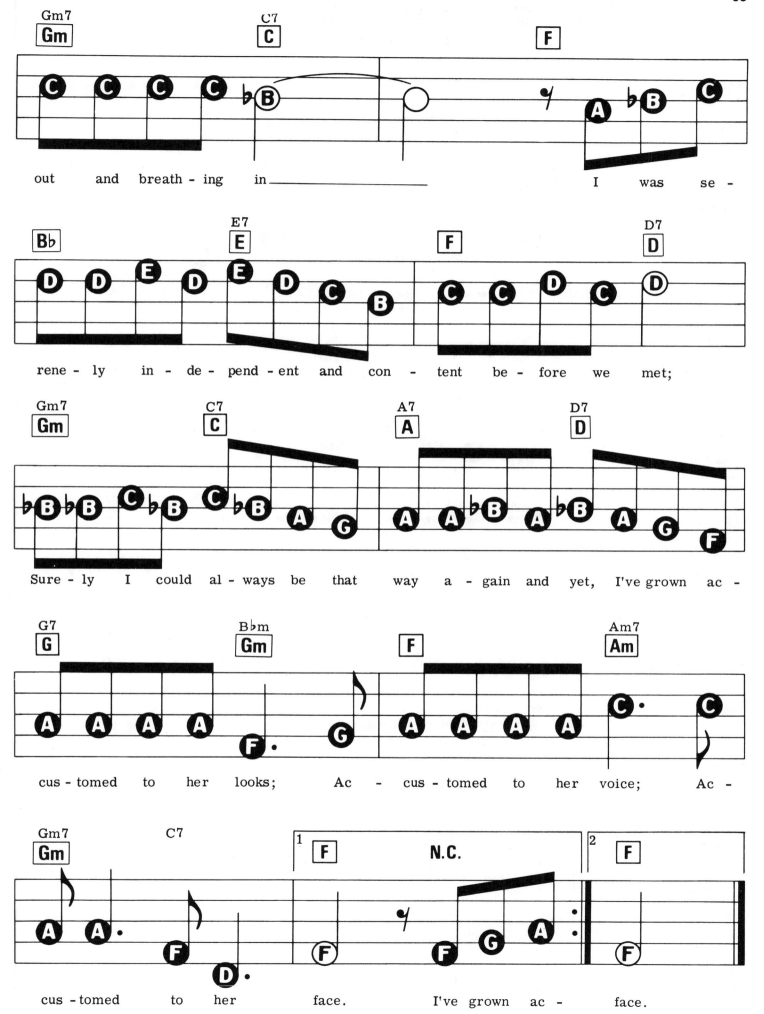

If Ever I Would Leave You

(From "CAMELOT")

Registration 5
Rhythm: Fox Trot or Ballad

Words by Alan Jay Lerner
Music by Frederick Loewe

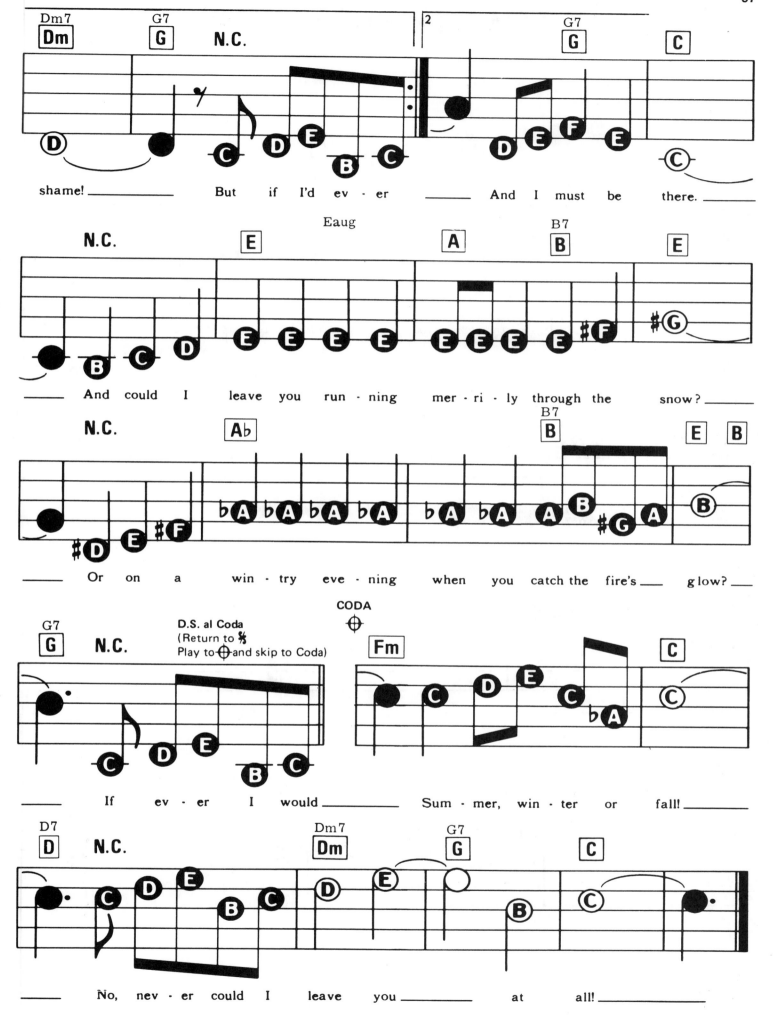

If I Loved You
(From "CAROUSEL")

Registration 2
Rhythm: Ballad

Lyrics by Oscar Hammerstein II
Music by Richard Rodgers

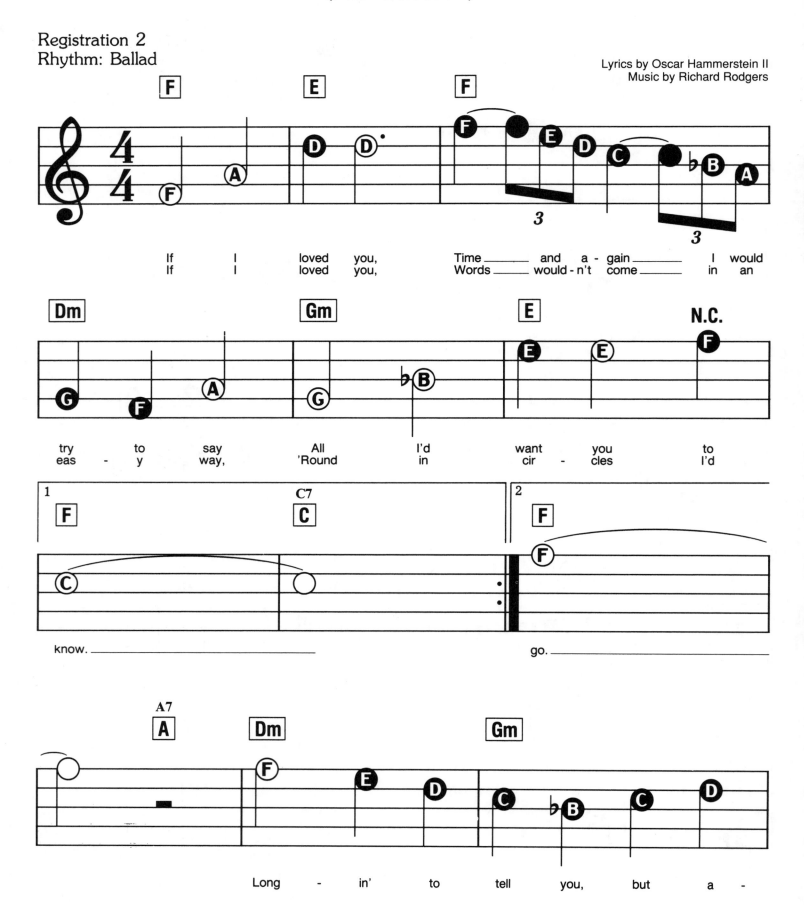

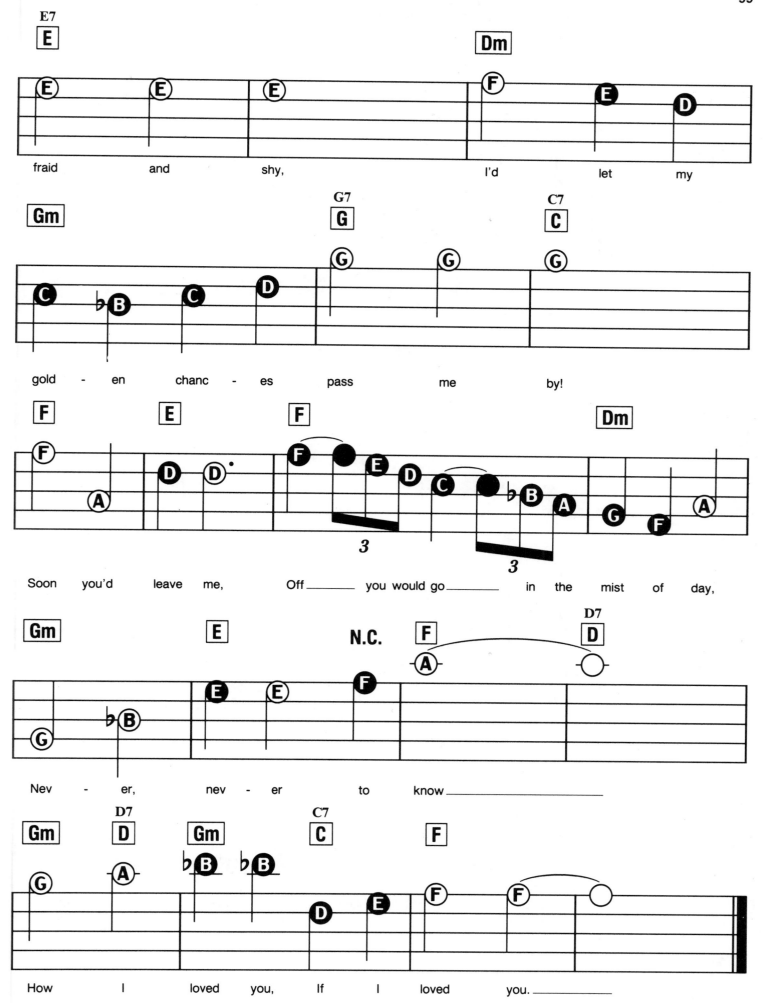

If I Ruled The World

(From "PICKWICK")

Registration 3
Rhythm: Swing

Words by Leslie Bricusse
Music by Cyril Ornadel

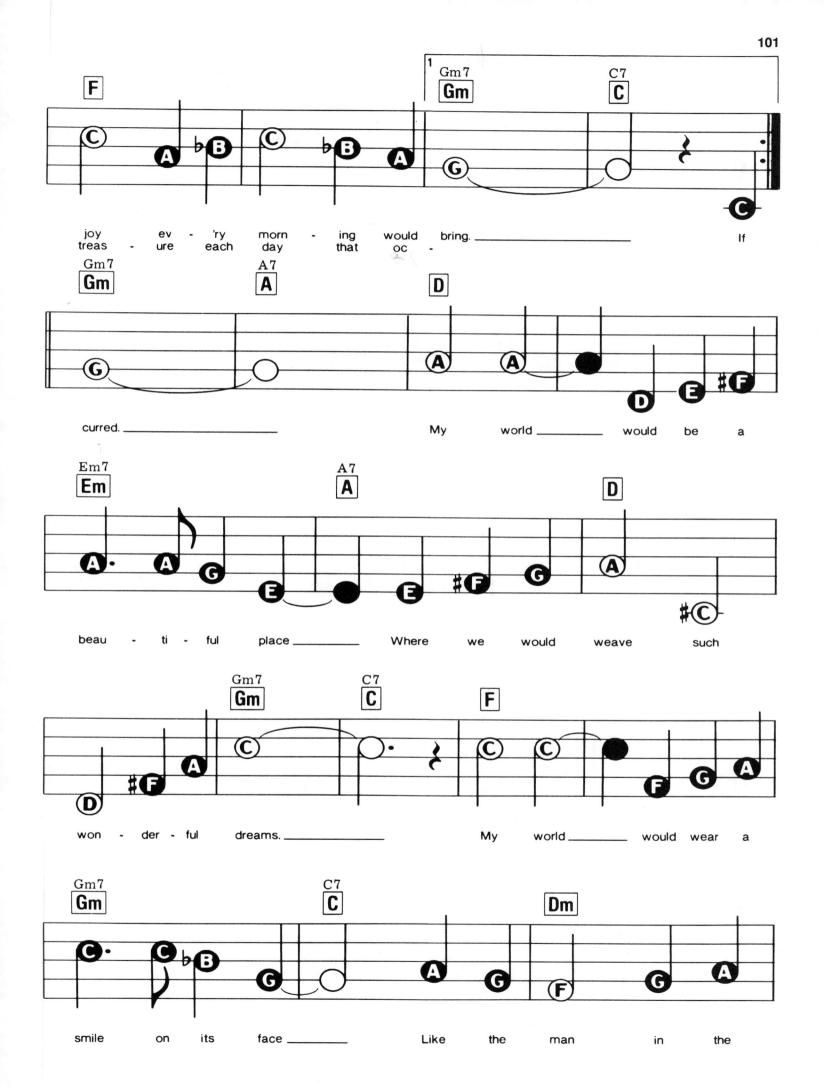

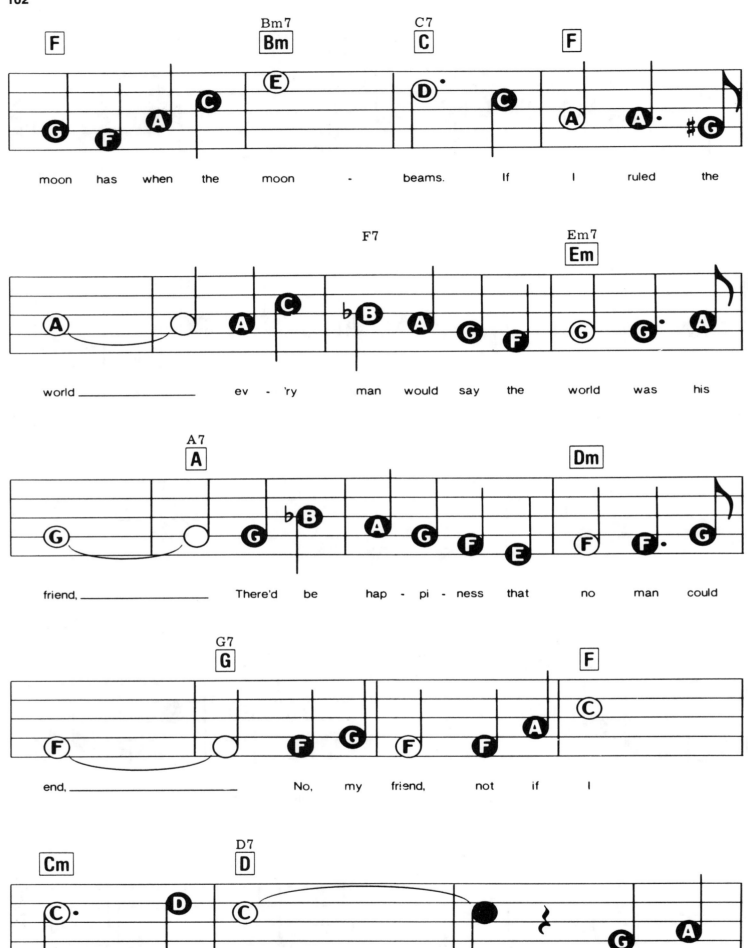

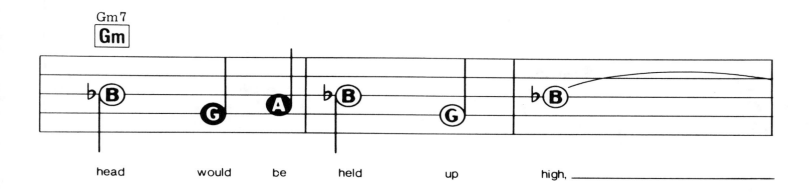

head would be held up high, _____

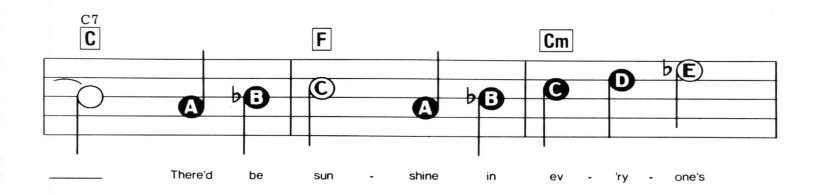

_____ There'd be sun - shine in ev - 'ry - one's

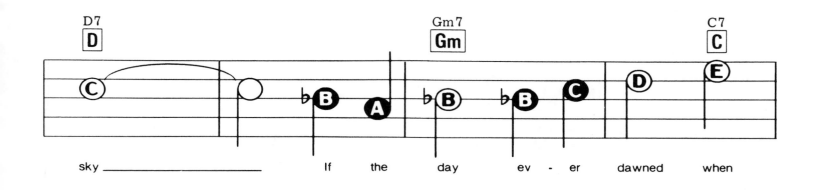

sky _____ If the day ev - er dawned when

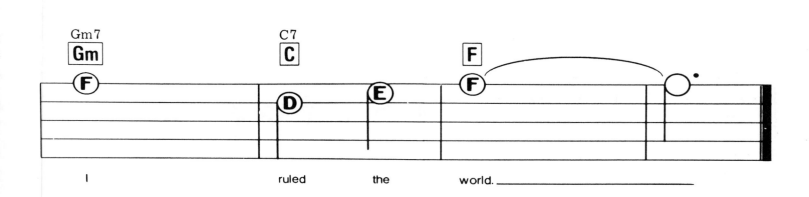

I ruled the world. _____

If I Were A Rich Man

(From the Musical "FIDDLER ON THE ROOF")

Words by Sheldon Harnick
Music by Jerry Bock

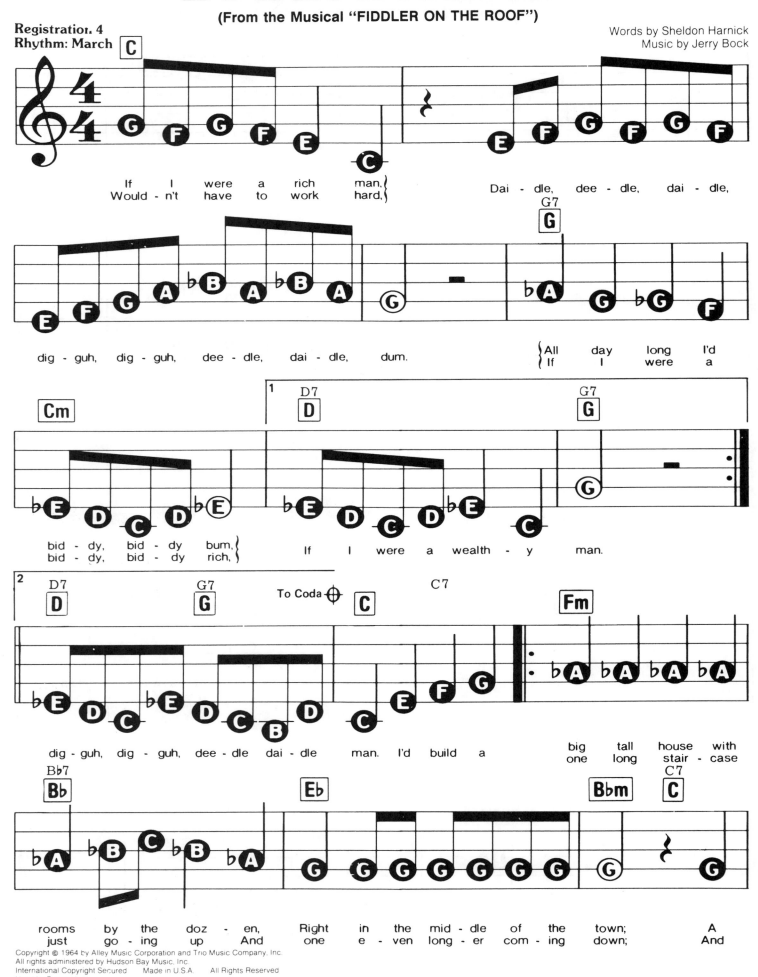

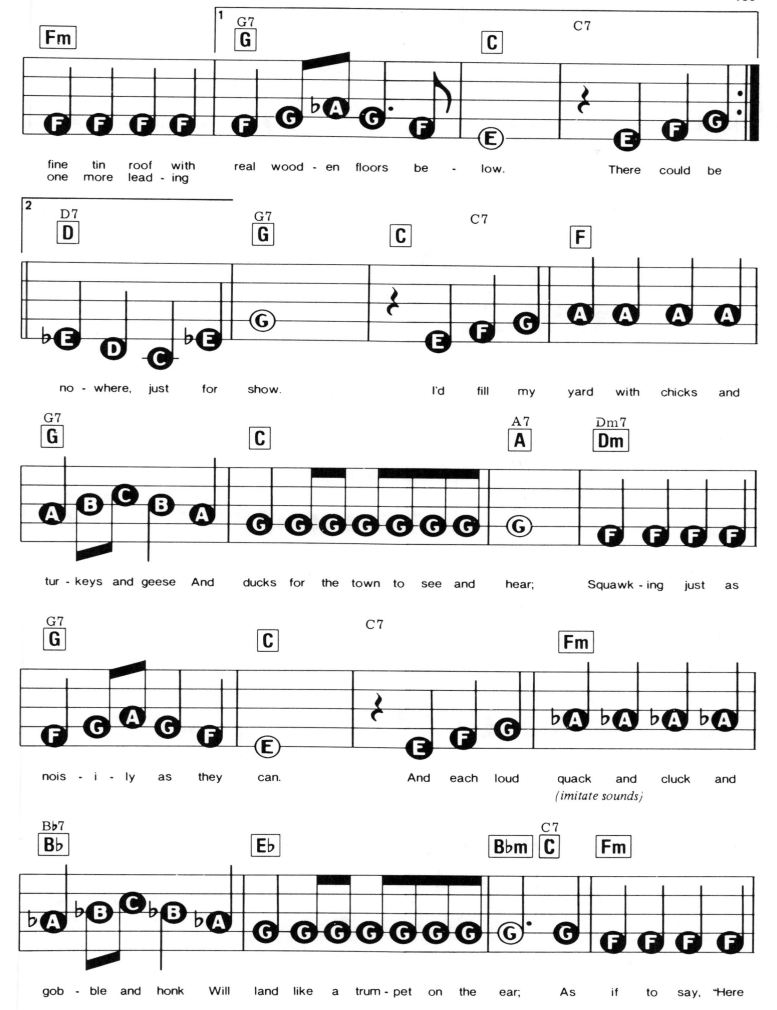

D.C. al Coda
(Return to beginning
Play to ⊕ and skip
to Coda)

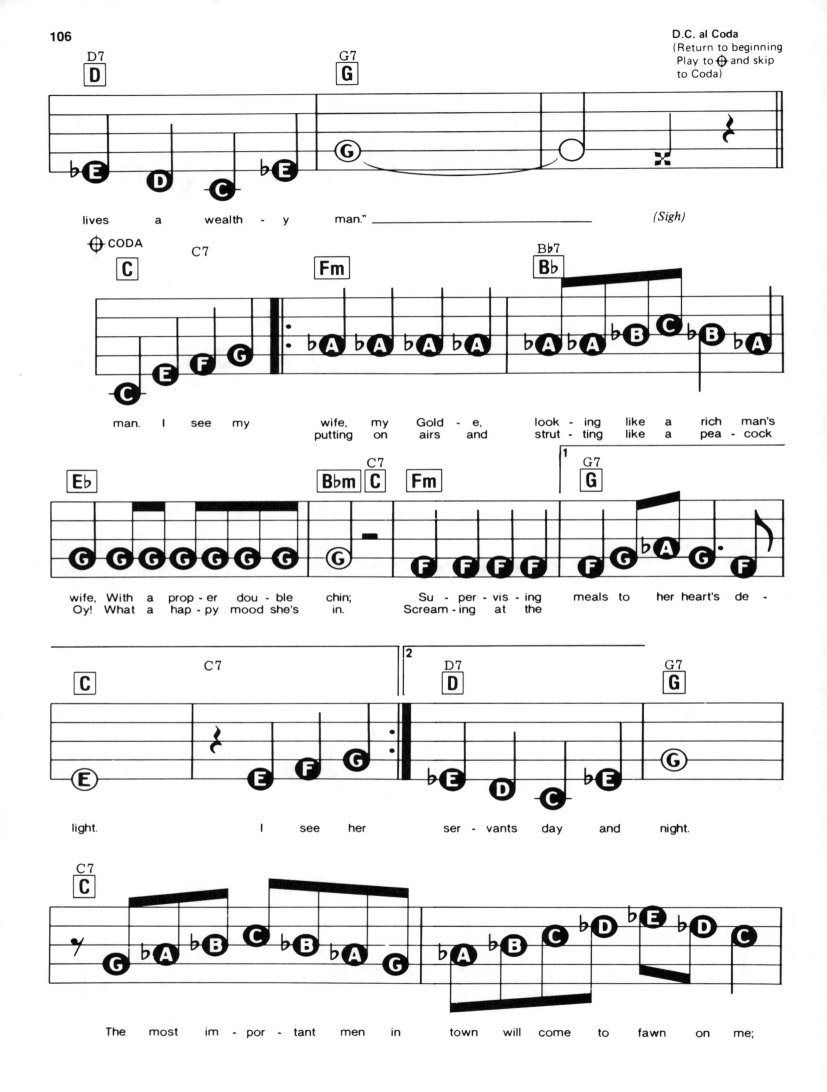

lives   a   wealth - y   man."   _____   *(Sigh)*

⊕ CODA

man.   I   see   my   wife,   my   Gold - e,   look - ing   like   a   rich   man's
putting   on   airs   and   strut - ting   like   a   pea - cock

wife,   With   a   prop - er   dou - ble   chin;   Su - per - vis - ing   meals   to   her   heart's   de -
Oy!   What   a   hap - py   mood   she's   in.   Scream - ing   at   the

light.   I   see   her   ser - vants   day   and   night.

The   most   im - por - tant   men   in   town   will   come   to   fawn   on   me;

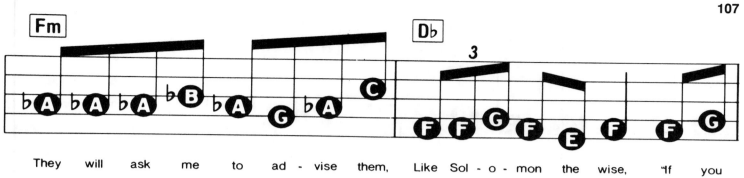

They will ask me to ad - vise them, Like Sol - o - mon the wise, "If you

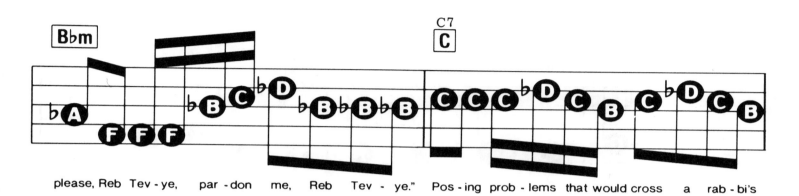

please, Reb Tev - ye, par - don me, Reb Tev - ye." Pos - ing prob - lems that would cross a rab - bi's

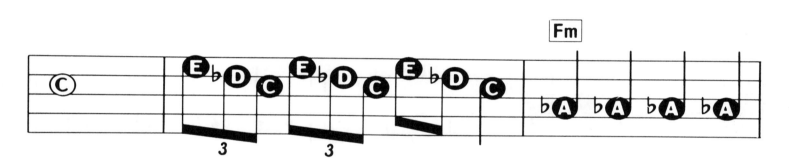

eyes. Boi, boi, boi. boi, boi, boi, boi, boi, boi. And it won't make

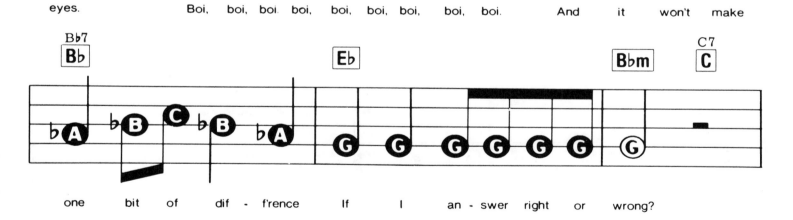

one bit of dif - f'rence If I an - swer right or wrong?

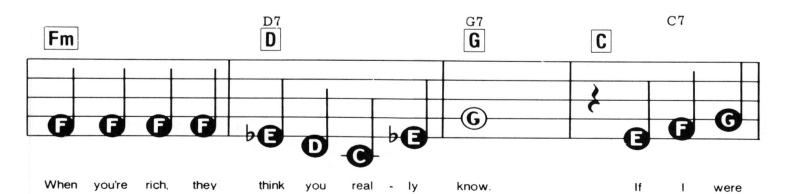

When you're rich, they think you real - ly know. If I were

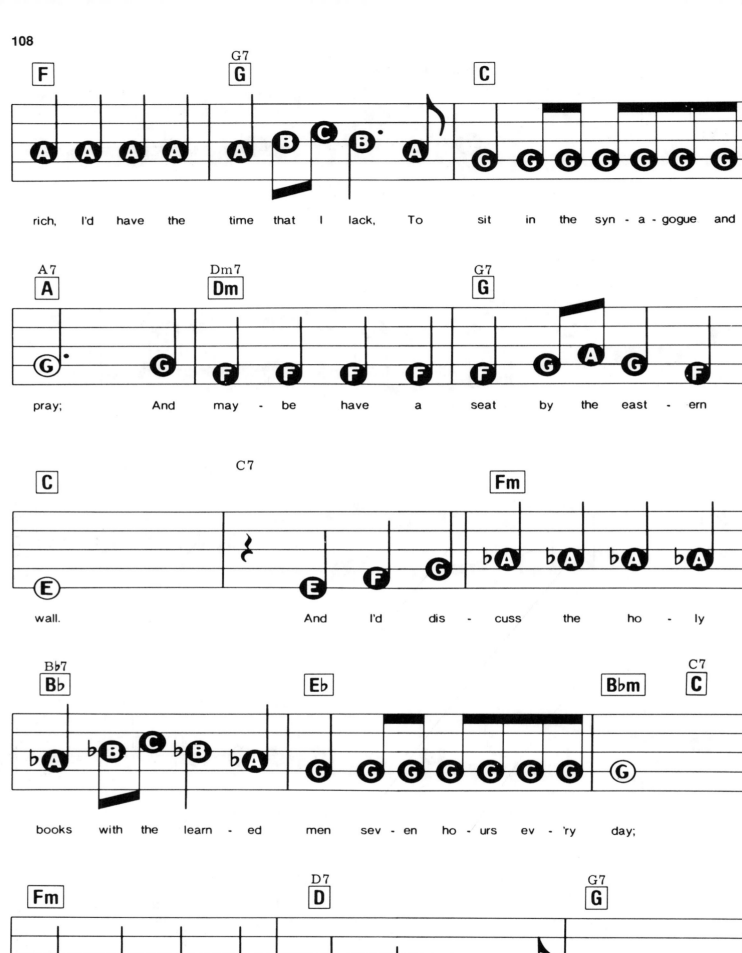

rich, I'd have the time that I lack, To sit in the syn-a-gogue and

pray; And may-be have a seat by the east-ern

wall. And I'd dis-cuss the ho-ly

books with the learn-ed men sev-en ho-urs ev-'ry day;

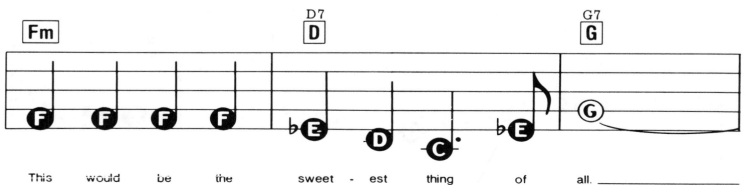

This would be the sweet-est thing of all. _____

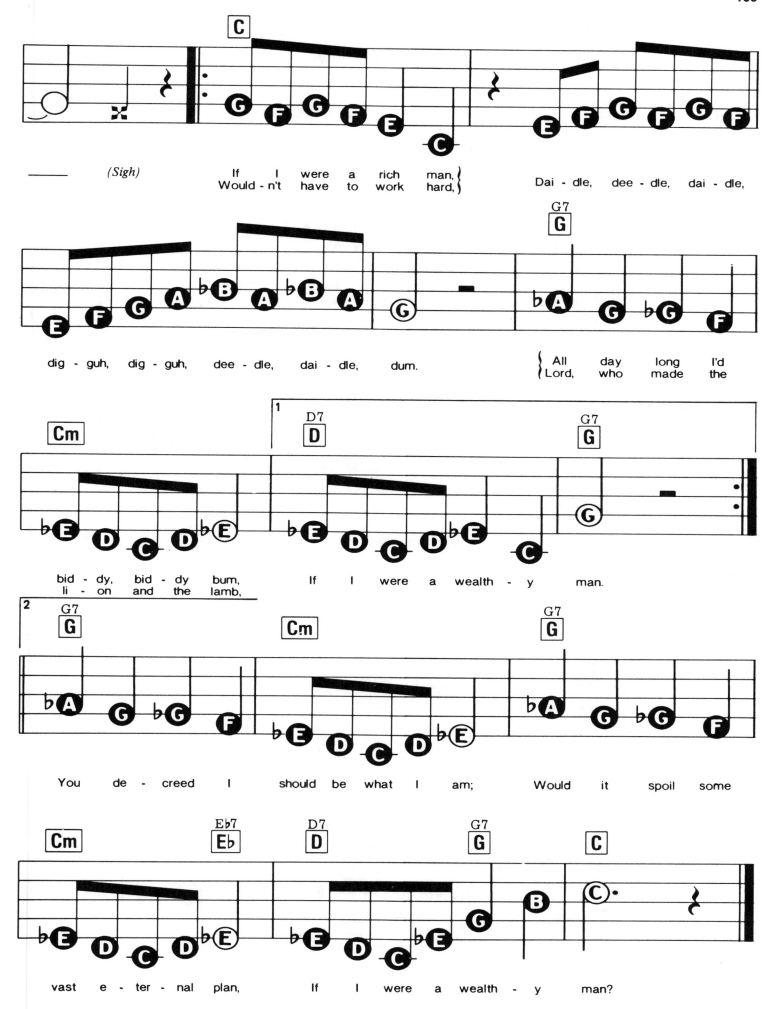

It Might As Well Be Spring

(From "STATE FAIR")

Lyrics by Oscar Hammerstein II
Music by Richard Rodgers

Registration 3
Rhythm: Ballad

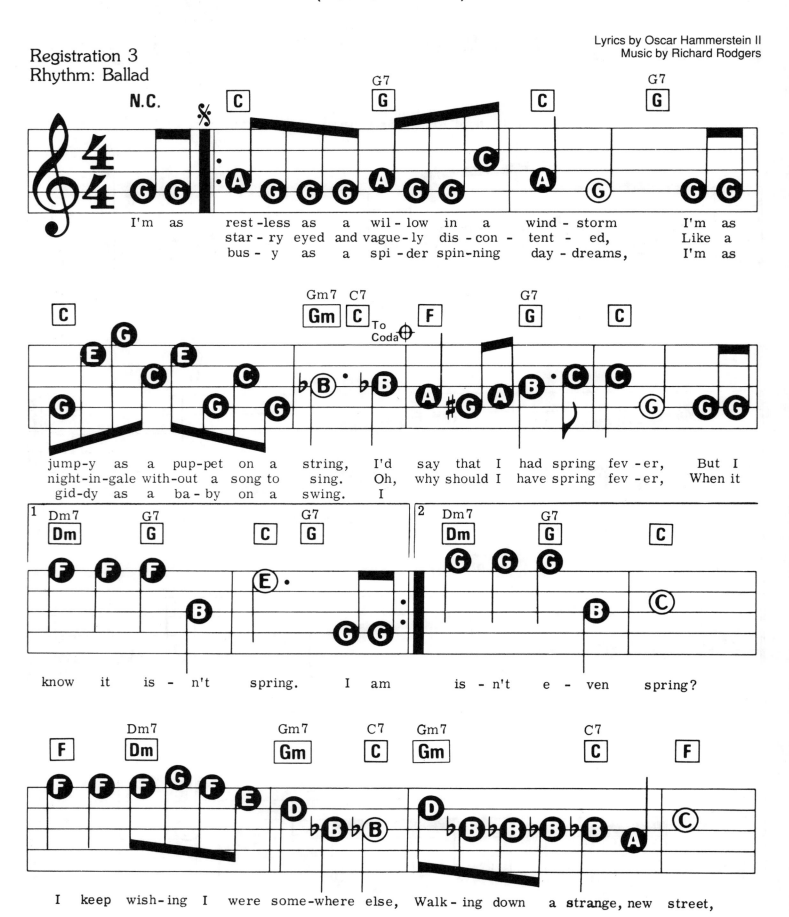

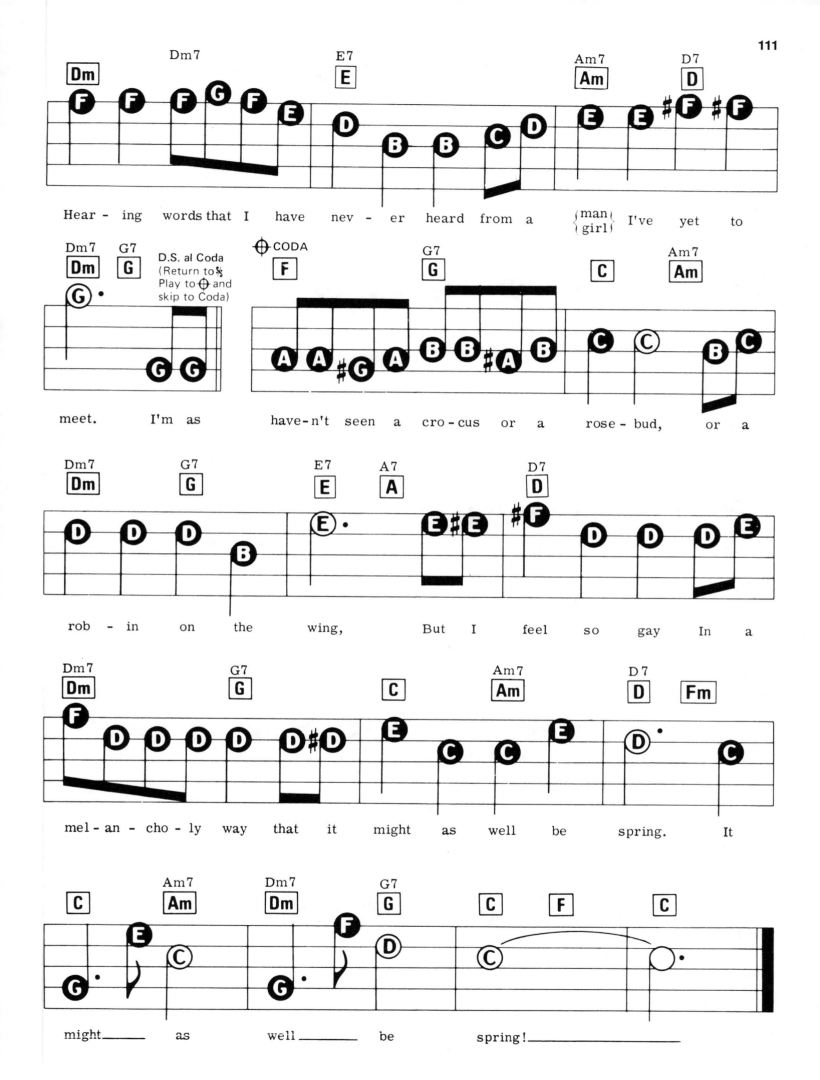

Just In Time

(From "BELLS ARE RINGING")

Words by Betty Comden
and Adolph Green
Music by Jule Styne

Registration 2
Rhythm: Latin

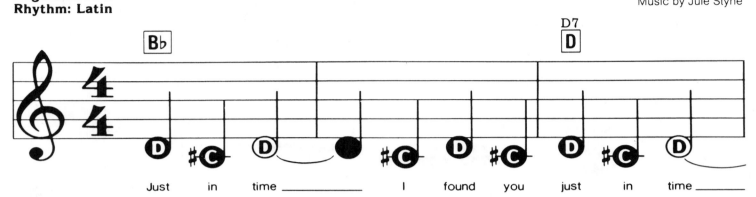

Just in time _____ I found you just in time _____

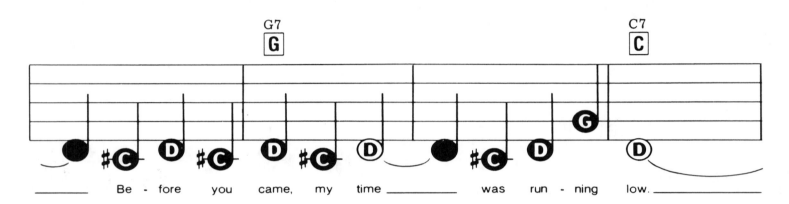

_____ Be - fore you came, my time _____ was run - ning low. _____

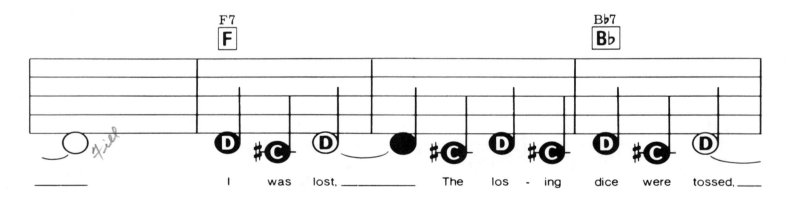

_____ I was lost, _____ The los - ing dice were tossed, _____

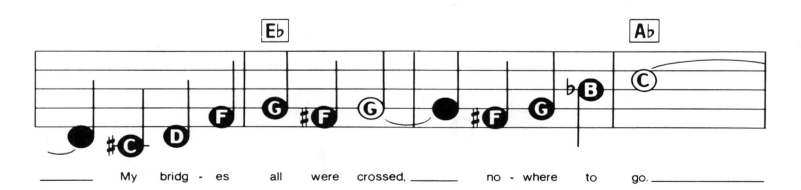

_____ My bridg - es all were crossed, _____ no - where to go. _____

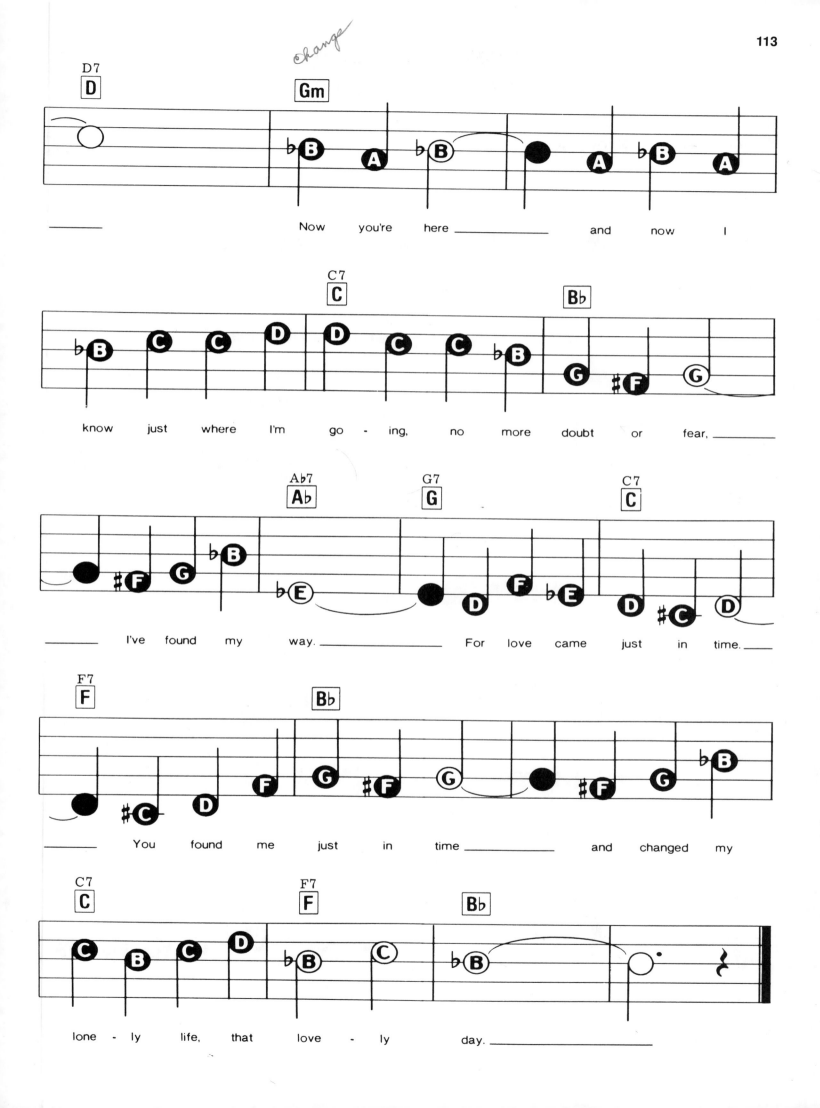

The Lady Is A Tramp

(From "BABES IN ARMS")

Registration 7
Rhythm: Fox Trot or Swing

Words by Lorenz Hart
Music by Richard Rodgers

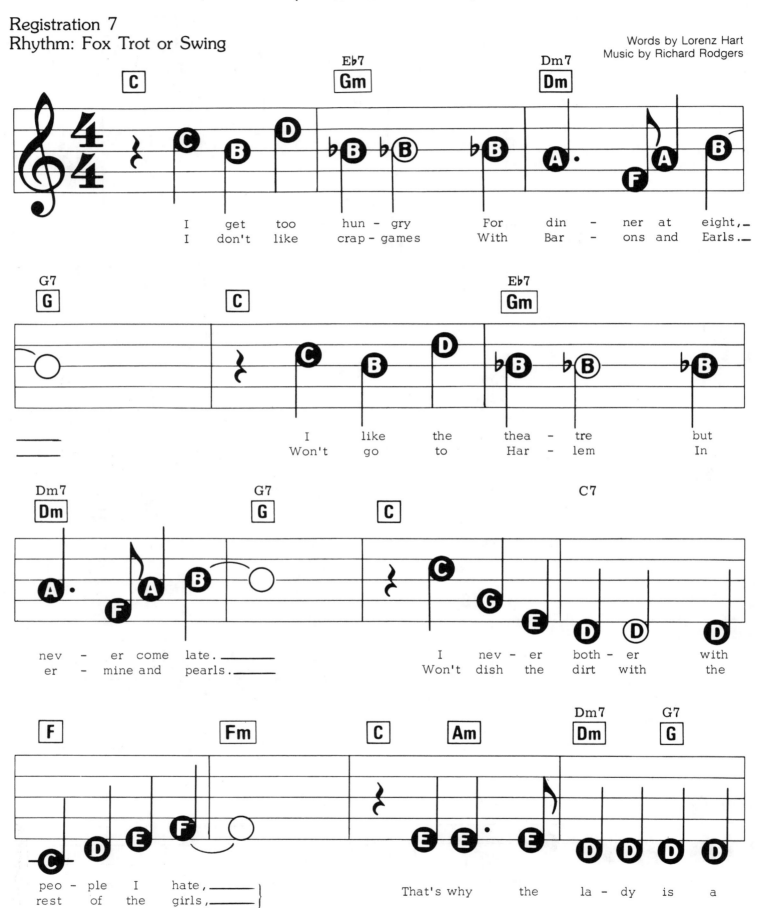

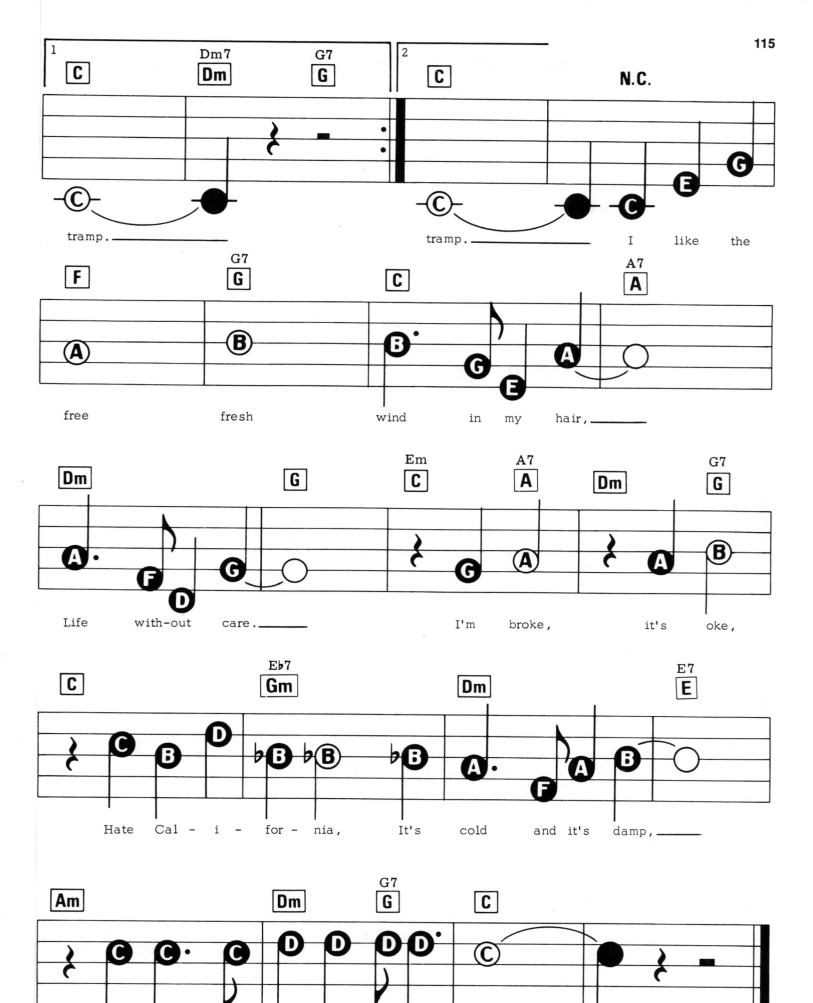

The Last Night Of The World

(From "MISS SAIGON")

Music by Claude-Michel Schonberg
Lyrics by Richard Maltby Jr. & Alain Boublil
Adapted from original French Lyrics by Alain Boublil

Registration 4
Rhythm: Rock or 8 Beat

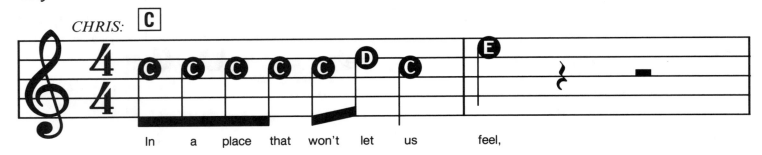

CHRIS: **C**

In a place that won't let us feel,

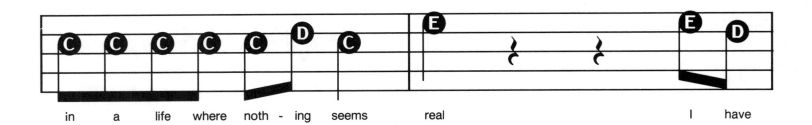

in a life where noth-ing seems real   I have

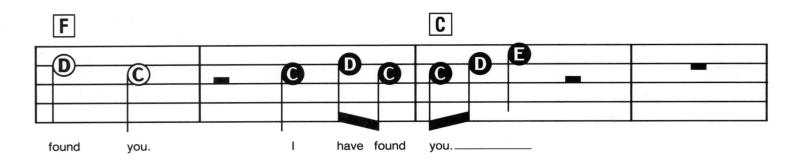

F   **C**

found you.   I have found you.____

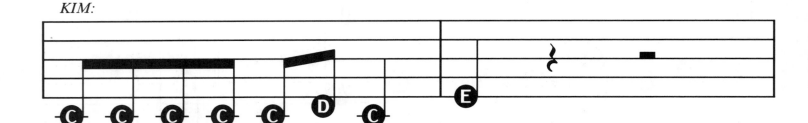

KIM:

In a world that's mov-ing too   fast,

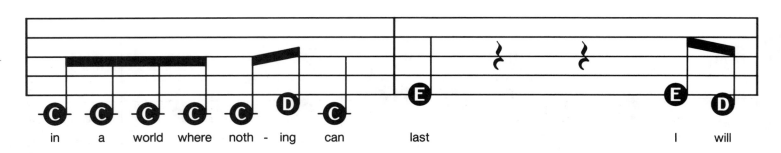

in a world where noth-ing can   last   I will

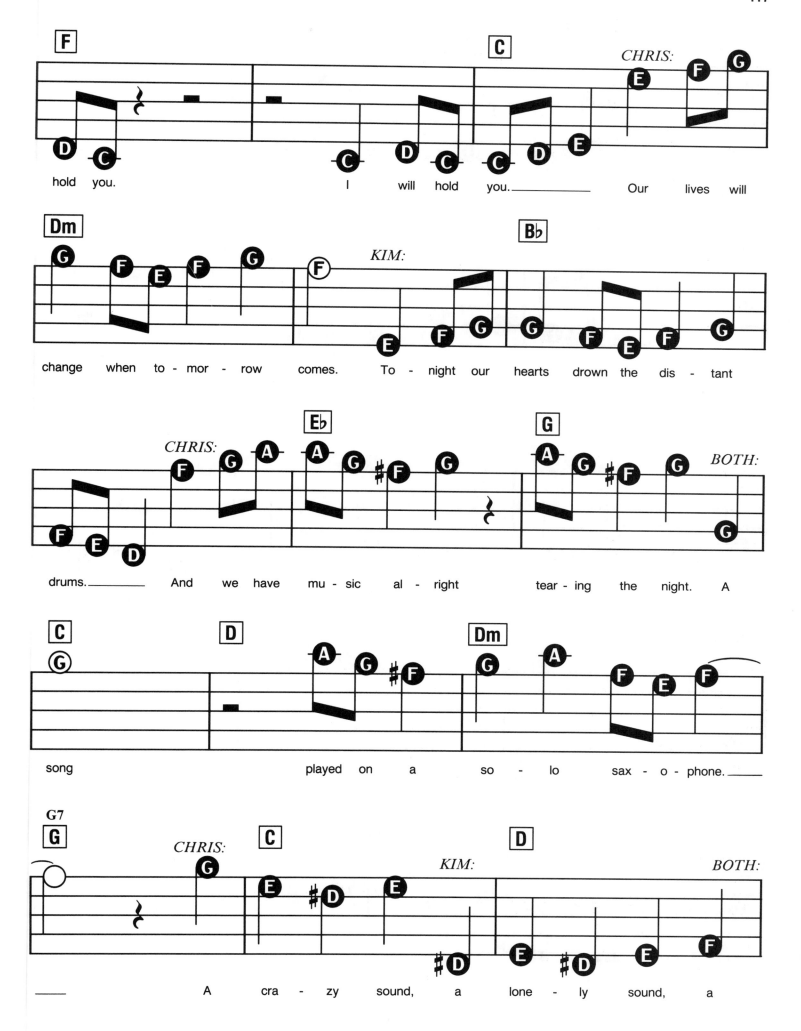

117

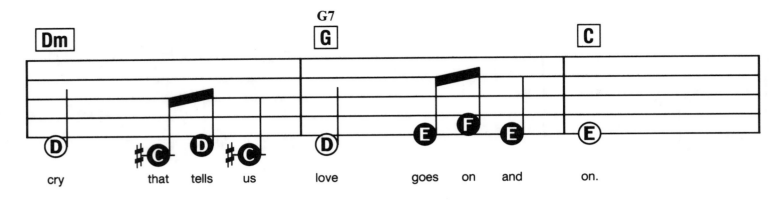

cry   that tells us   love   goes on and   on.

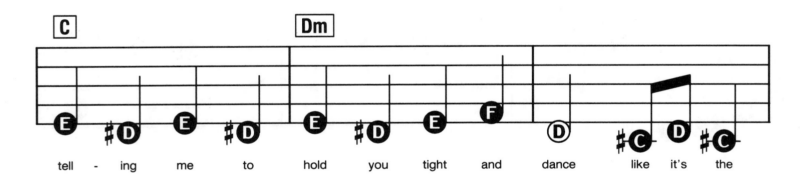

Played   on   a   so - lo   sax - o - phone,_____   it's

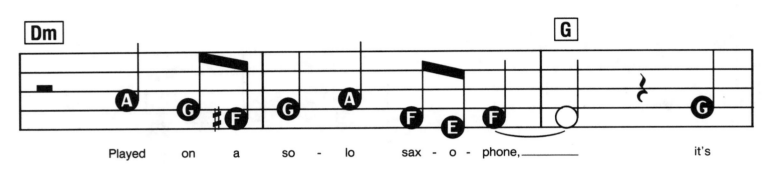

tell - ing   me   to   hold   you   tight   and   dance   like   it's   the

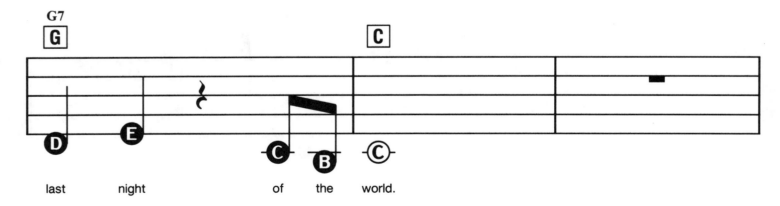

last   night   of   the   world.

CHRIS:

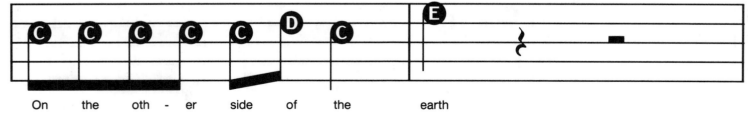

On   the   oth - er   side   of   the   earth

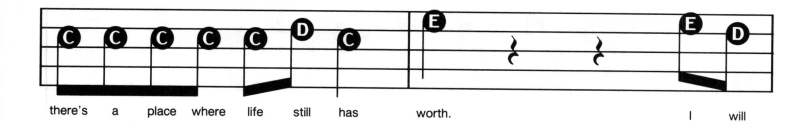

there's a place where life still has worth. I will

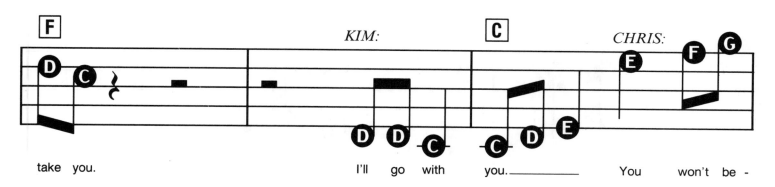

take you. *KIM:* I'll go with you._____ *CHRIS:* You won't be -

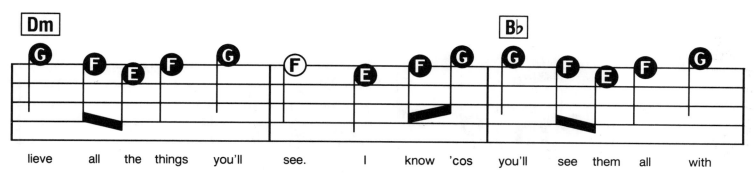

lieve all the things you'll see. I know 'cos you'll see them all with

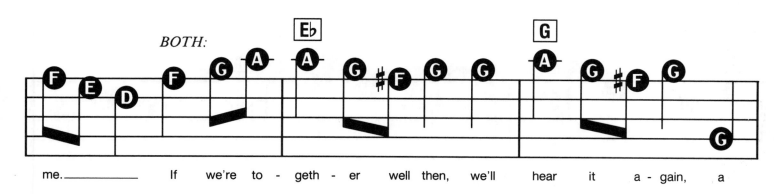

BOTH: me._____ If we're to - geth - er well then, we'll hear it a - gain, a

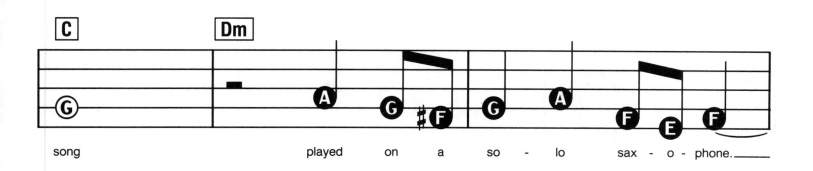

song played on a so - lo sax - o - phone._____

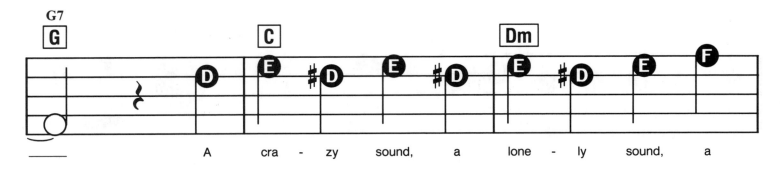

A cra - zy sound, a lone - ly sound, a

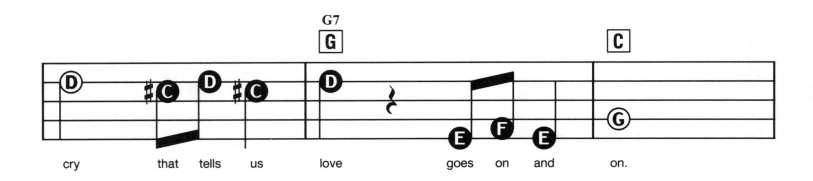

cry that tells us love goes on and on.

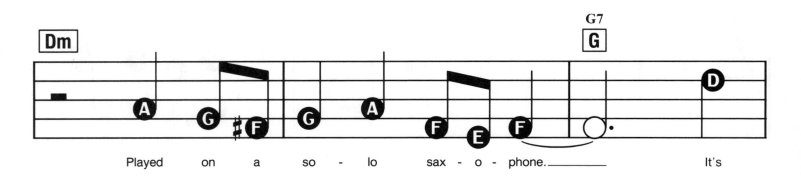

Played on a so - lo sax - o - phone._____ It's

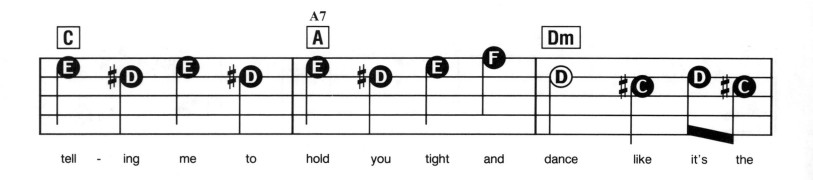

tell - ing me to hold you tight and dance like it's the

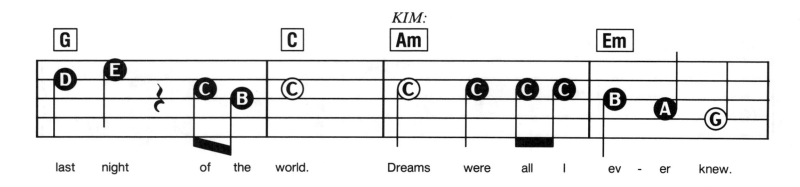

KIM:

last night of the world. Dreams were all I ev - er knew.

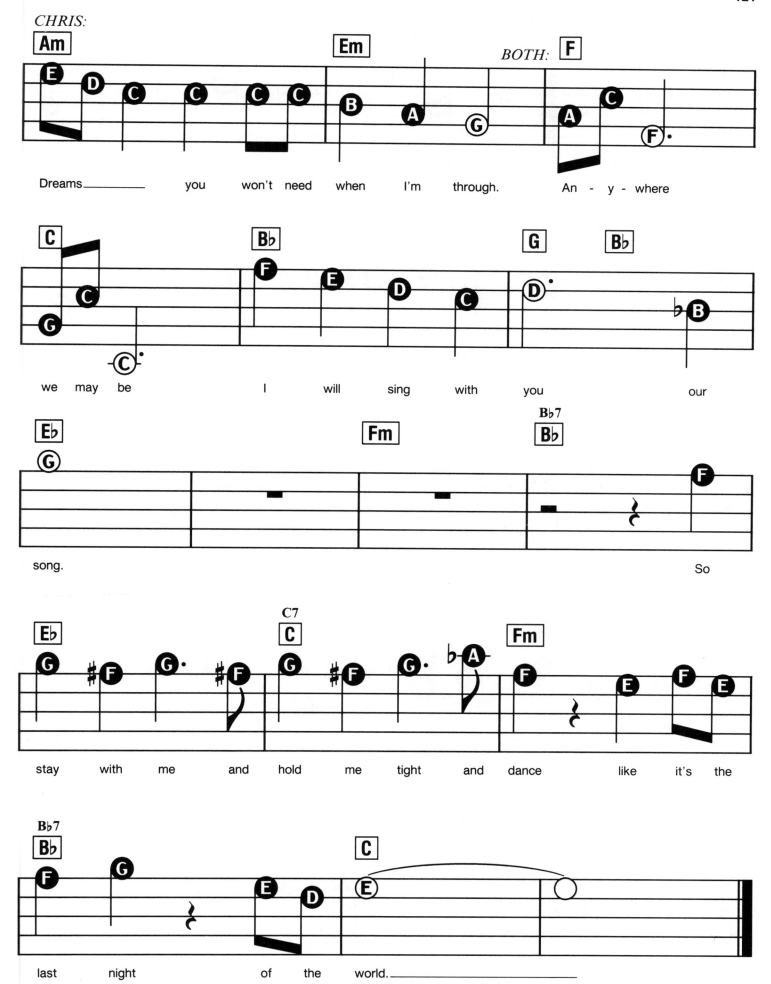

Look To The Rainbow

Registration 2
Rhythm: Waltz

(From "FINIAN'S RAINBOW")

Words by E.Y. Harburg
Music by Burton Lane

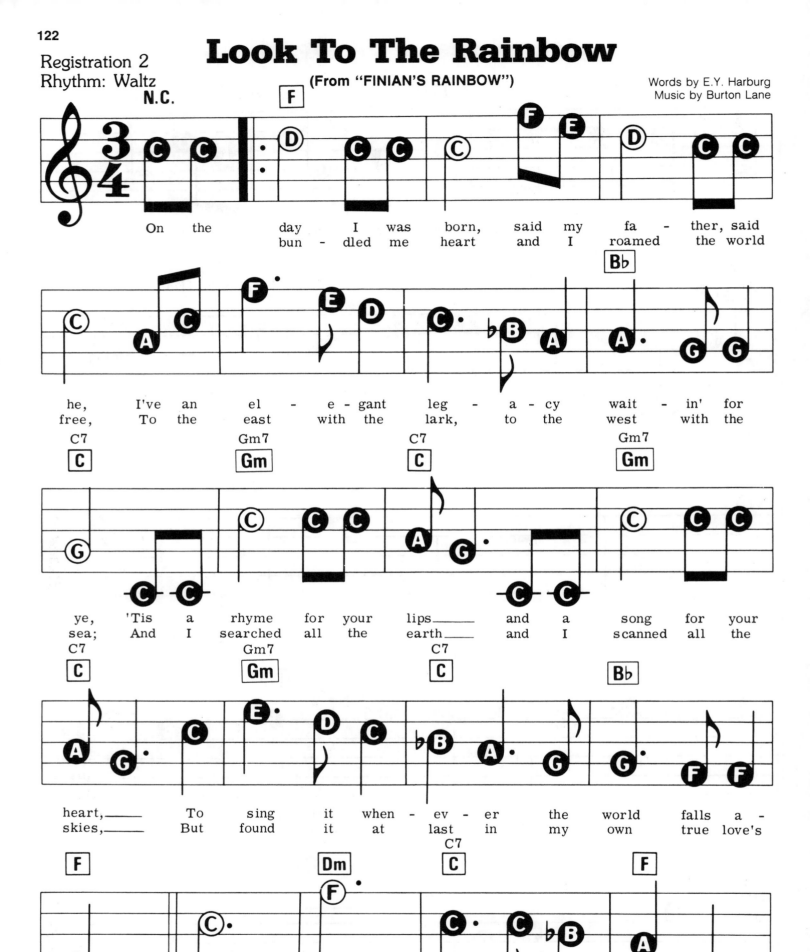

On the day I was born, said my fa - ther, said
bun - dled me heart and I roamed the world

he, I've an el - e - gant leg - a - cy wait - in' for
free, To the east with the lark, to the west with the

ye, 'Tis a rhyme for your lips_____ and a song for your
sea; And I searched all the earth_____ and I scanned all the

heart,_____ To sing it when - ev - er the world falls a -
skies,_____ But I found it at last in my own true love's

part. }
eyes. } Look, look, look to the rain - bow,

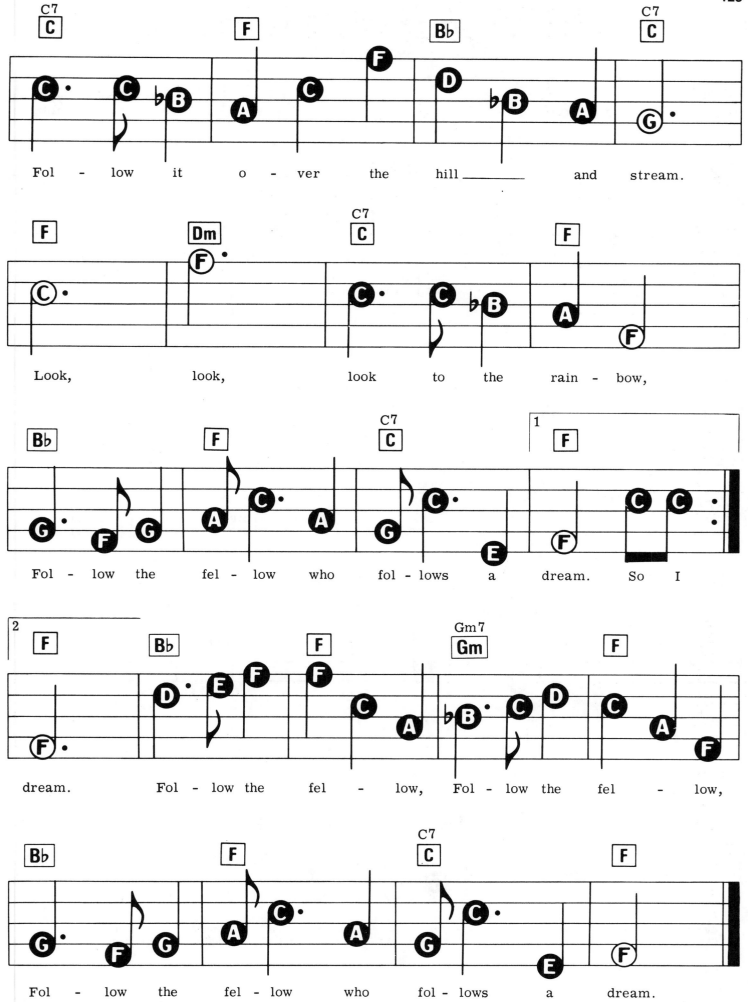

Love Changes Everything

(From "ASPECTS OF LOVE")

Registration 2
Rhythm: Rock or 8 Beat

Music by Andrew Lloyd Webber
Lyrics by Don Black and Charles Hart

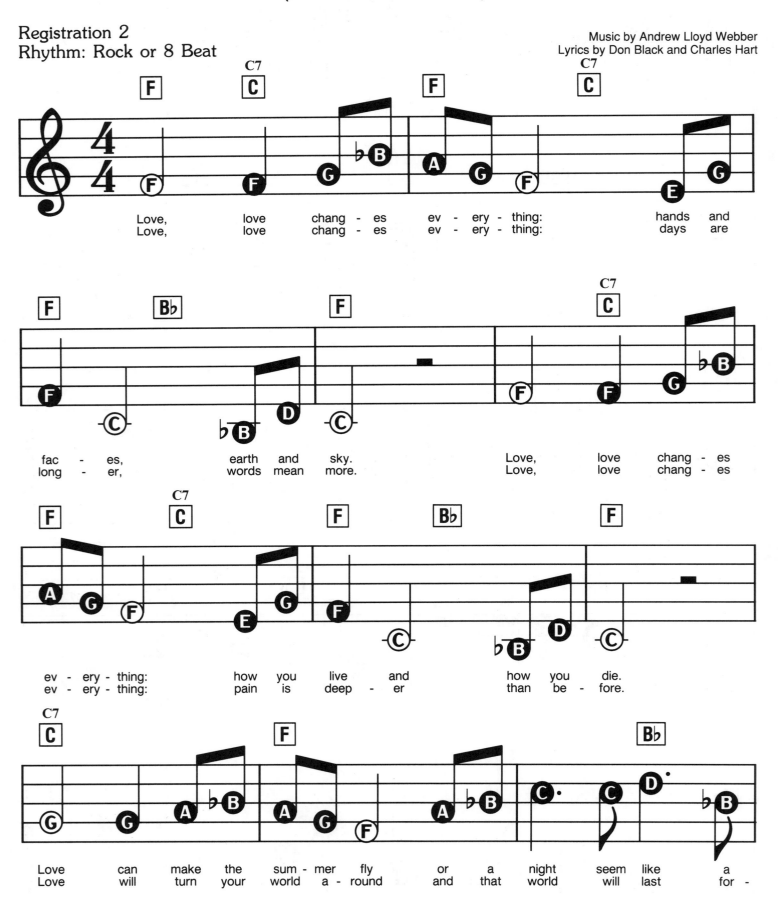

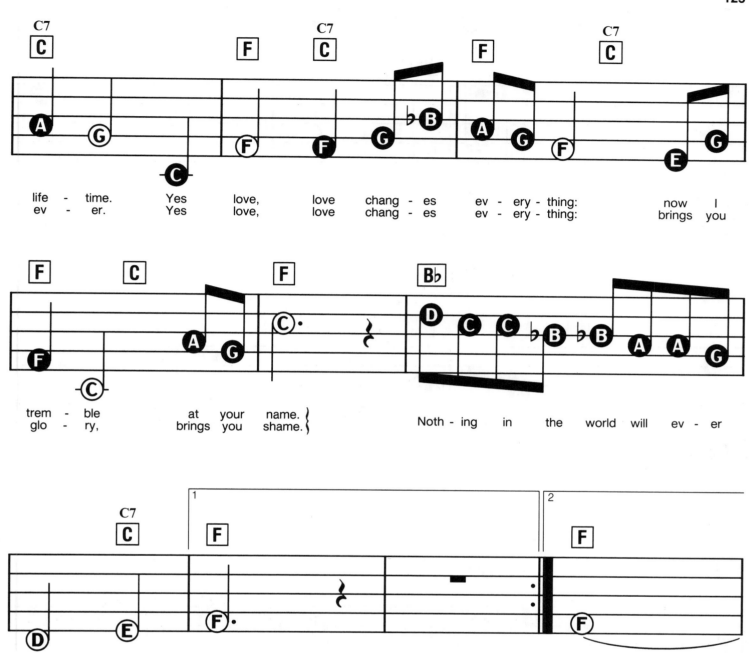

life - time.   Yes   love,   love   chang - es   ev - ery - thing: now   I
ev - er.   Yes   love,   love   chang - es   ev - ery - thing: brings   you

trem - ble   at   your   name. ⎱
glo - ry,   brings you   shame. ⎰

Noth - ing   in   the   world   will   ev - er

be   the   same.

same._____

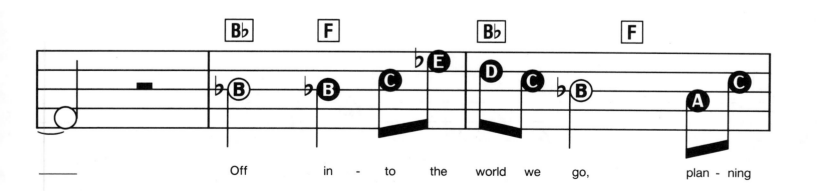

Off   in - to   the   world   we   go,   plan - ning

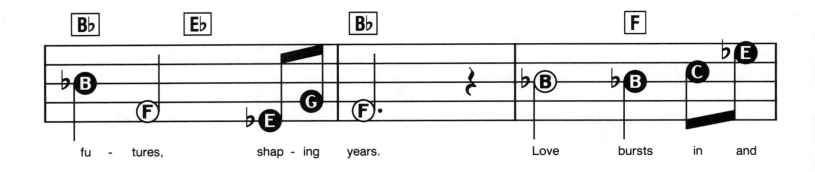

fu - tures, shap - ing years. Love bursts in and

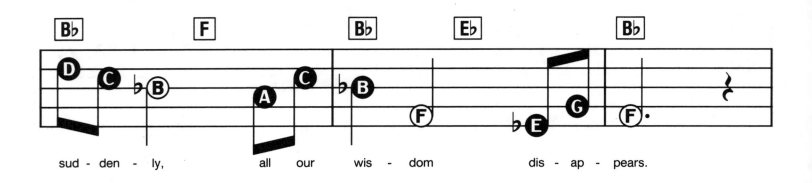

sud - den - ly, all our wis - dom dis - ap - pears.

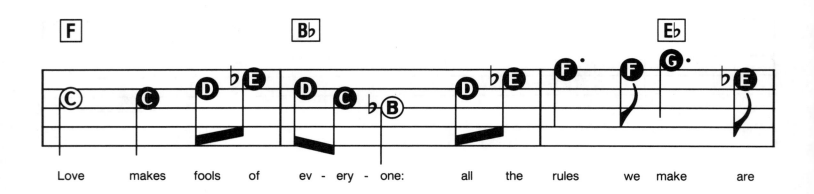

Love makes fools of ev - ery - one: all the rules we make are

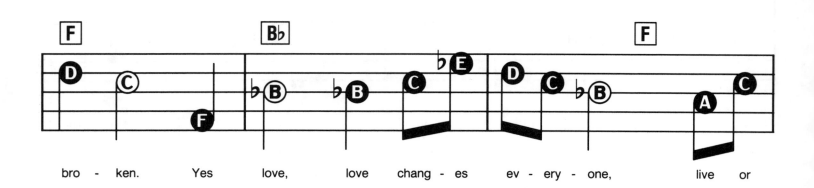

bro - ken. Yes love, love chang - es ev - ery - one, live or

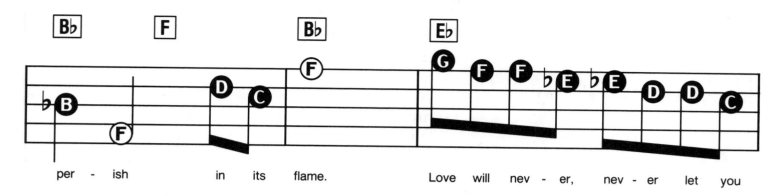

per - ish in its flame. Love will nev - er, nev - er let you

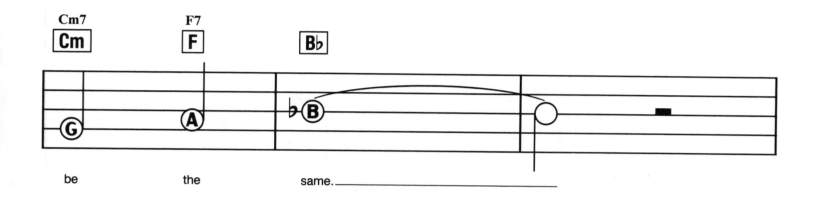

be the same._____

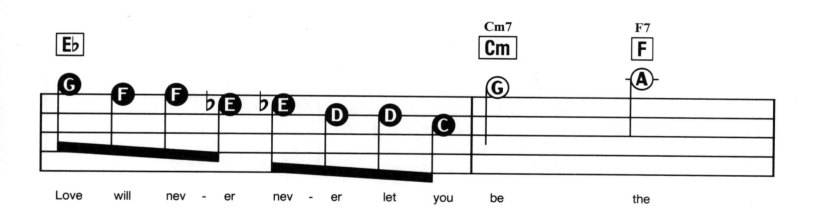

Love will nev - er nev - er let you be the

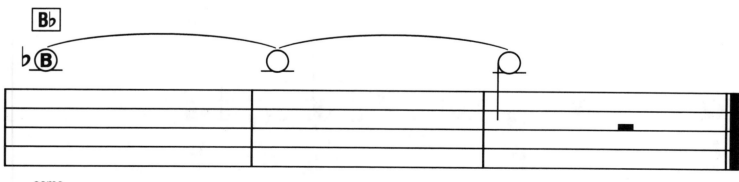

same._____

Luck Be A Lady

(From "GUYS AND DOLLS")

Registration 4
Rhythm: Fox Trot or Swing

Words and Music by
Frank Loesser

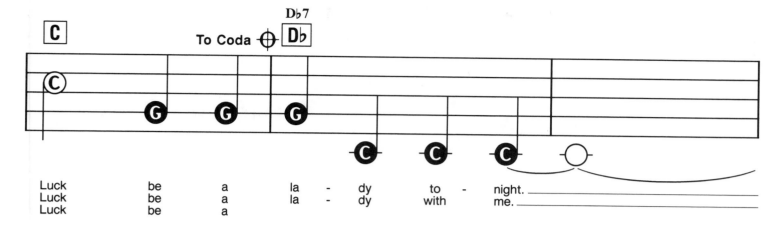

Luck be a la - dy to - night.
Luck be a a la - dy with me.
Luck be a a

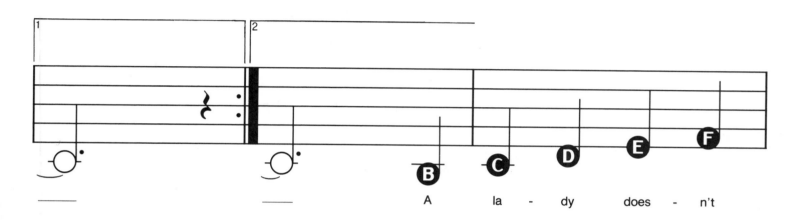

A la - dy does - n't

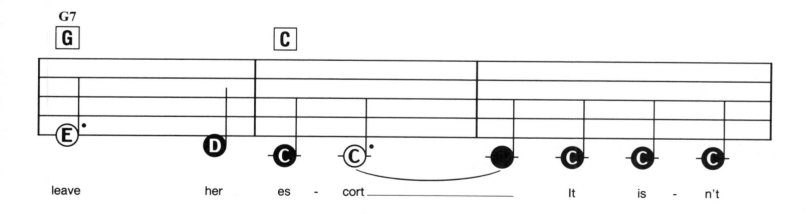

leave her es - cort   It is - n't

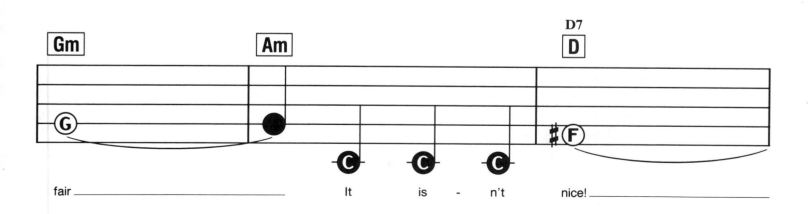

fair   It is - n't nice!

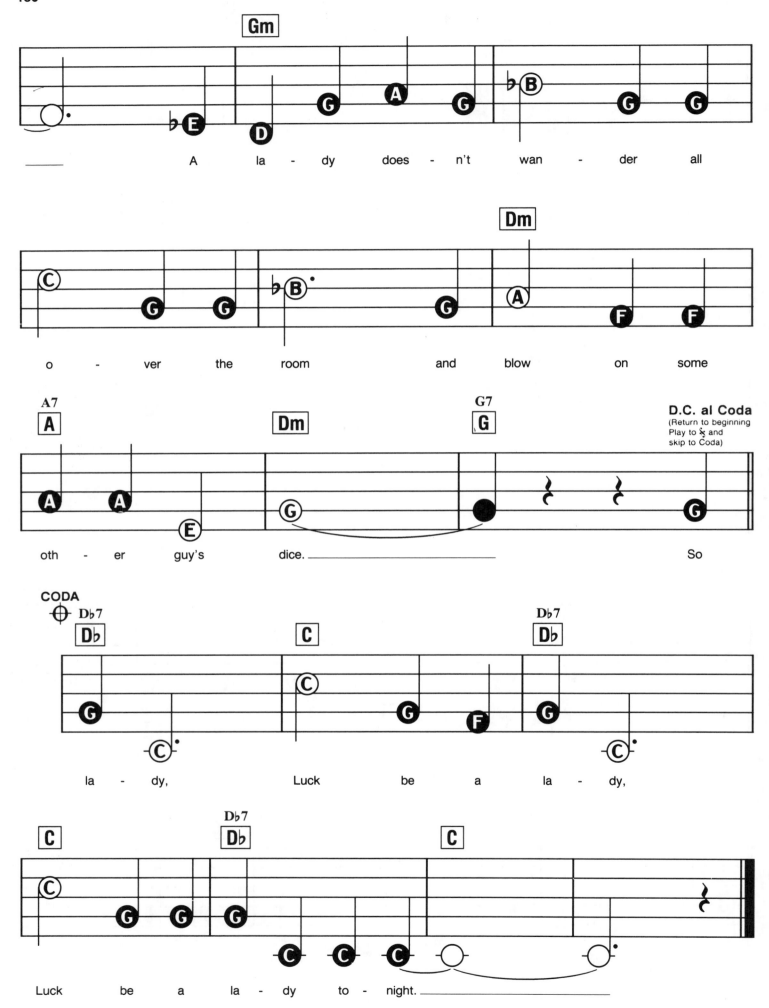

Not A Day Goes By
(From "MERRILY WE ROLL ALONG")

Registration 3

Words and Music by
Stephen Sondheim

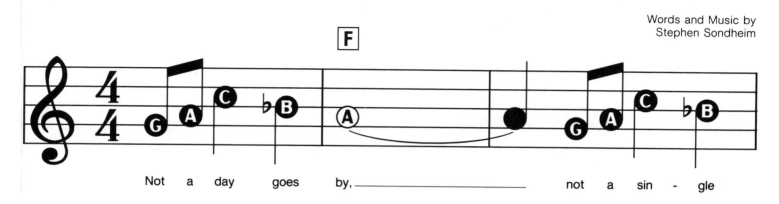

Not a day goes by, _____ not a sin - gle

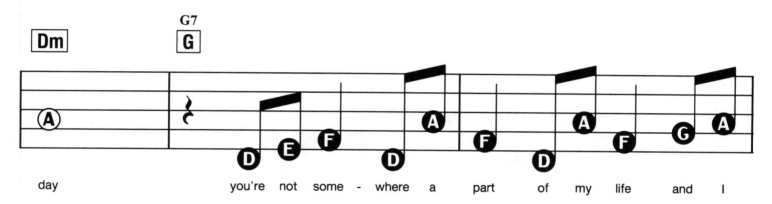

day you're not some - where a part of my life and I

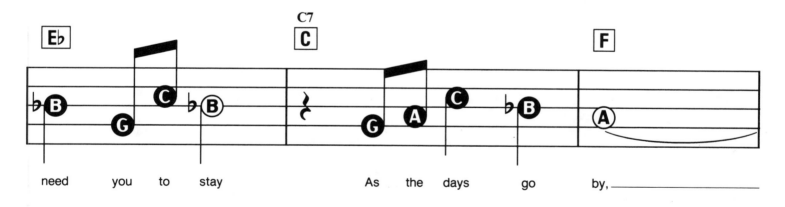

need you to stay As the days go by, _____

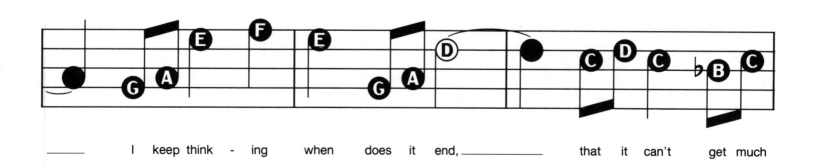

I keep think - ing when does it end, _____ that it can't get much

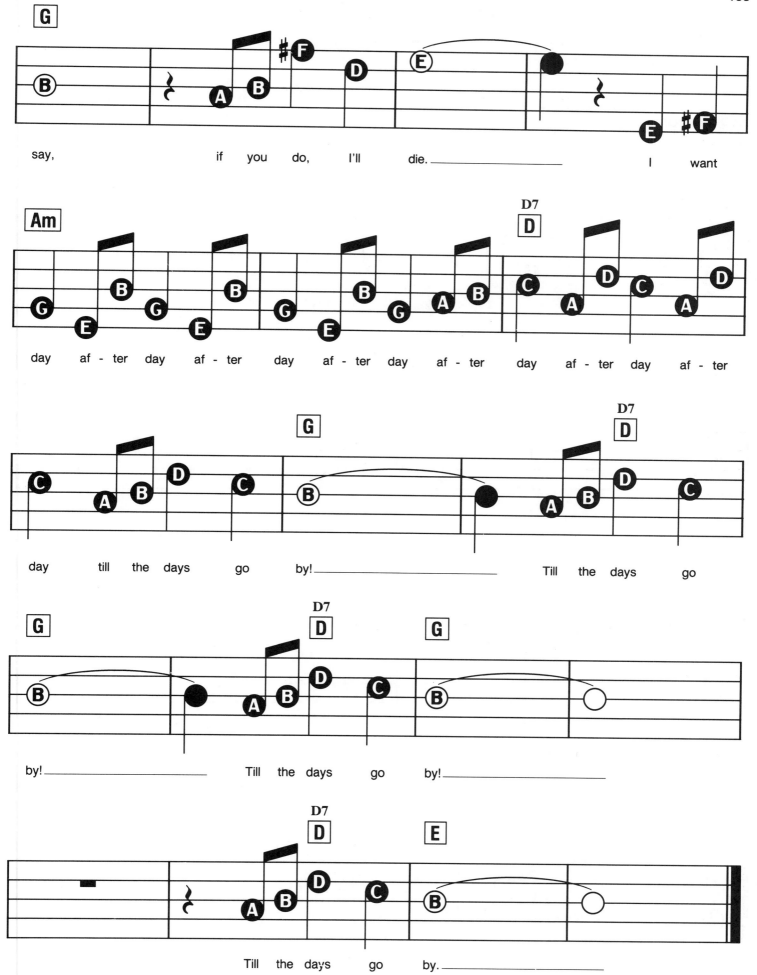

Make Believe

(From "SHOW BOAT")

Registration 10
Rhythm: Ballad or Fox Trot

Lyrics by Oscar Hammerstein II
Music by Jerome Kern

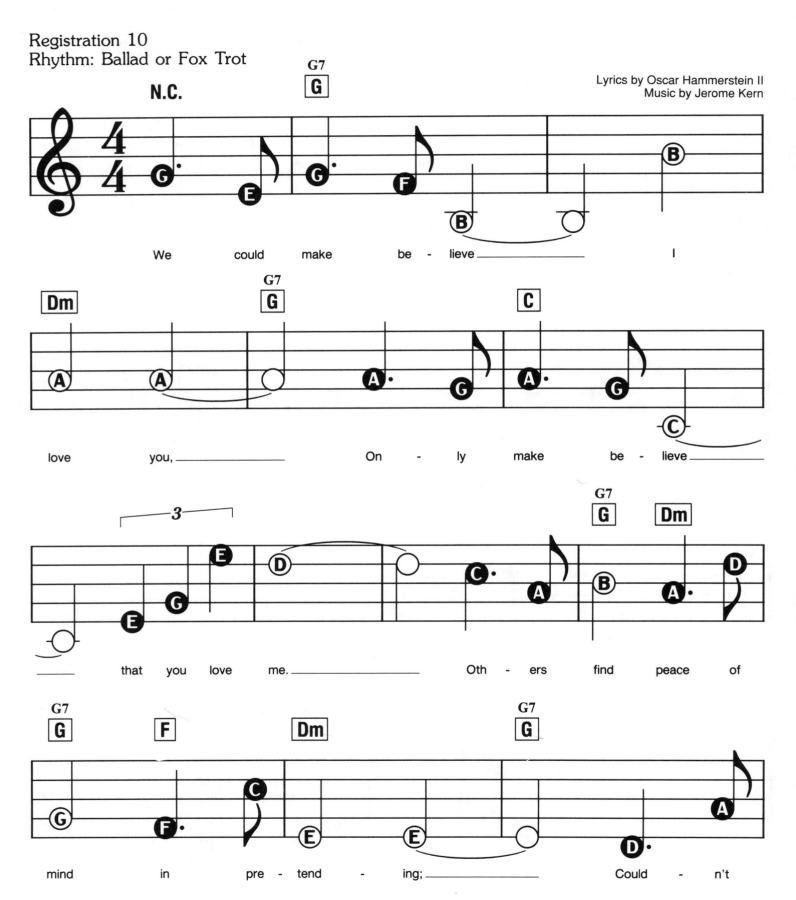

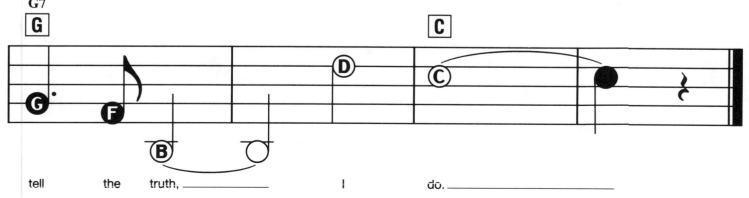

Memory

(From "CATS")

Registration 3
Rhythm: 6/8 March

Music by Andrew Lloyd Webber
Text by Trevor Nunn after T.S. Eliot

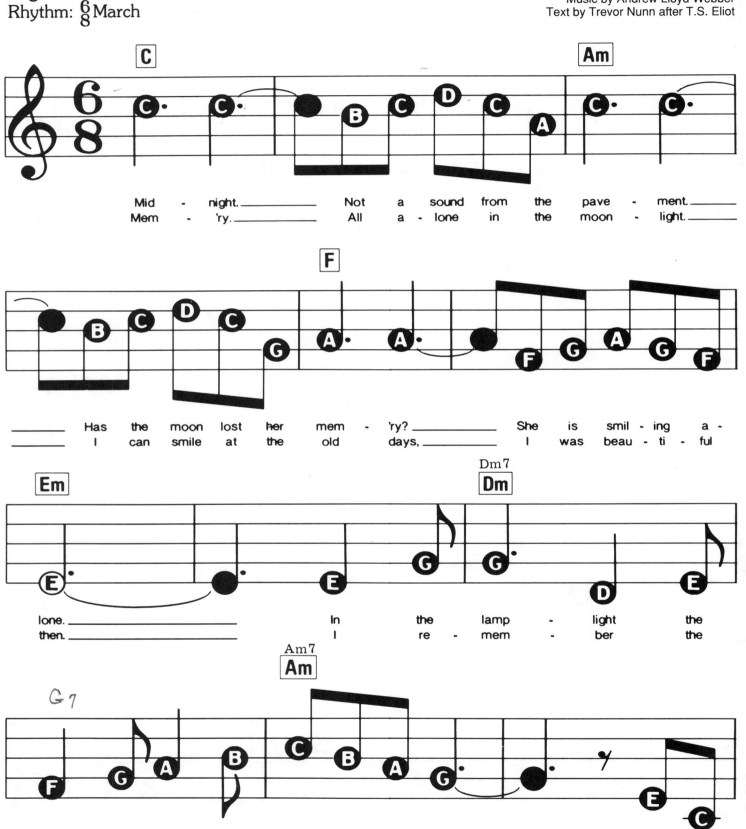

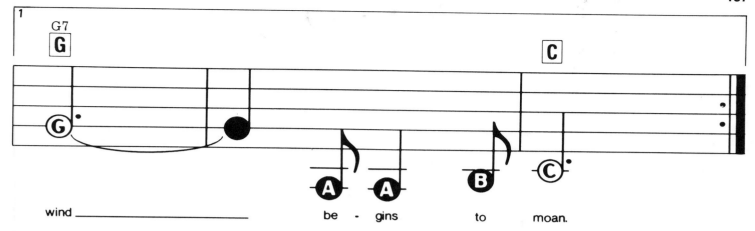

wind _____ be - gins to moan.

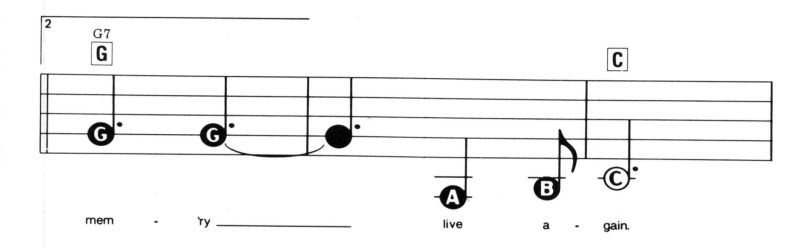

mem - 'ry _____ live a - gain.

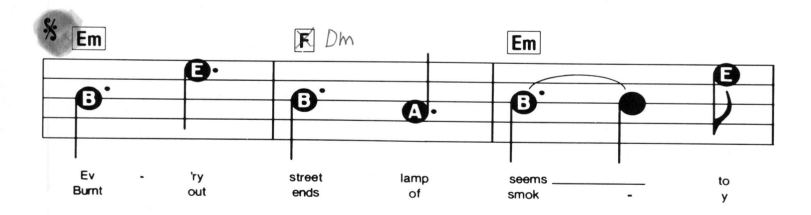

Ev - 'ry street lamp seems _____ to
Burnt out ends of smok - y

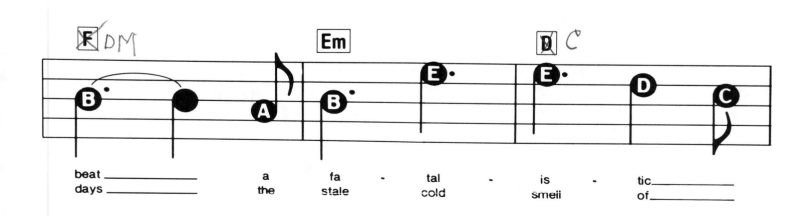

beat _____ a fa - tal - is - tic _____
days _____ the stale cold smell of _____

138

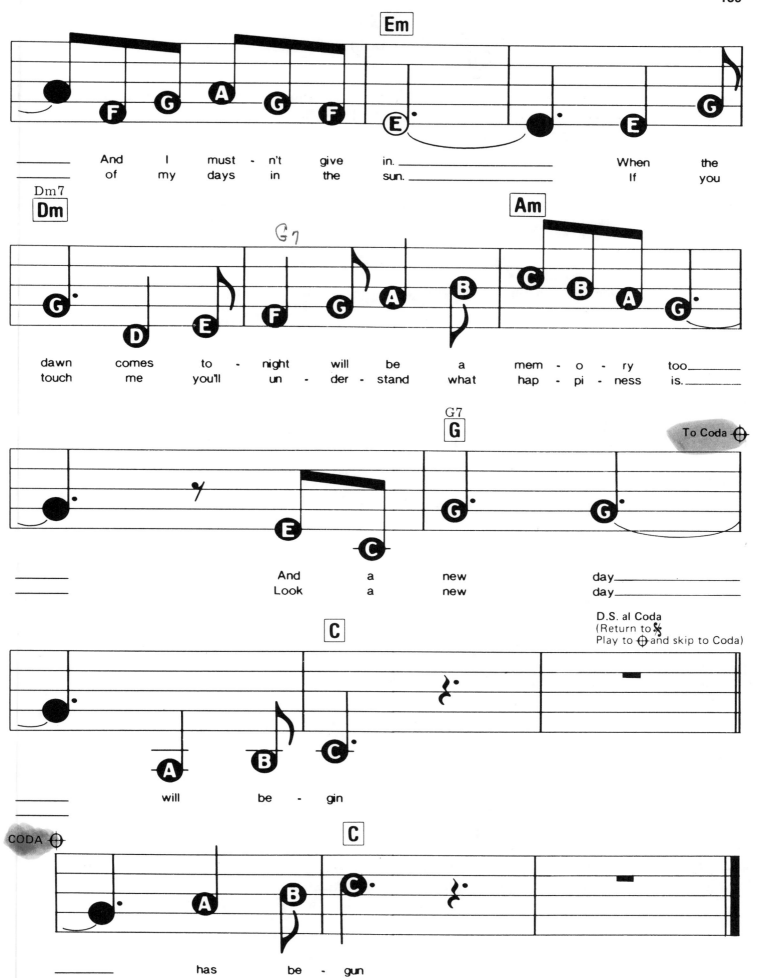

My Cup Runneth Over

(From "I DO! I DO!")

Words by Tom Jones
Music by Harvey Schmidt

Registration 3
Rhythm: Waltz

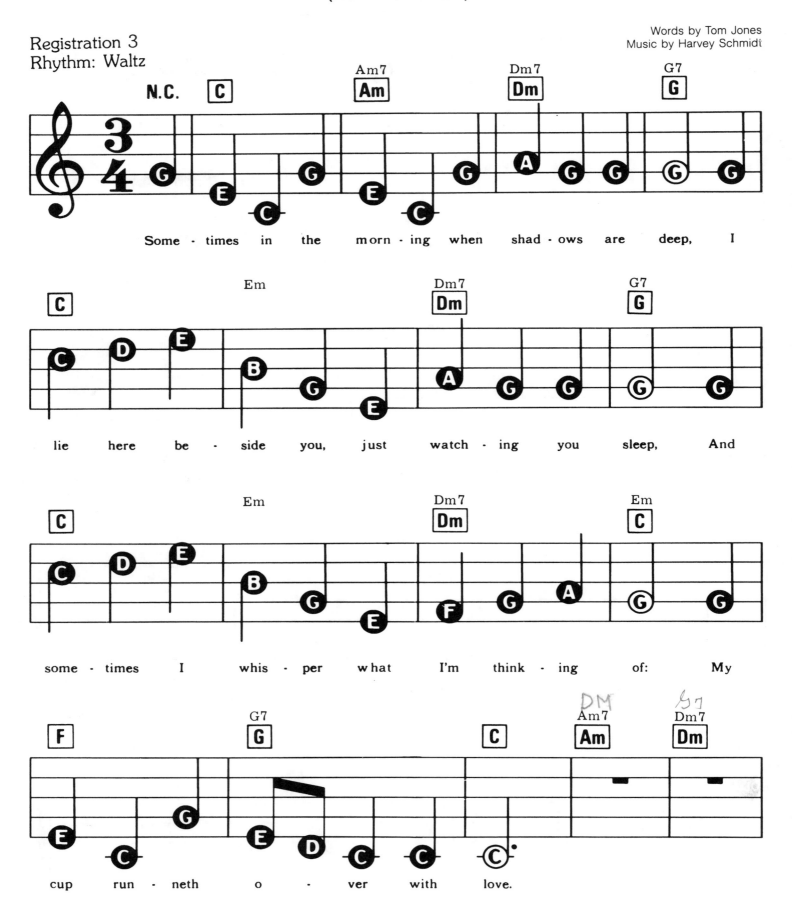

Some - times in the morn - ing when shad - ows are deep, I

lie here be - side you, just watch - ing you sleep, And

some - times I whis - per what I'm think - ing of: My

cup run - neth o - ver with love.

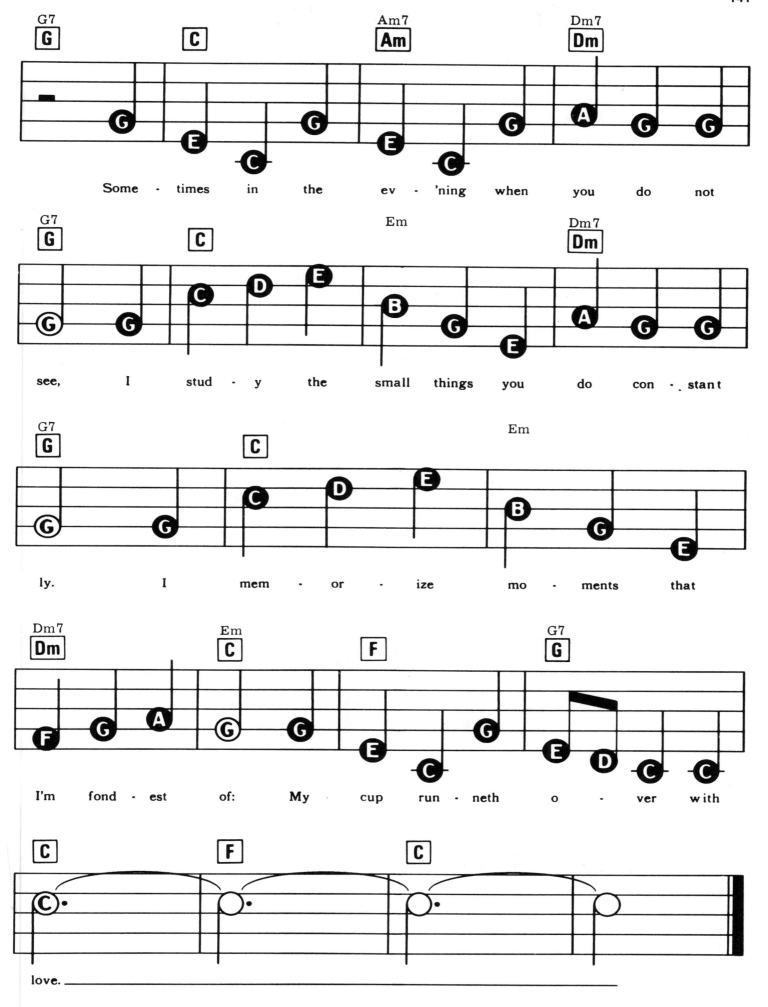

My Favorite Things

(From "THE SOUND OF MUSIC")

Lyrics by Oscar Hammerstein II
Music by Richard Rodgers

Registration 9
Rhythm: Waltz

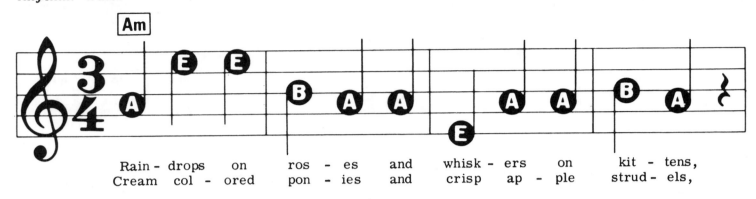

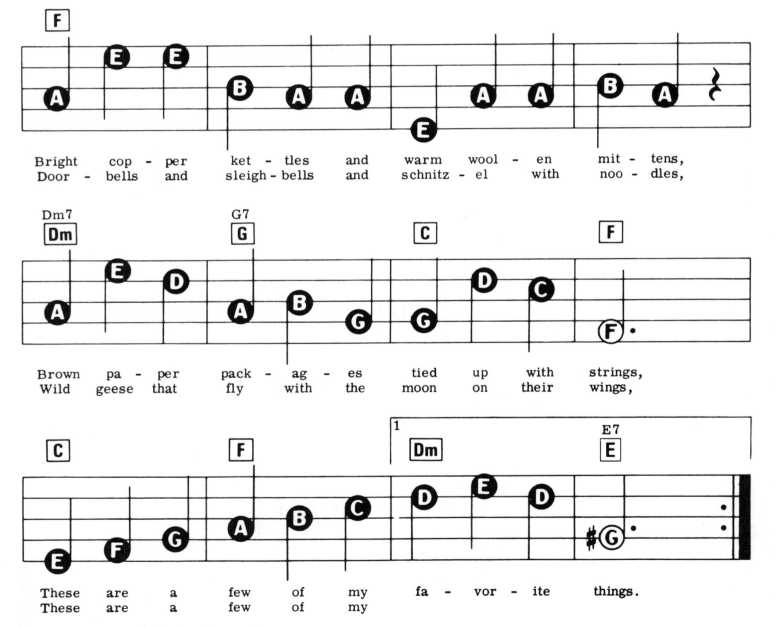

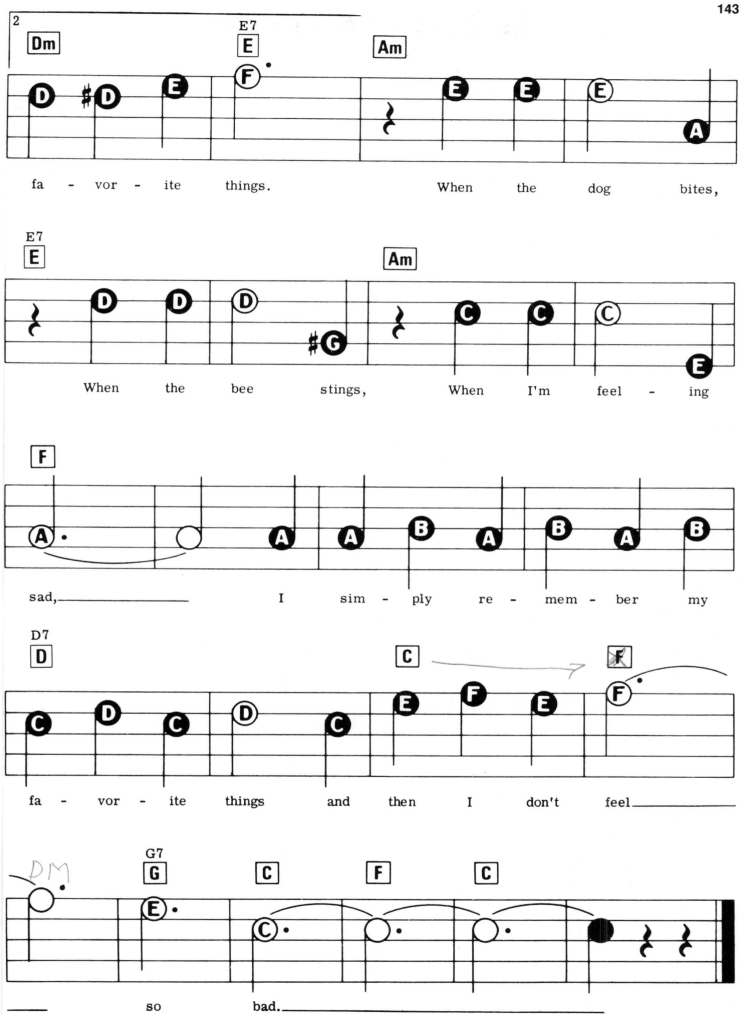

My Funny Valentine

(From "BABES IN ARMS")

Registration 1
Rhythm: Ballad

Words by Lorenz Hart
Music by Richard Rodgers

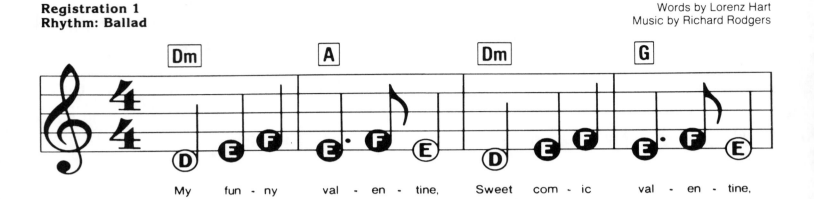

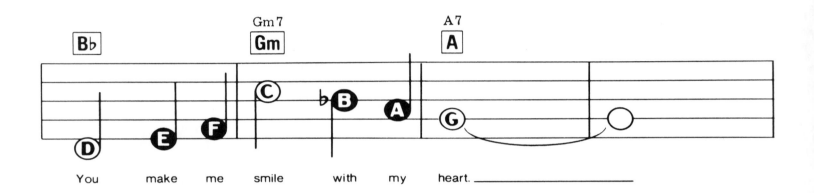

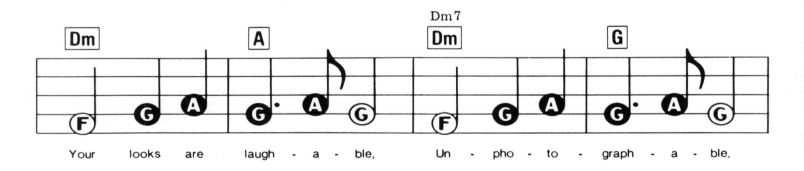

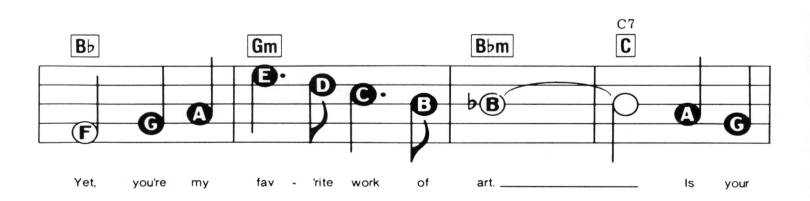

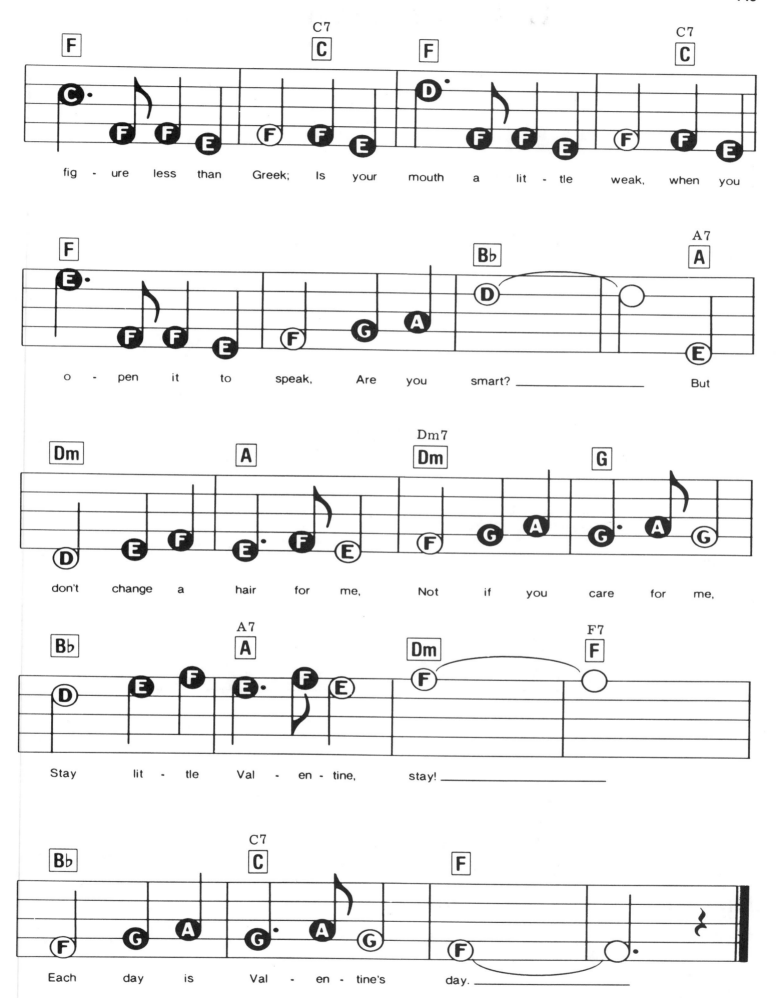

Oh, What A Beautiful Mornin'

(From "OKLAHOMA!")

Registration 5
Rhythm: Waltz

Lyrics by Oscar Hammerstein II
Music by Richard Rodgers

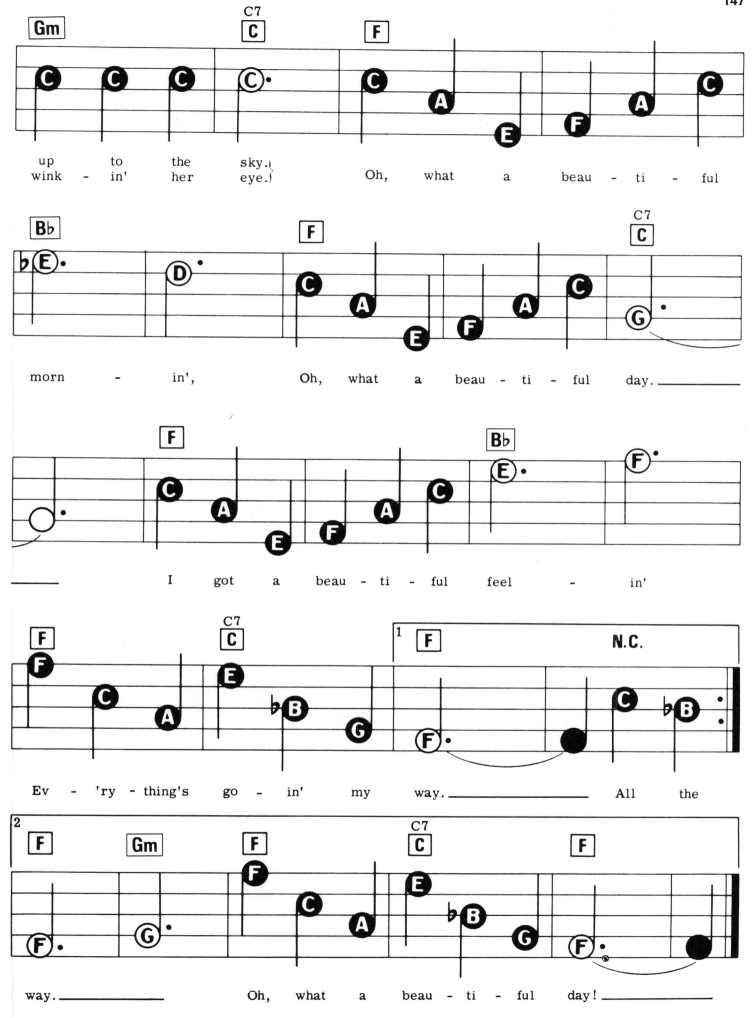

Ol' Man River

(From "SHOW BOAT")

Registration 5
Rhythm: Ballad or Fox Trot

Words by Oscar Hammerstein II
Music by Jerome Kern

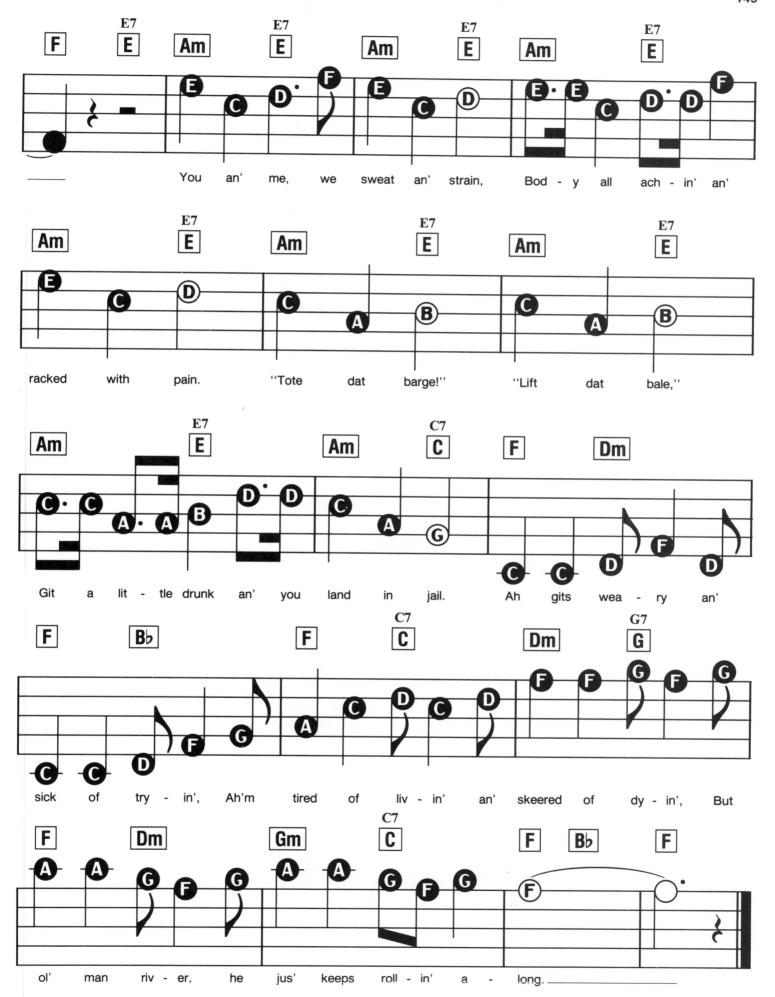

On A Clear Day
(You Can See Forever)
(From "ON A CLEAR DAY YOU CAN SEE FOREVER")

Words by Alan Jay Lerner
Music by Burton Lane

Registration 1
Rhythm: Fox Trot

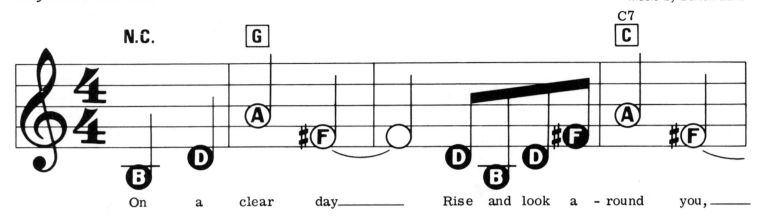

On a clear day____ Rise and look a - round you,____

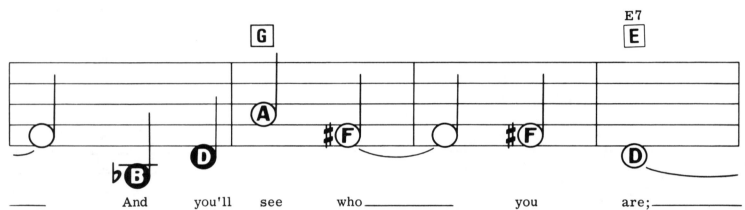

____ And you'll see who_____ you are;_____

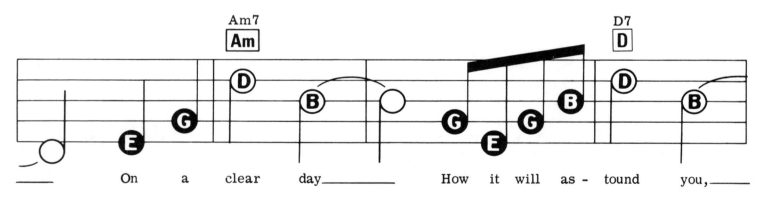

____ On a clear day_____ How it will as - tound you,____

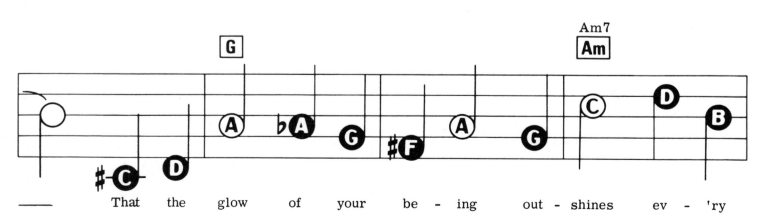

____ That the glow of your be - ing out - shines ev - 'ry

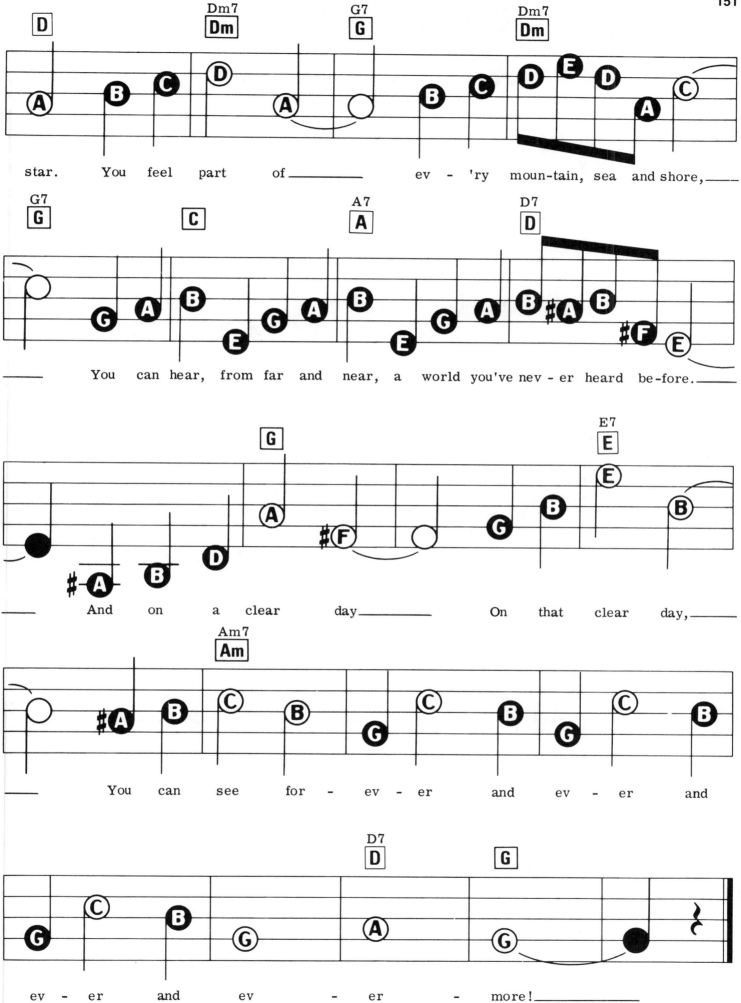

On The Street Where You Live

(From "MY FAIR LADY")

Registration 4
Rhythm: Beguine

Words by Alan Jay Lerner
Music by Frederick Loewe

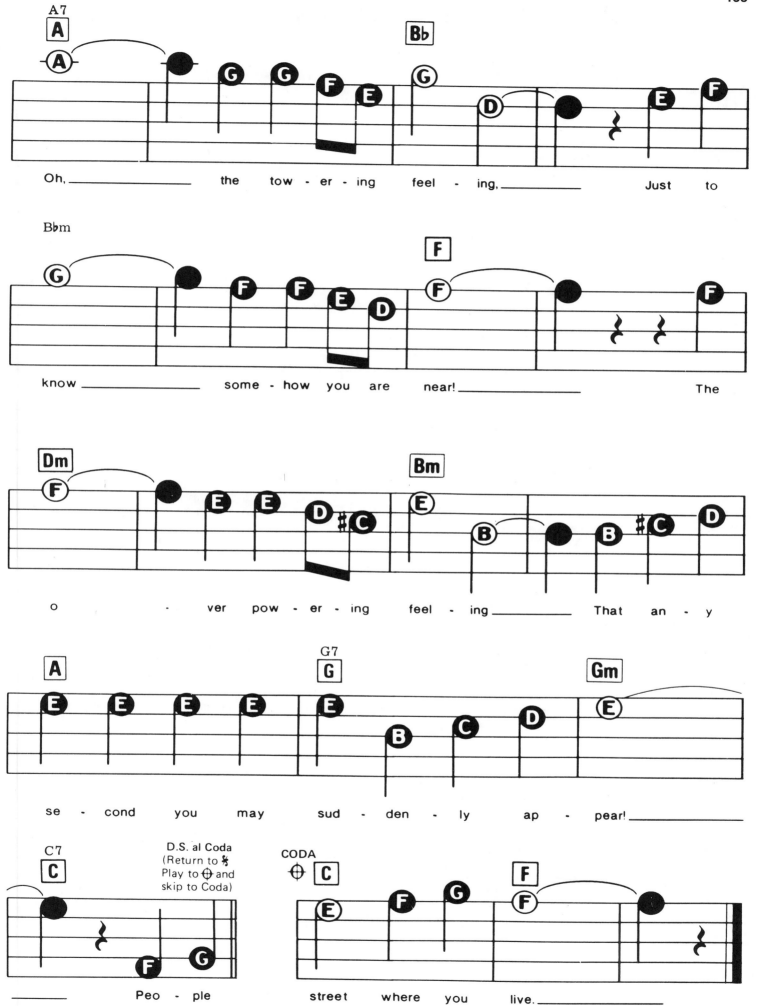

Oklahoma

(From "OKLAHOMA!")

Lyrics by Oscar Hammerstein II
Music by Richard Rodgers

Registration 5
Rhythm: Fox Trot or Swing

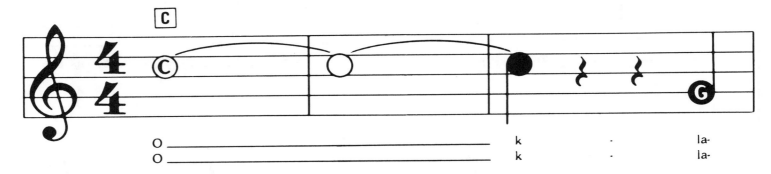

O _____ k - la-
O _____ k - la-

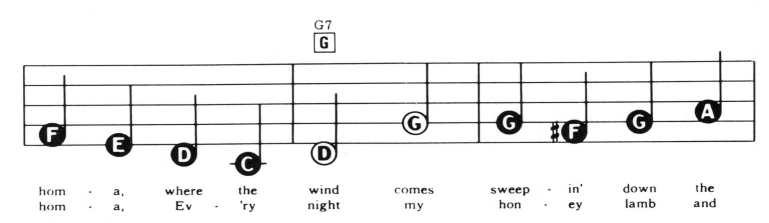

hom - a, where the wind comes sweep - in' down the
hom - a, Ev - 'ry night comes my hon - ey lamb and

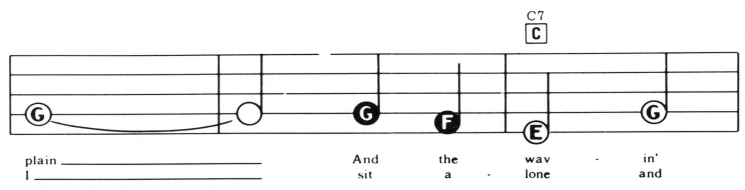

plain _____ And the wav - in'
I _____ sit a - lone and

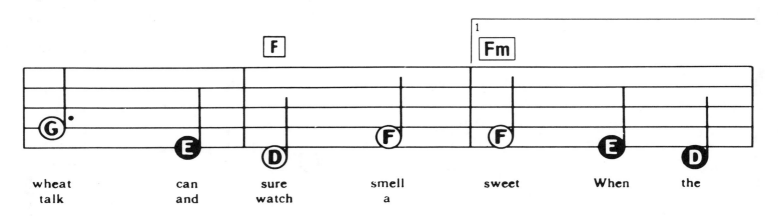

wheat can sure smell a sweet When the
talk and watch a

155

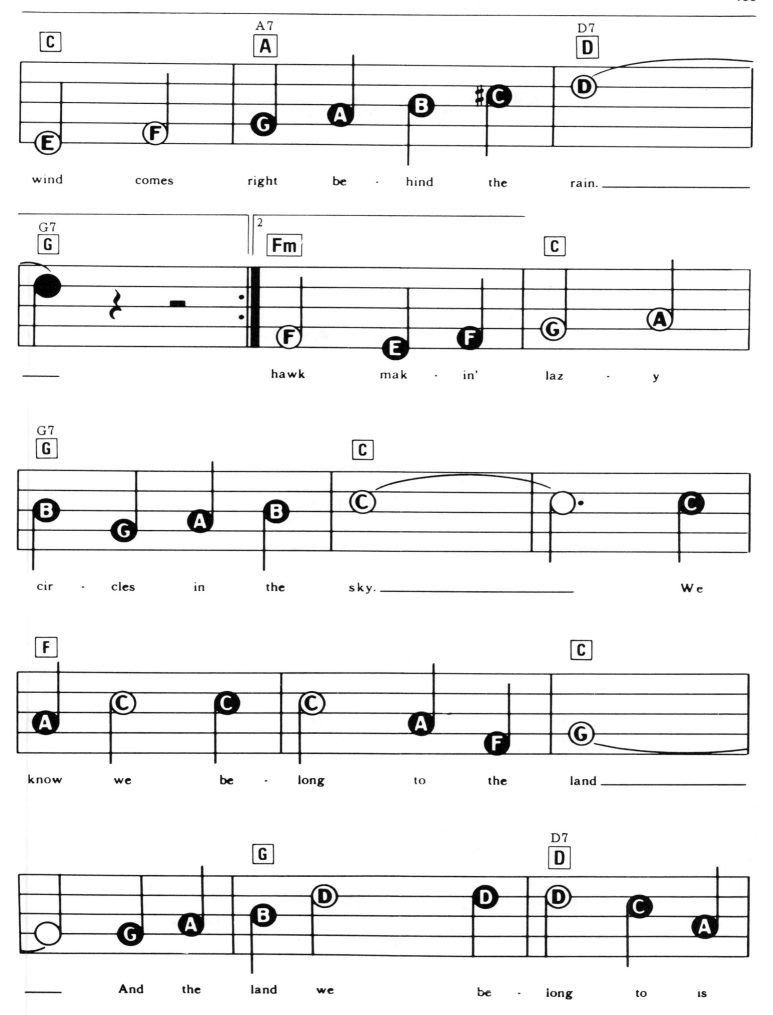

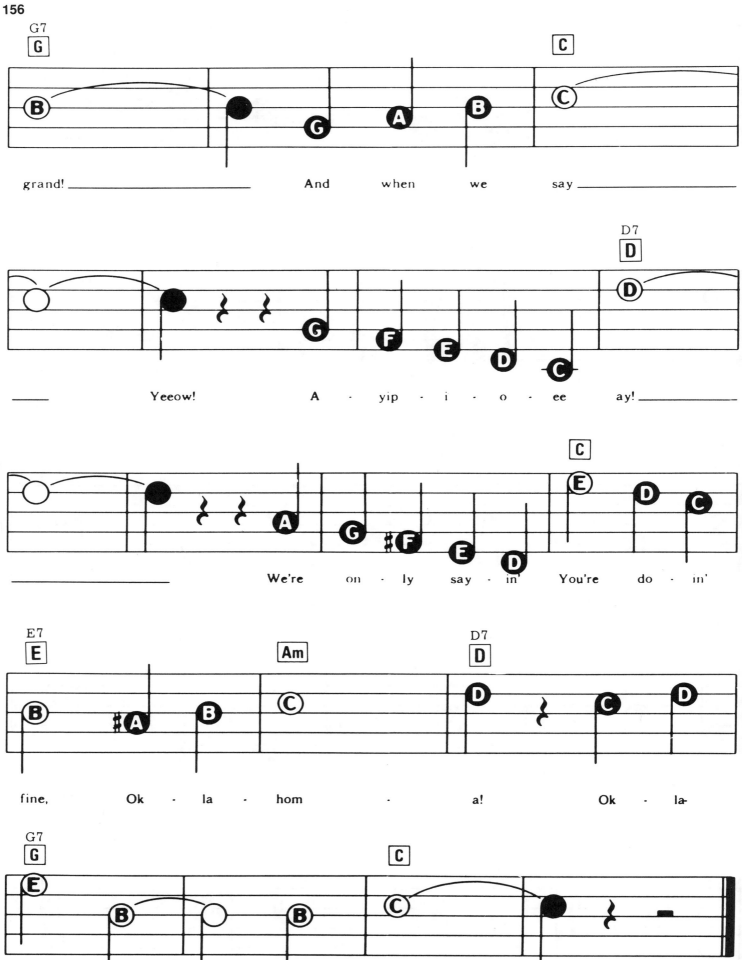

People

(From "FUNNY GIRL")

Words by Bob Merrill
Music by Jule Styne

Registration 1
Rhythm: Ballad or Fox Trot

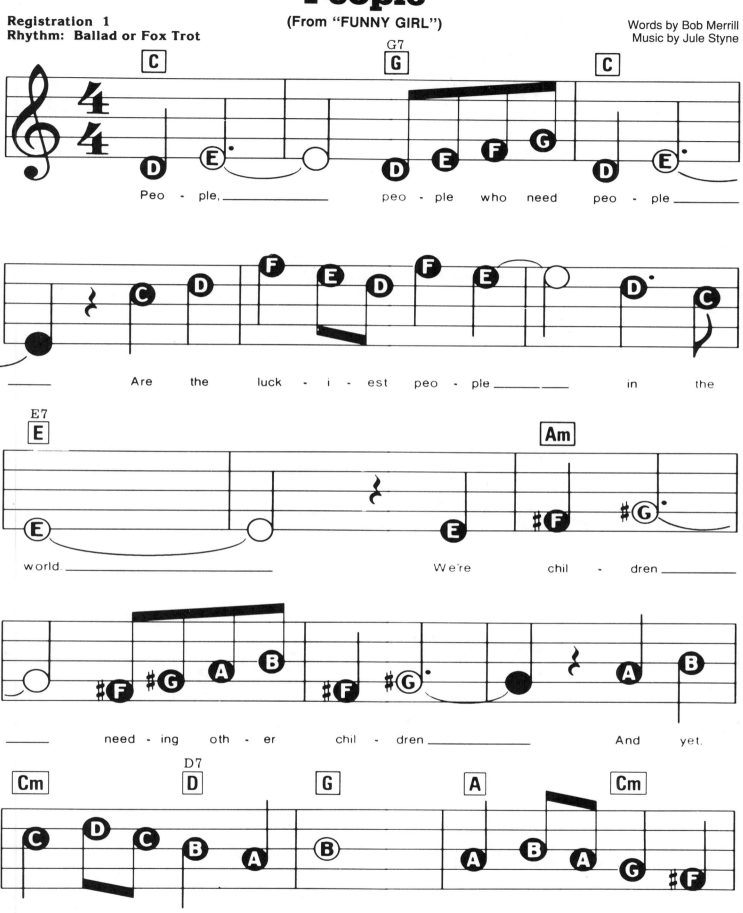

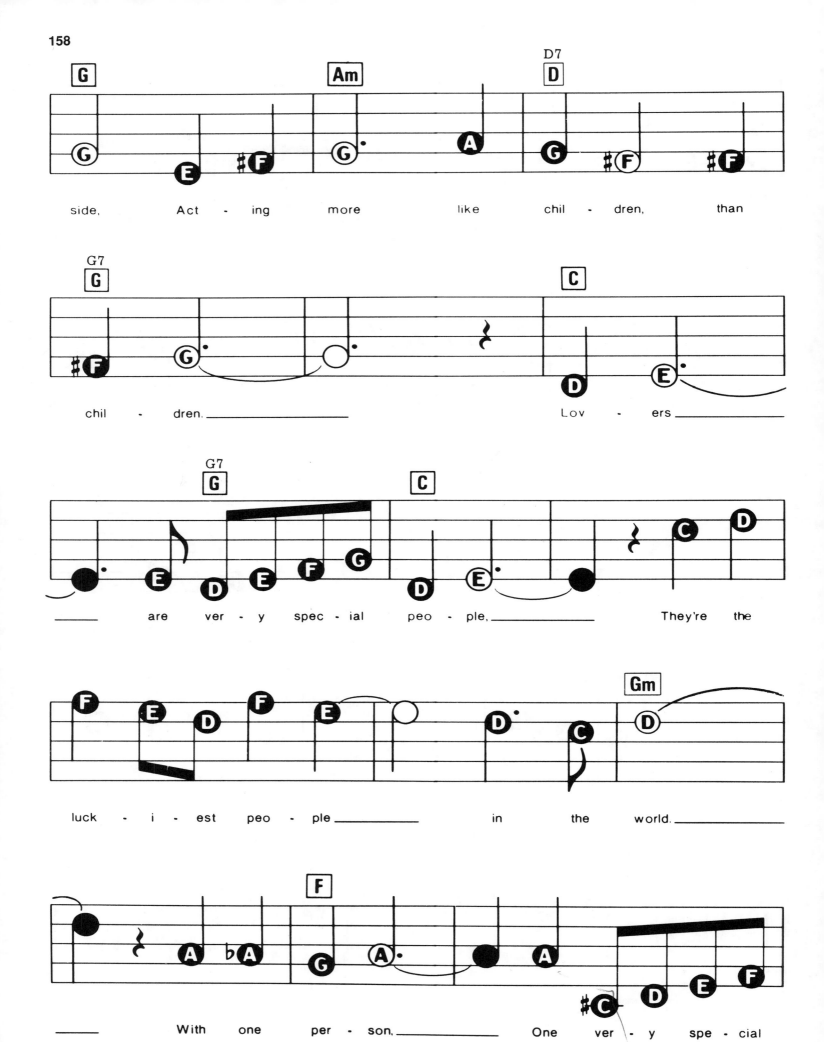

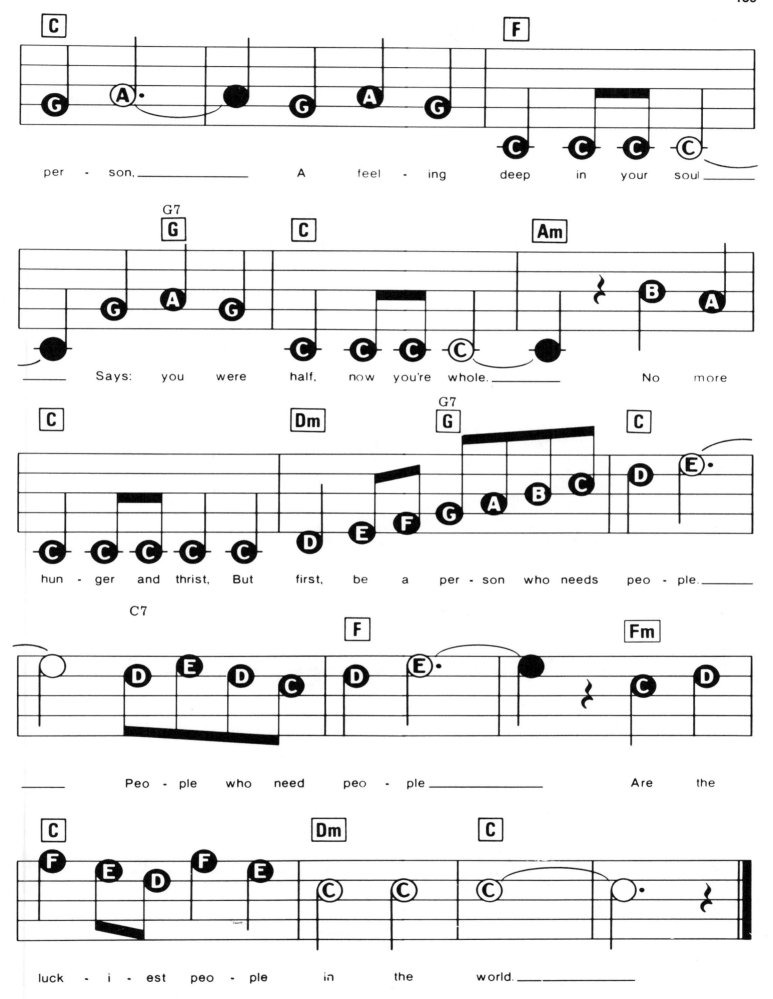

People Will Say We're In Love

(From "OKLAHOMA!")

Registration 5
Rhythm: Beguine

Lyrics by Oscar Hammerstein II
Music by Richard Rodgers

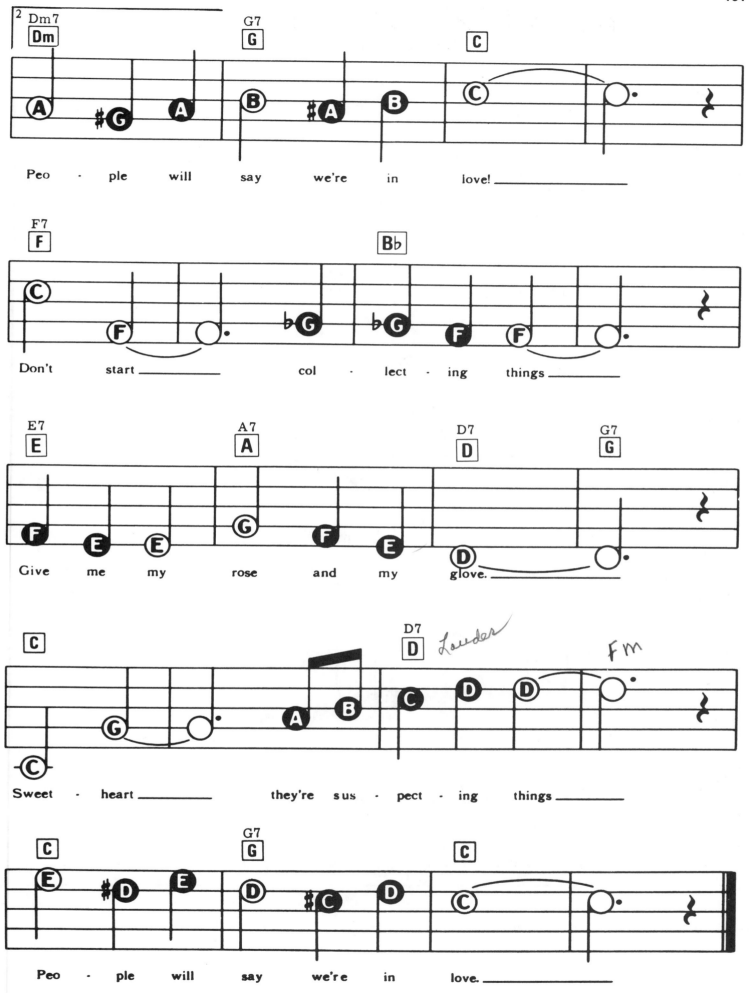

Send In The Clowns

(From the musical "A LITTLE NIGHT MUSIC")

Registration 10
Rhythm: Slow Rock or Ballad

Music and Lyrics by STEPHEN SONDHEIM

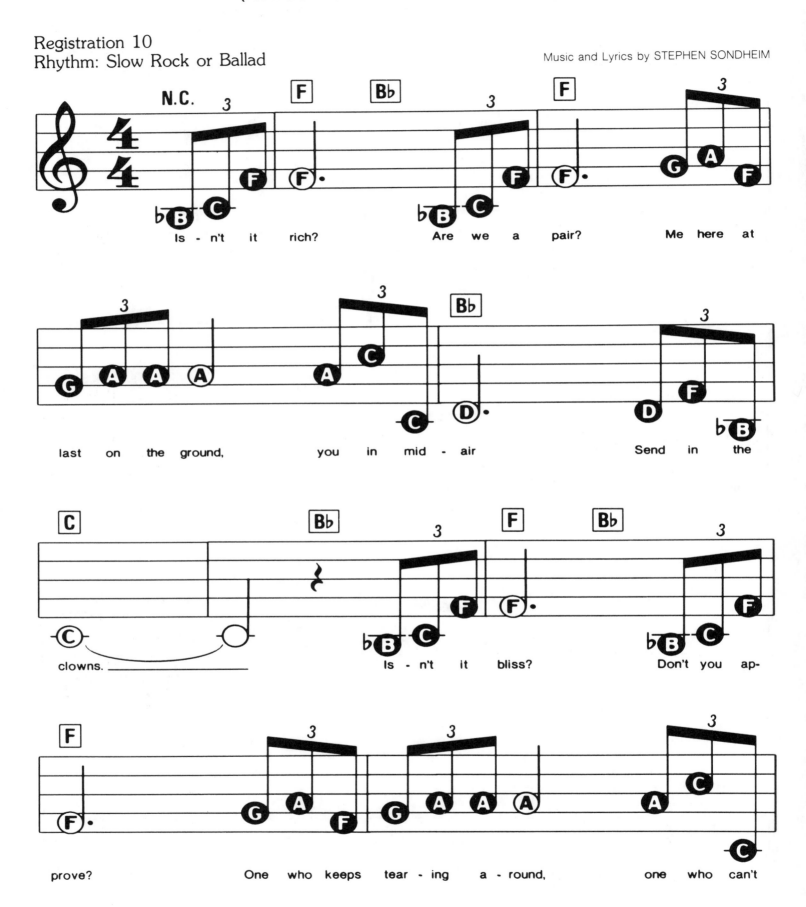

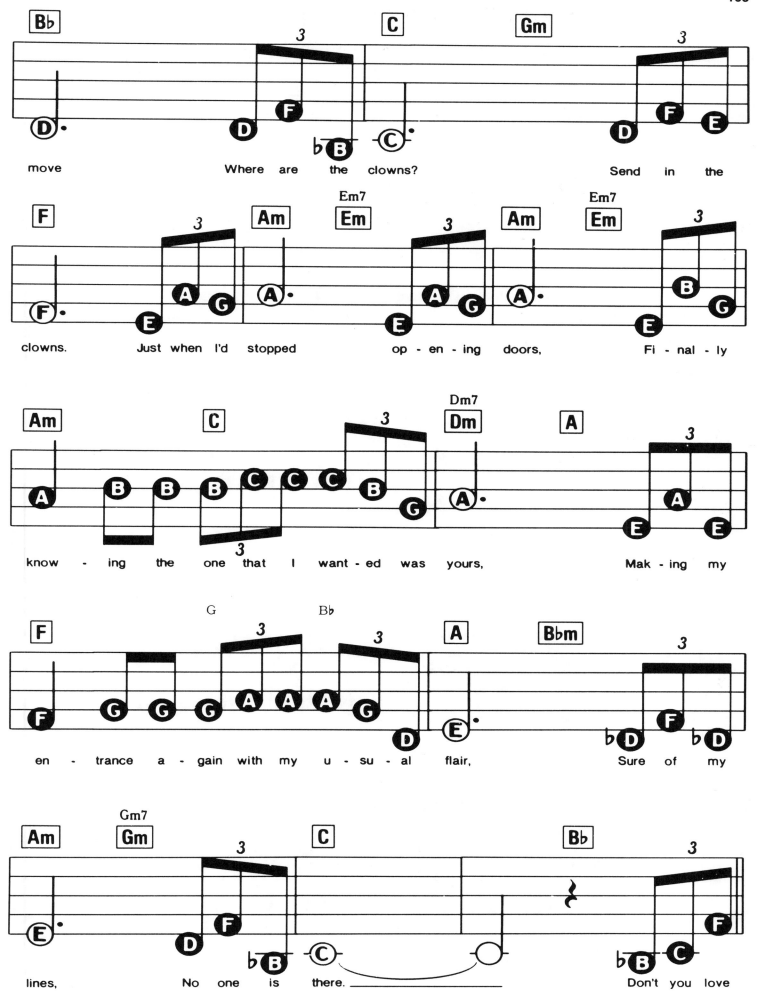

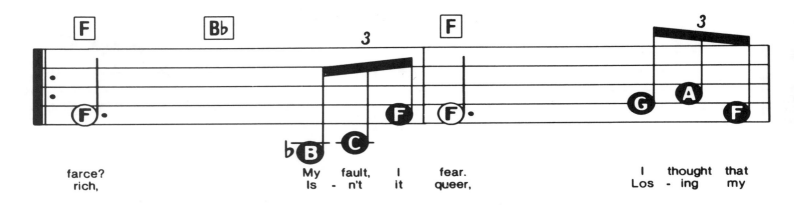

farce?
rich,

My fault, I fear.
Is - n't it queer,

I thought that
Los - ing my

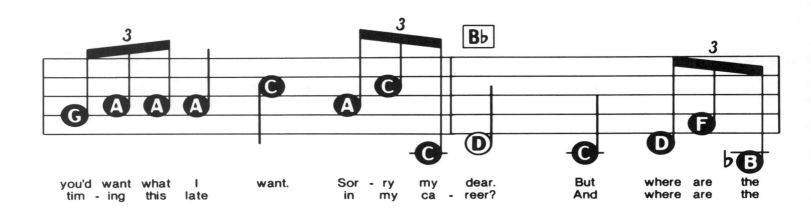

you'd want what I want.
tim - ing this late

Sor - ry my dear.
in my ca - reer?

But
And

where are the
where are the

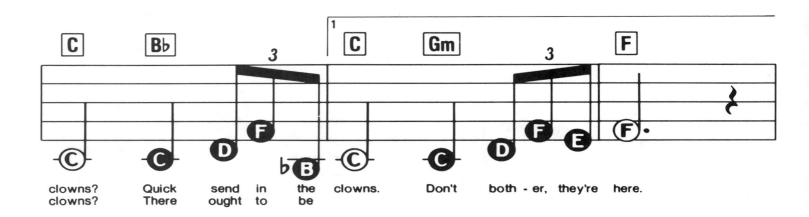

clowns?
clowns?

Quick
There

send
ought

in
to

the
be

clowns.

Don't

both - er, they're here.

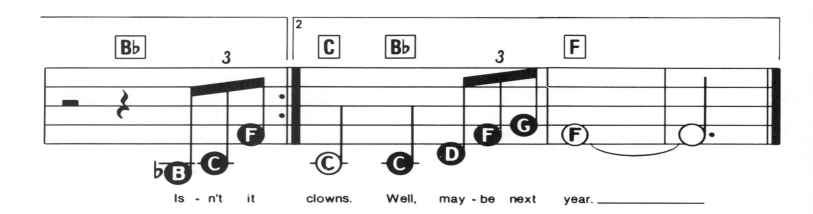

Is - n't it

clowns.

Well, may - be next year. _____

Small World

(From "GYPSY")

Registration 9
Rhythm: Fox Trot or Swing

Words by Stephen Sondheim
Music by Jule Styne

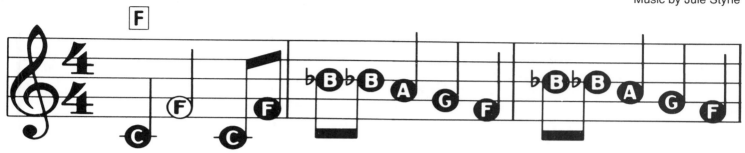

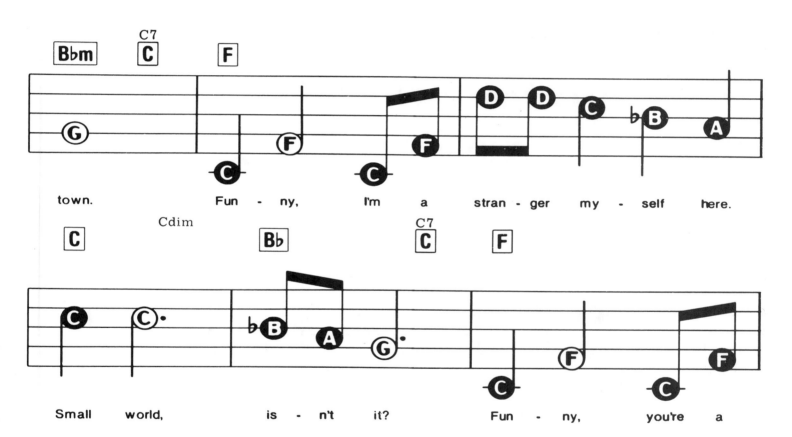

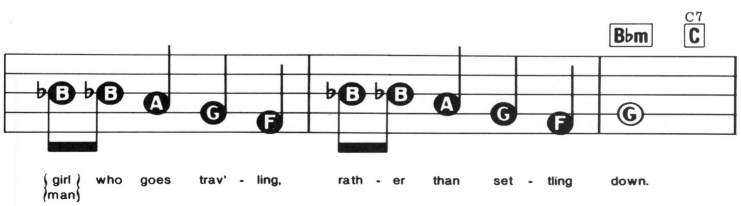

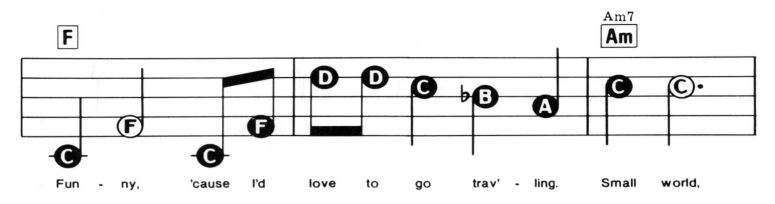

Fun - ny, 'cause I'd love to go trav' - ling. Small world,

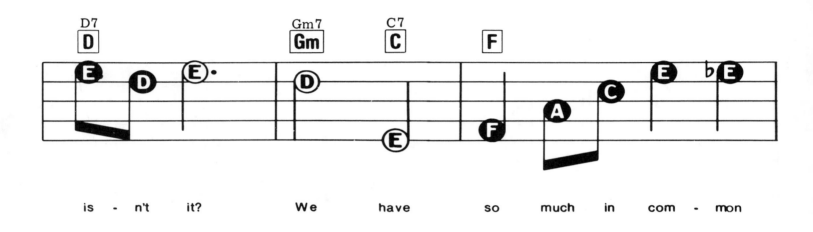

is - n't it? We have so much in com - mon

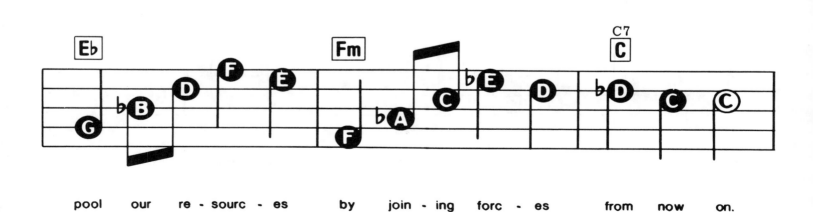

It's a phe - nom - e - non. We could

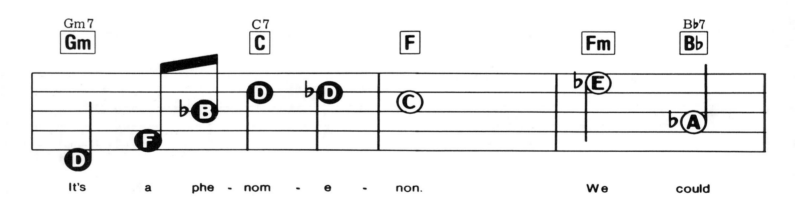

pool our re - sourc - es by join - ing forc - es from now on.

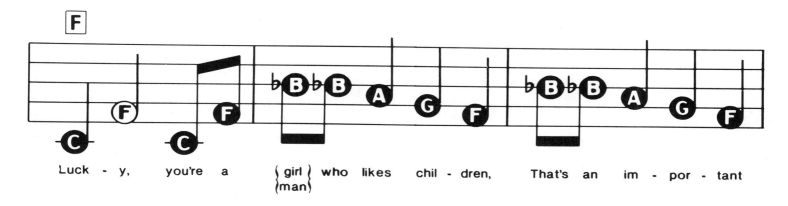

Luck - y, you're a {girl}{man} who likes chil - dren, That's an im - por - tant

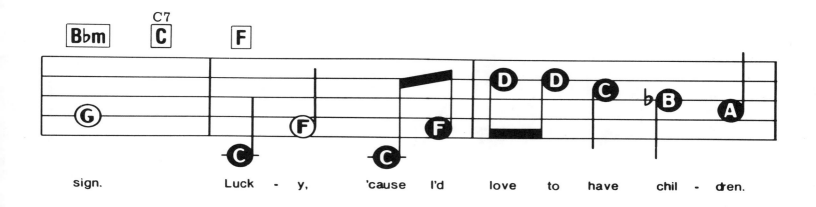

sign.   Luck - y,   'cause I'd   love   to   have   chil - dren.

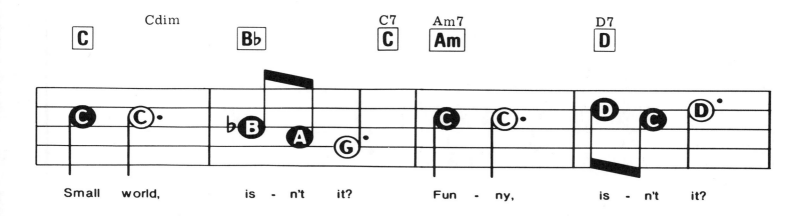

Small   world,   is - n't   it?   Fun - ny,   is - n't   it?

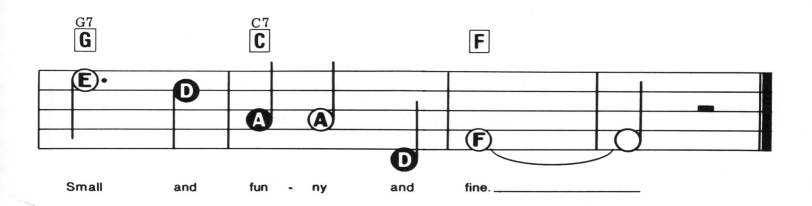

Small   and   fun - ny   and   fine. _____

September Song

(From the Musical Play "KNICKERBOCKER HOLIDAY")

Registration 2
Rhythm: Fox Trot

Words by Maxwell Anderson
Music by Kurt Weil

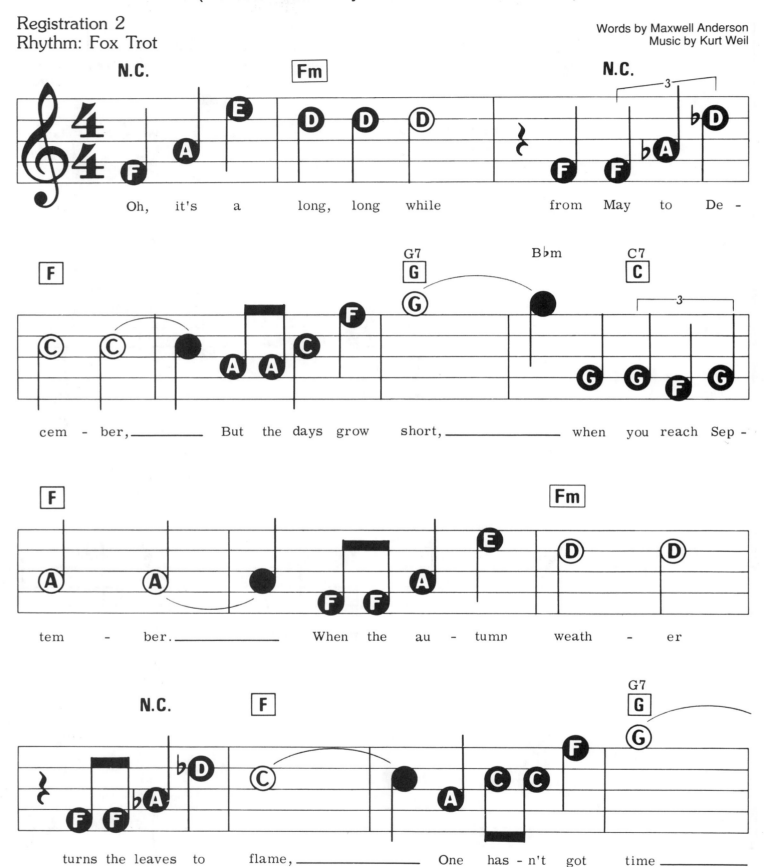

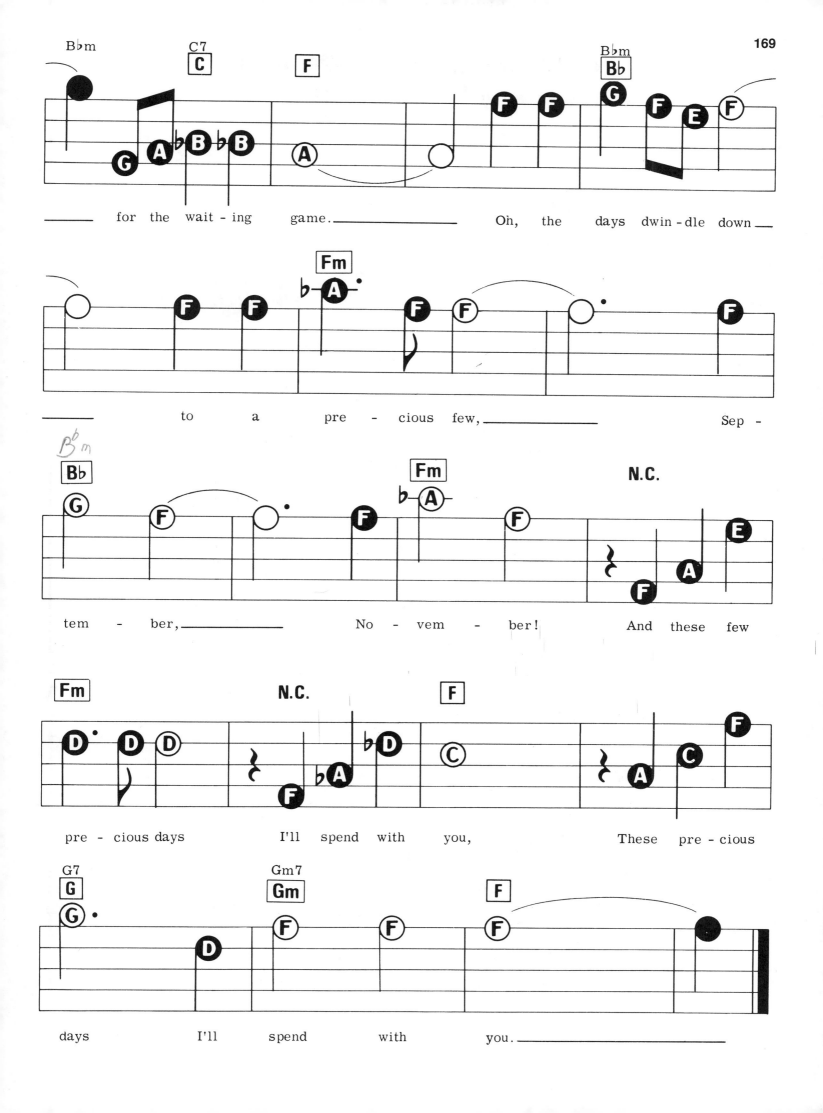

Seventy Six Trombones

(From "THE MUSIC MAN")

Registration 5
Rhythm: ⁶⁄₈ March

By Meredith Willson

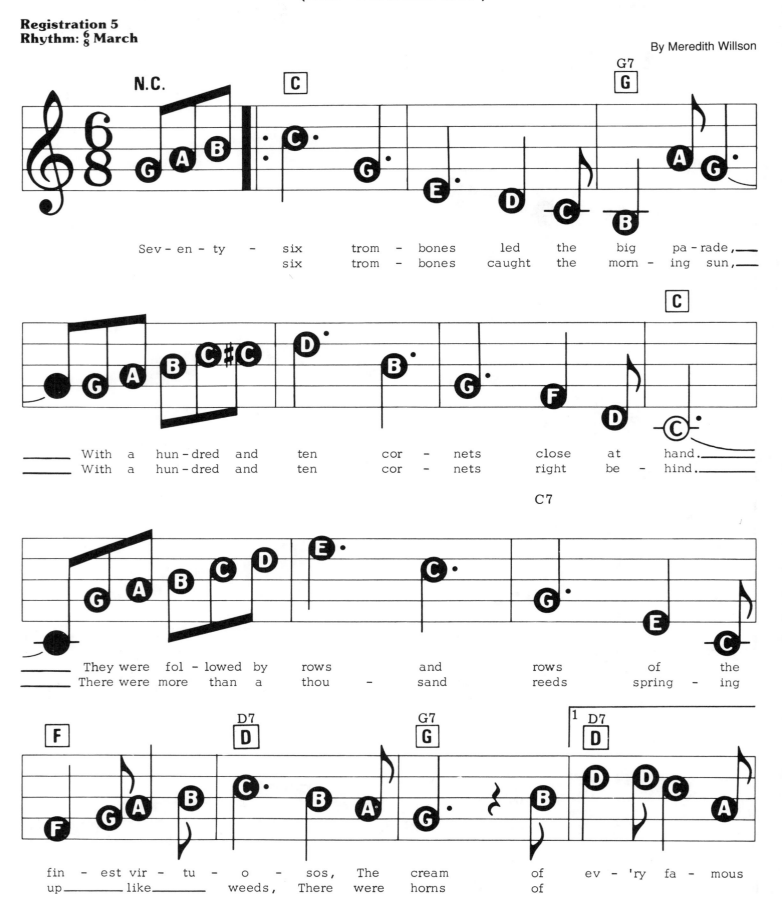

Sev - en - ty - six trom - bones led the big pa - rade,___
six trom - bones caught the morn - ing sun,___

___ With a hun - dred and ten cor - nets close at hand.___
With a hun - dred and ten cor - nets right be - hind.___

___ They were fol - lowed by rows and rows of the
There were more than a thou - sand reeds spring - ing

fin - est vir - tu - o - sos, The cream of ev - 'ry fa - mous
up___ like___ weeds, There were horns of

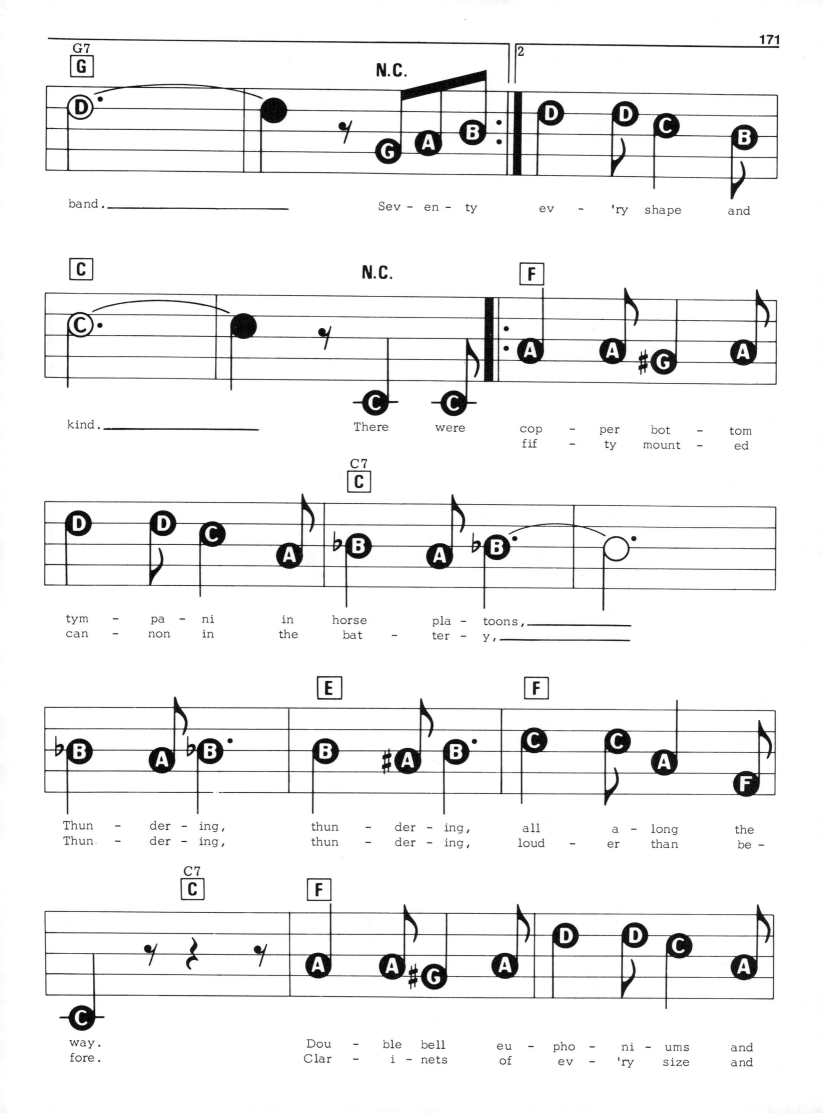

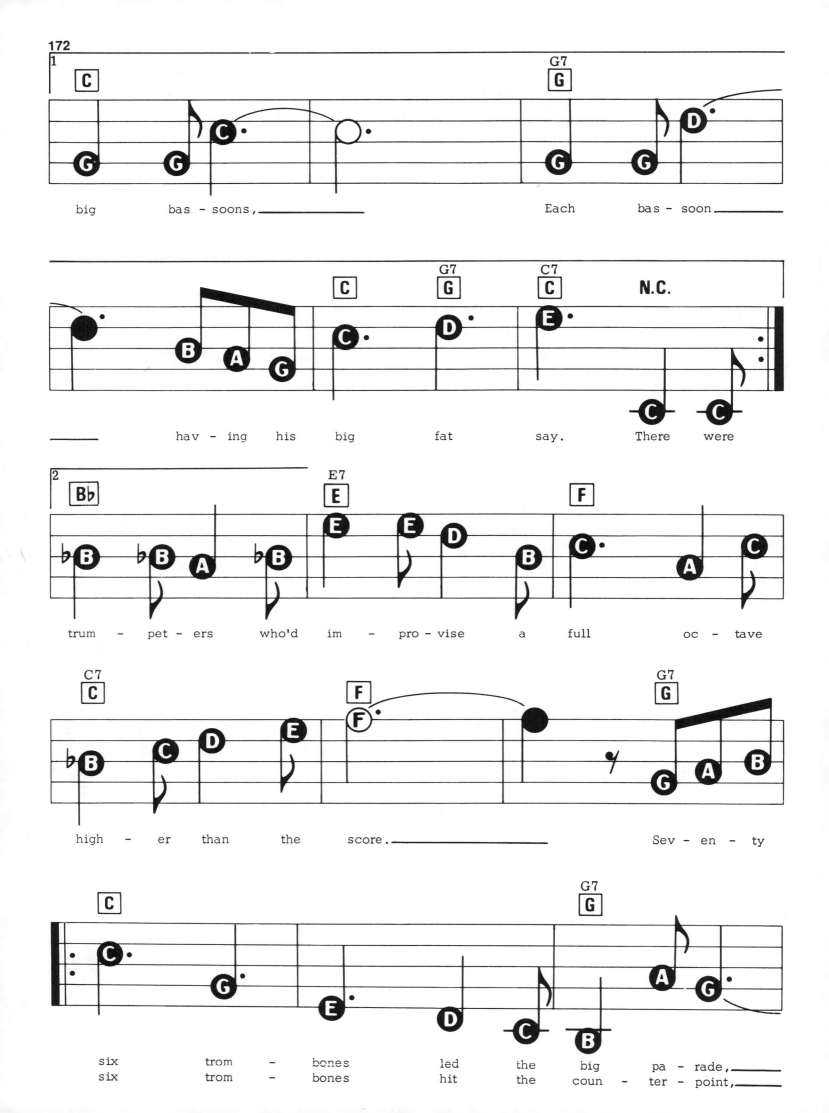

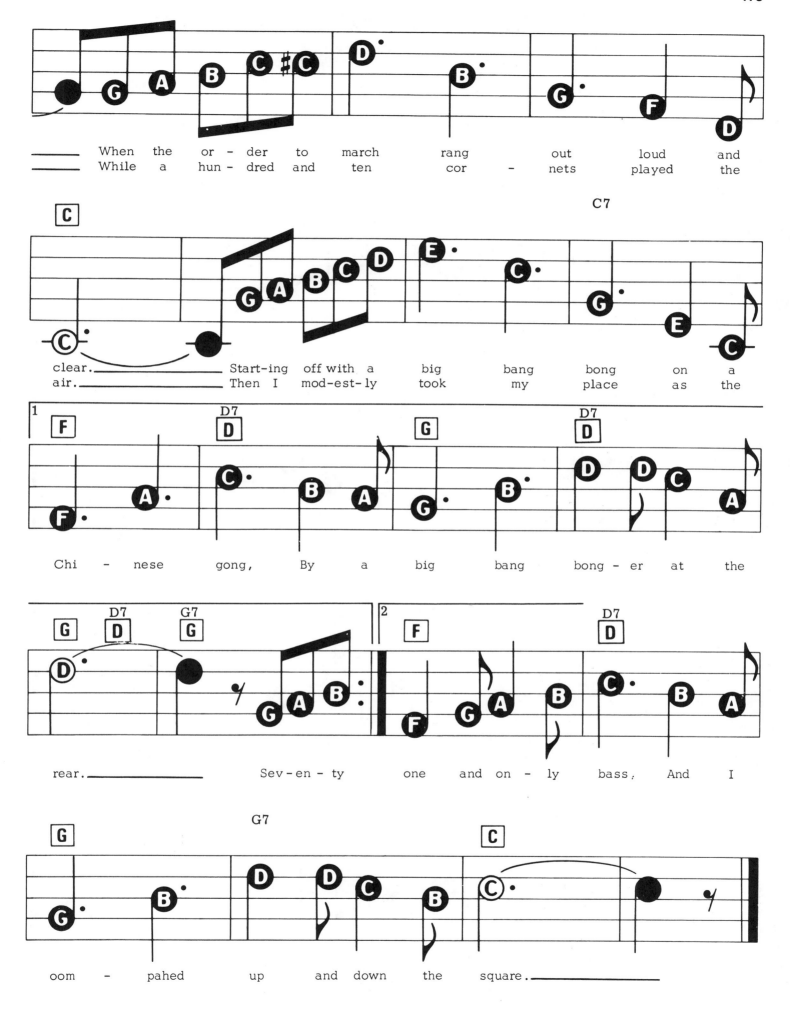

Smoke Gets In Your Eyes

(From "ROBERTA")

Words by Otto Harbach
Music by Jerome Kern

Registration 10
Rhythm: Ballad or Fox Trot

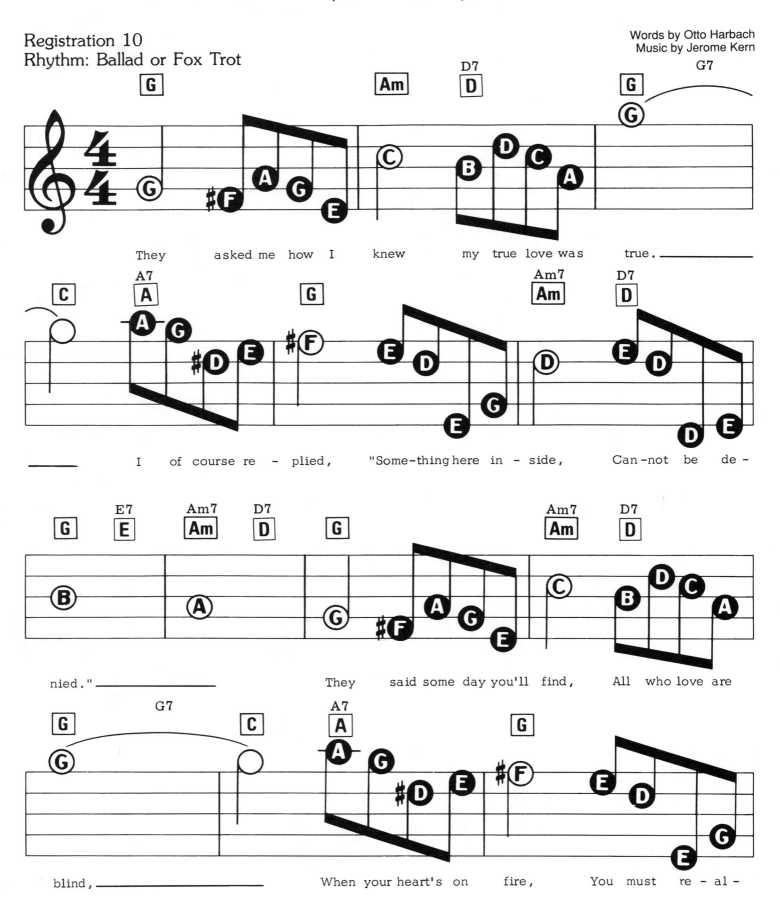

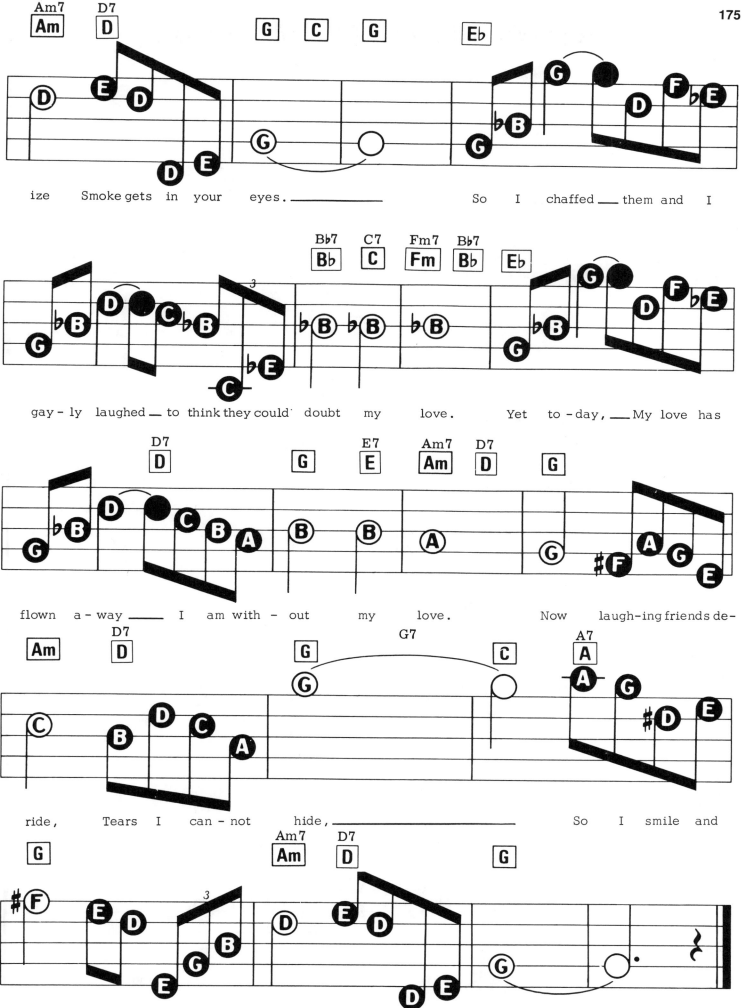

Some Enchanted Evening

(From "SOUTH PACIFIC")

Registration 1
Rhythm: Fox Trot

Lyrics by Oscar Hammerstein II
Music by Richard Rodgers

Some en-chant-ed eve-ning_____ You may see a stran-ger,_____
Some en-chant-ed eve-ning_____ When you find your true love,_____

You may see a stran-ger_____ A - cross a crowd-ed room
When you feel her call you_____ A - cross a crowd-ed room

And some-how you know,_____ You know e - ven then_____
Then fly to her side_____ And make her your

That some-where you'll see her a - gain and a -

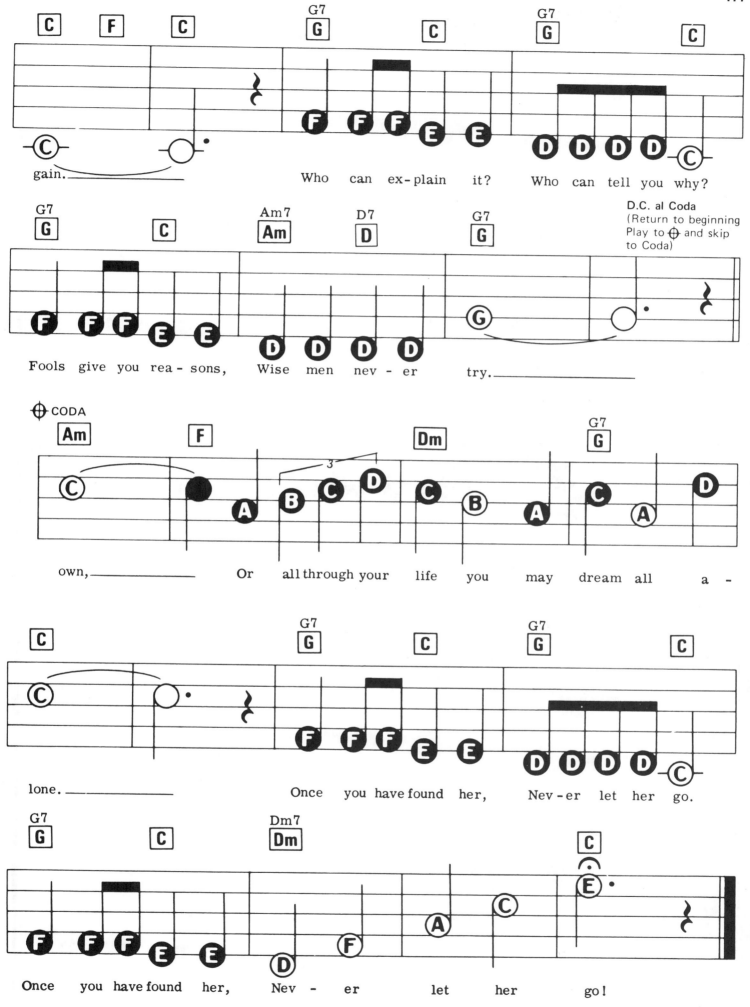

The Sound Of Music

(From "THE SOUND OF MUSIC")

Lyrics by Oscar Hammerstein II
Music by Richard Rodgers

Registration 5
Rhythm: Fox Trot

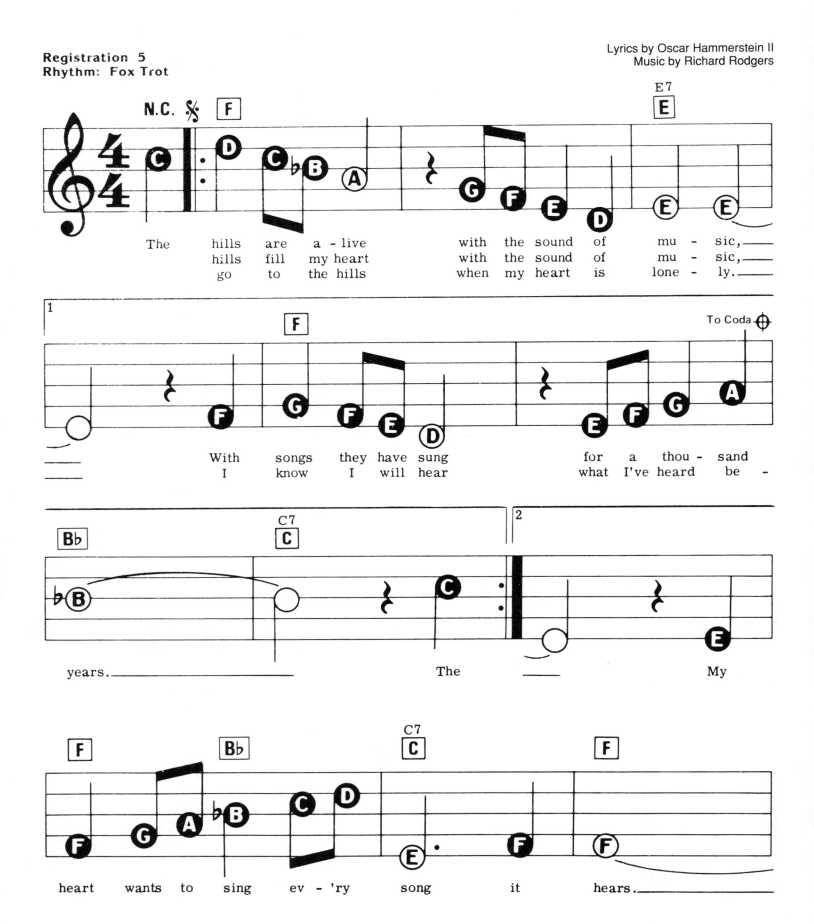

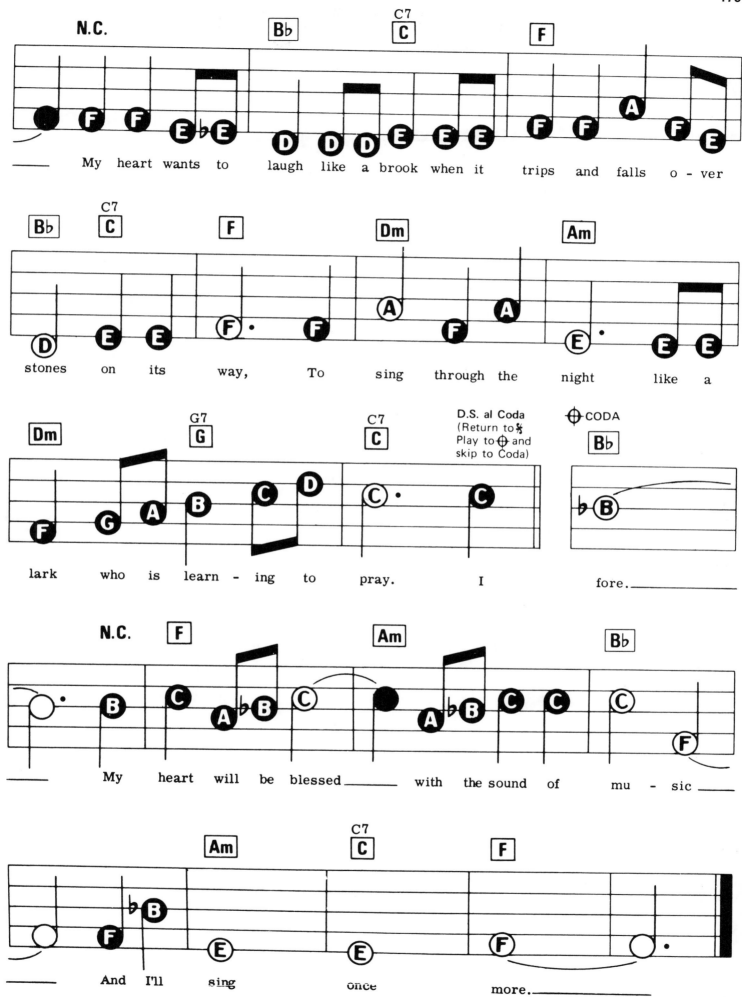

Summertime

(From "PORGY AND BESS")

Registration 10
Rhythm: Ballad or Blues

Words by DuBose Heyward
Music by George Gershwin

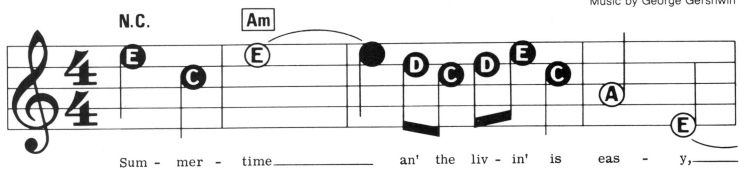

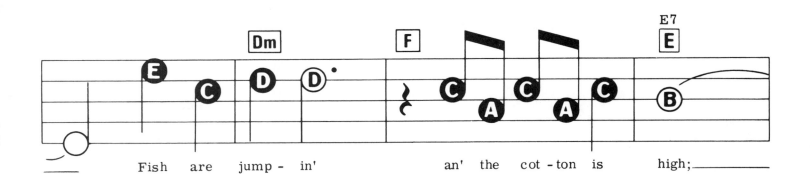

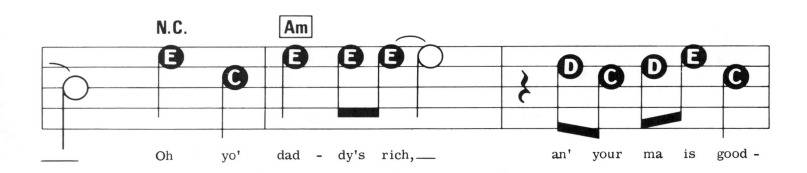

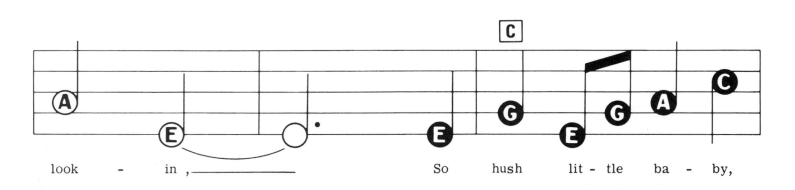

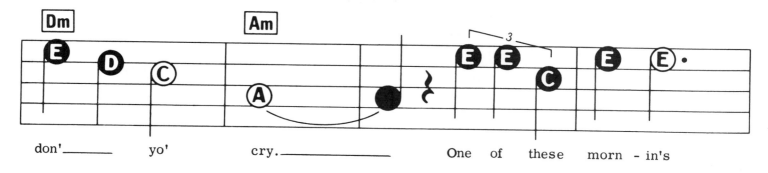

don'_____ yo'   cry._____   One of these morn - in's

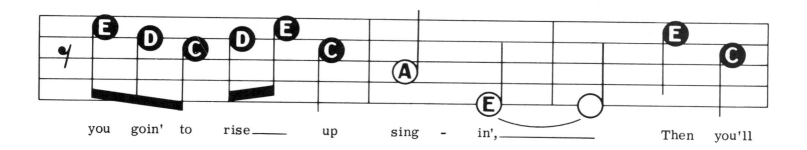

you goin' to rise____ up sing - in',_____   Then you'll

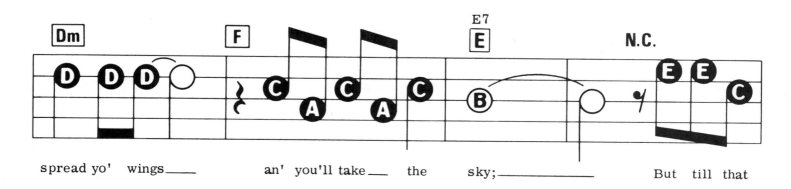

spread yo' wings____   an' you'll take___ the   sky;_____   But till that

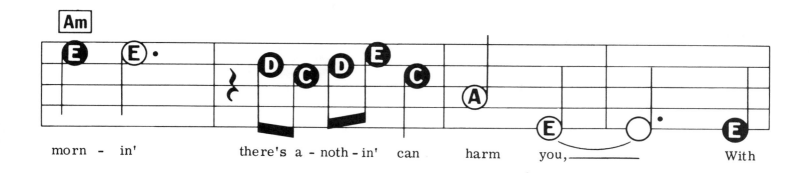

morn - in'   there's a - noth - in' can   harm   you,_____   With

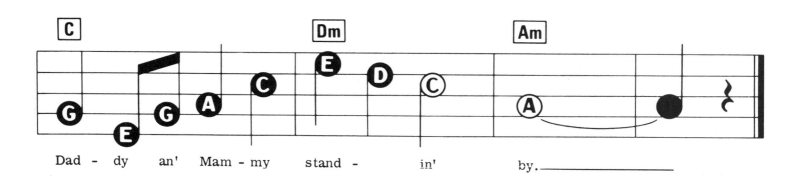

Dad - dy an' Mam - my   stand - in'   by._____

This Nearly Was Mine

(From "SOUTH PACIFIC")

Registration 3
Rhythm: Waltz

Lyrics by Oscar Hammerstein II
Music by Richard Rodgers

One   dream in my heart,_____
One   girl for my dream,_____
Now,   now I'm a - lone,_____

One   love to be liv - ing for,_____
One   part - ner in par - a - dise,_____
Still   dream - ing of par - a - dise,_____

One   love to be liv - ing for
This   prom - ise of par - a - dise
Still   say - ing that

This   near - ly was mine.
This   near - ly was mine._____

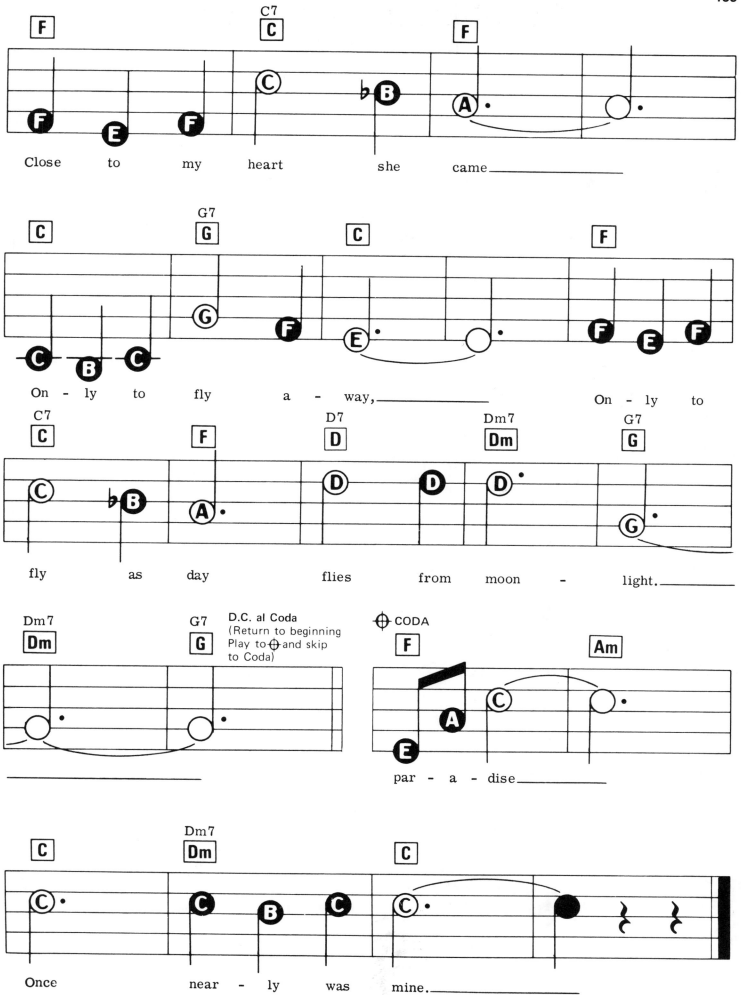

Till There Was You

(From "THE MUSIC MAN")

Registration 2
Rhythm: Ballad

By Meredith Willson

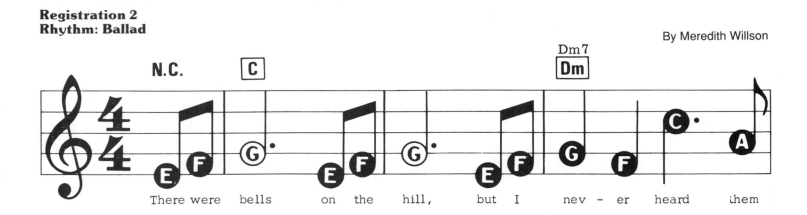

There were bells on the hill, but I nev - er heard them

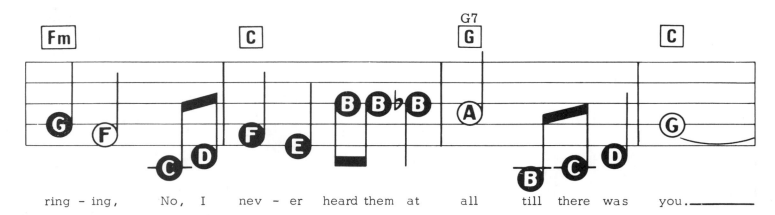

ring - ing, No, I nev - er heard them at all till there was you._____

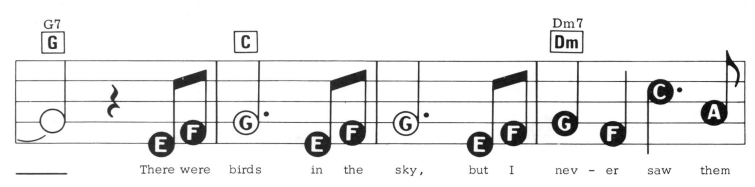

_____ There were birds in the sky, but I nev - er saw them

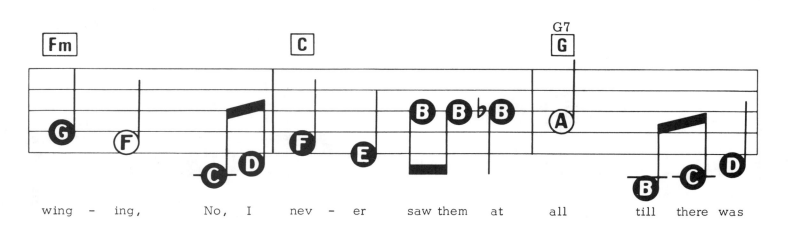

wing - ing, No, I nev - er saw them at all till there was

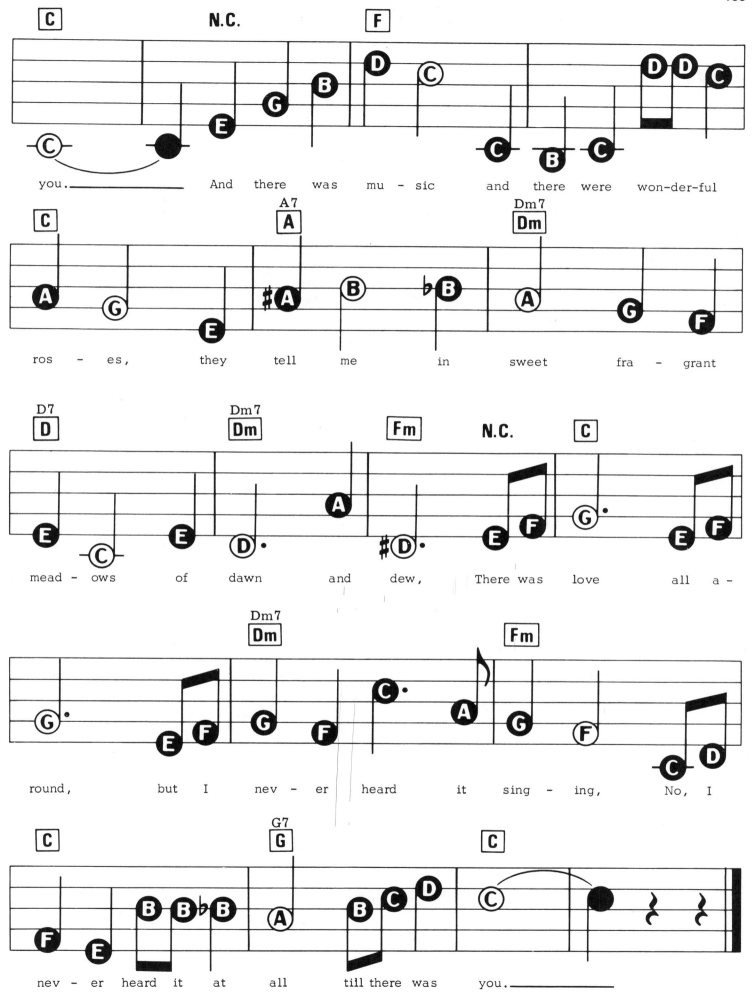

Try To Remember
(From "THE FANTASTICKS")

Words by Tom Jones
Music by Harvey Schmidt

Registration 10
Rhythm: Waltz

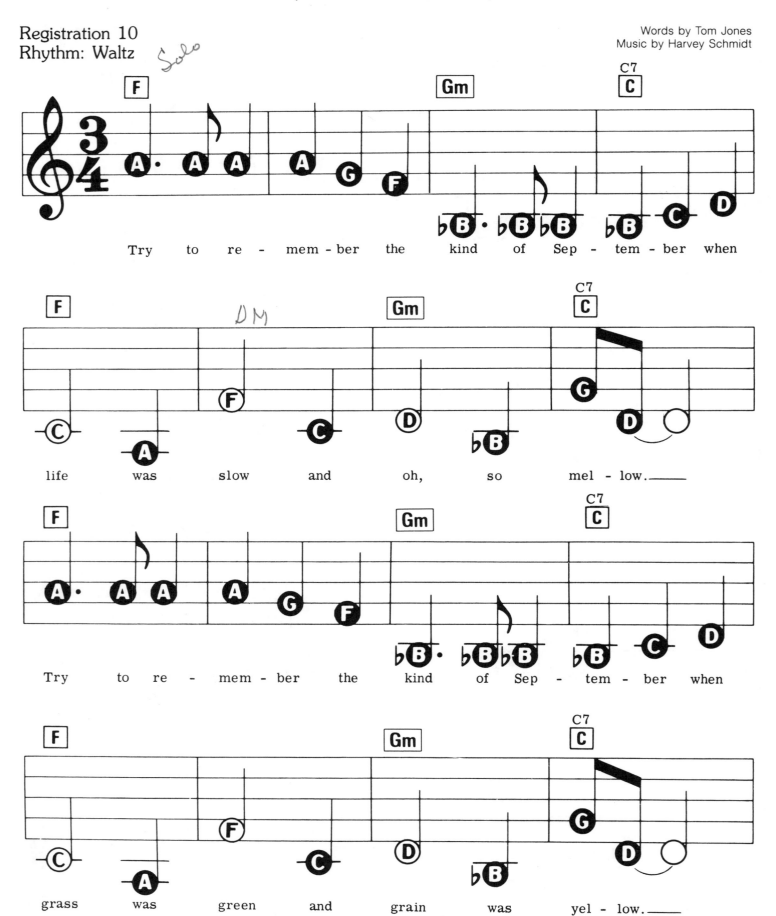

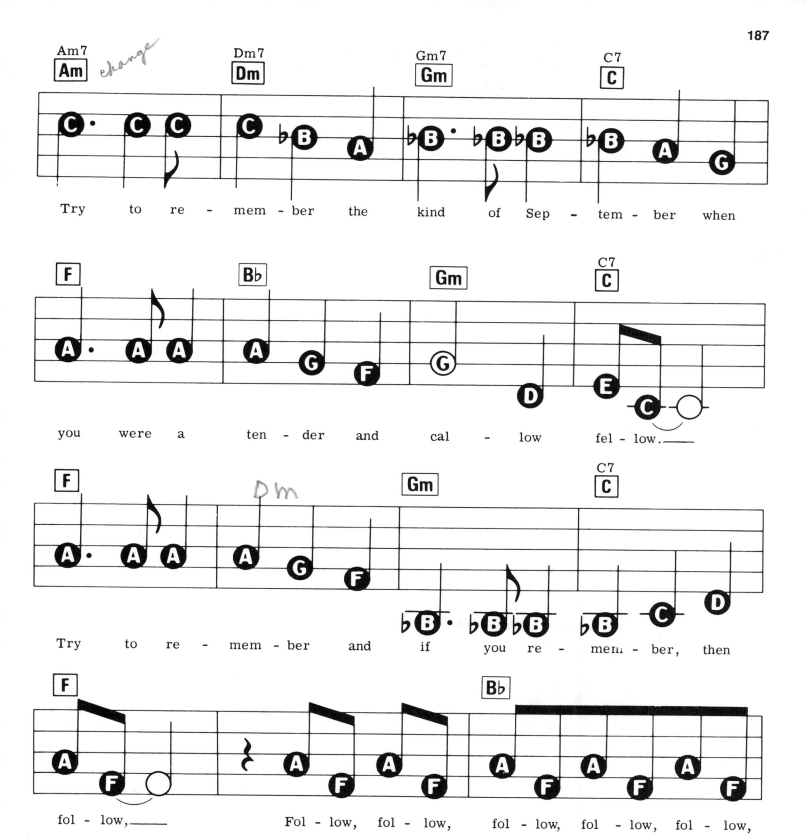

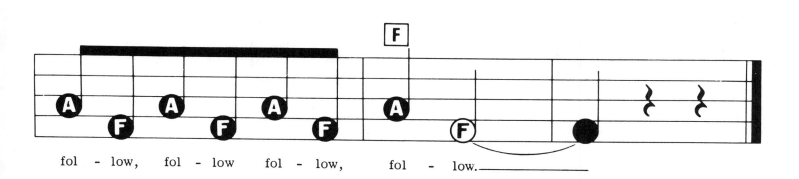

Unexpected Song

Registration 1
Rhythm: Rock or 8 Beat

Music by Andrew Lloyd Webber
Lyrics by Don Black

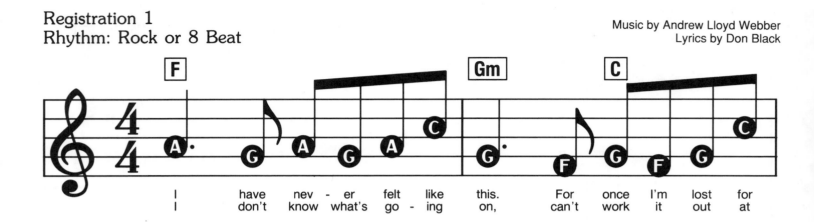

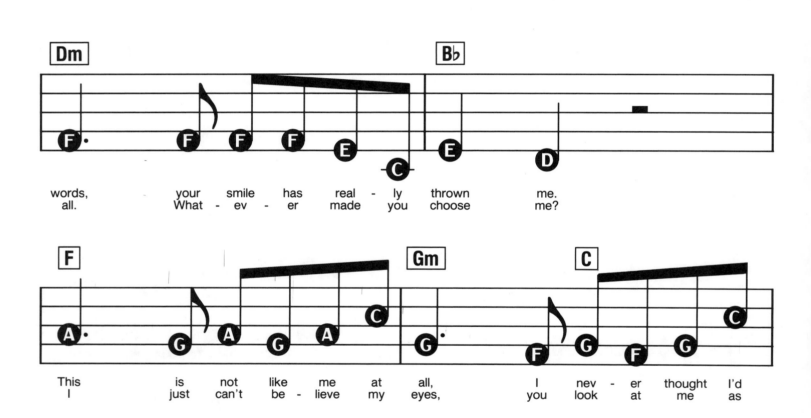

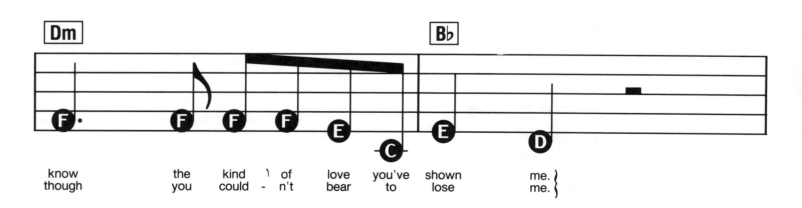

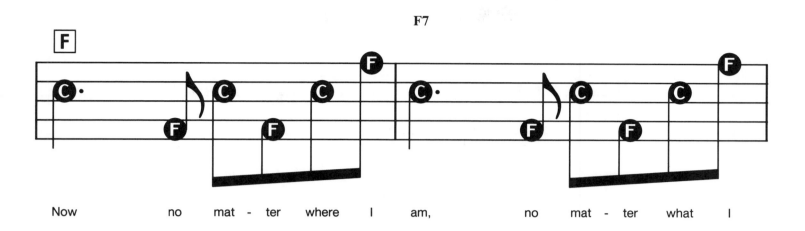

Now no mat - ter where I am, no mat - ter what I

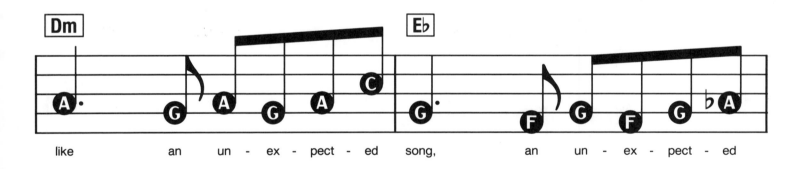

do, I see your face ap - pear - ing

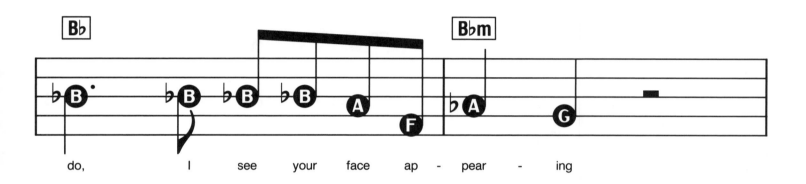

like an un - ex - pect - ed song, an un - ex - pect - ed

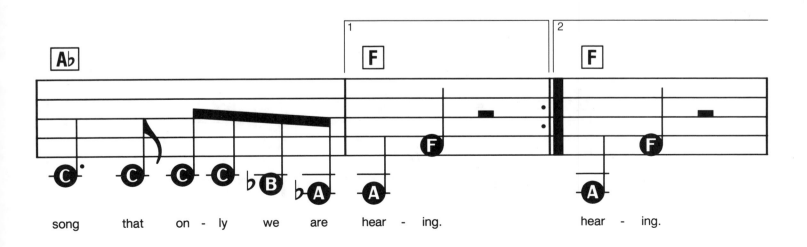

song that on - ly we are hear - ing. hear - ing.

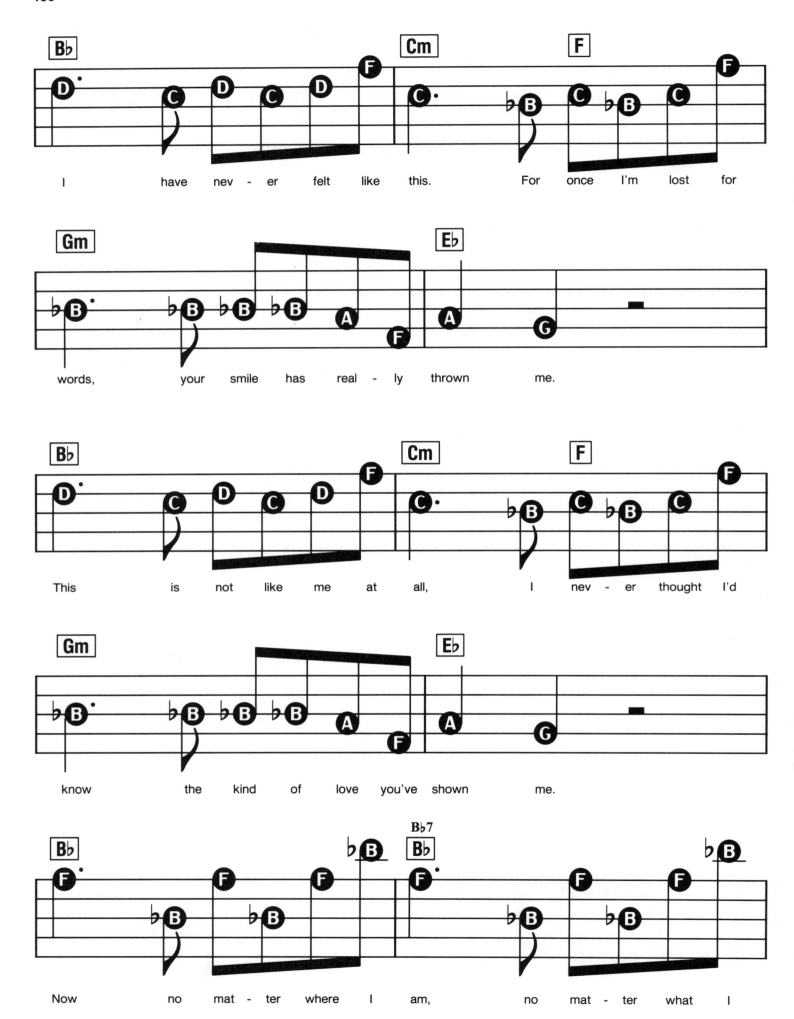

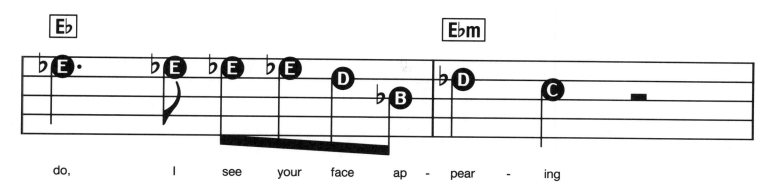

do, I see your face ap - pear - ing

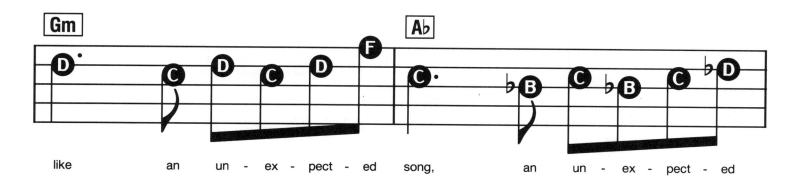

like an un - ex - pect - ed song, an un - ex - pect - ed

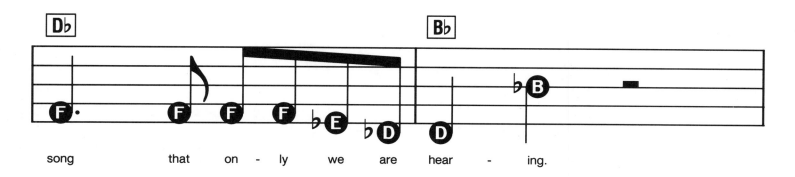

song that on - ly we are hear - ing.

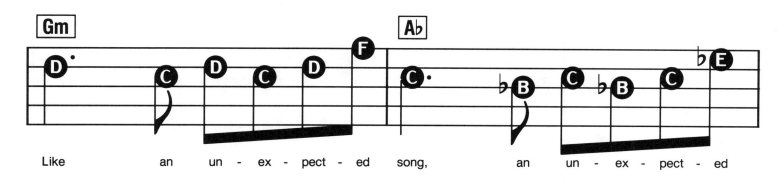

Like an un - ex - pect - ed song, an un - ex - pect - ed

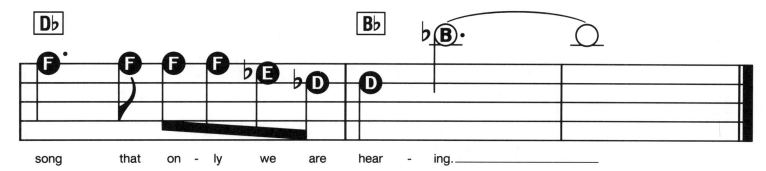

song that on - ly we are hear - ing.

What Kind Of Fool Am I?

(From the Musical Production "STOP THE WORLD — I WANT TO GET OFF")

Registration 2
Rhythm: Fox Trot

Words and Music by Leslie Bricusse
and Anthony Newley

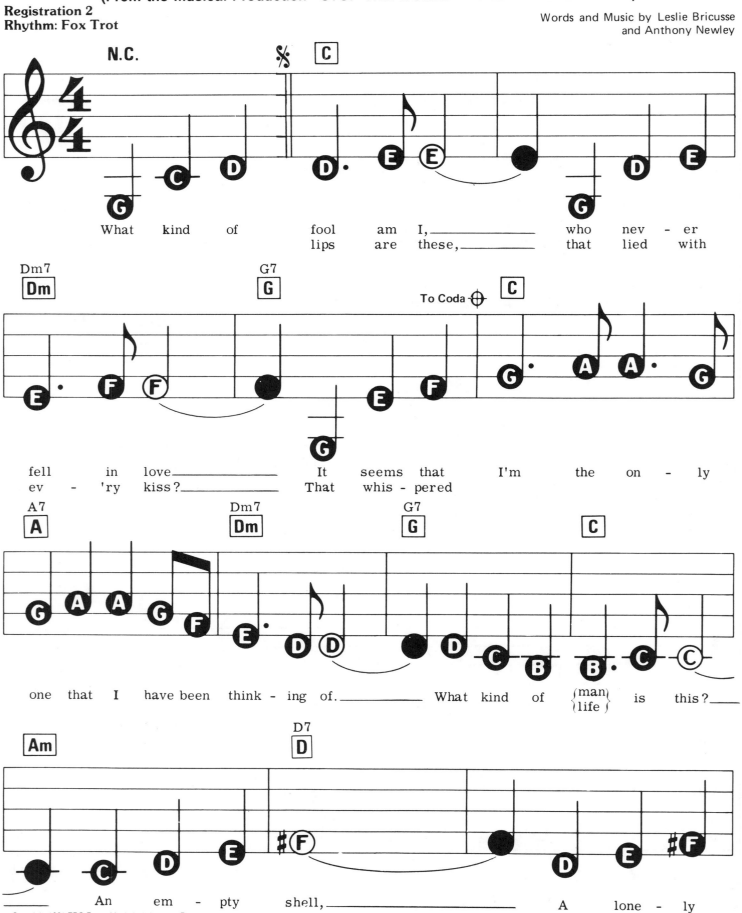

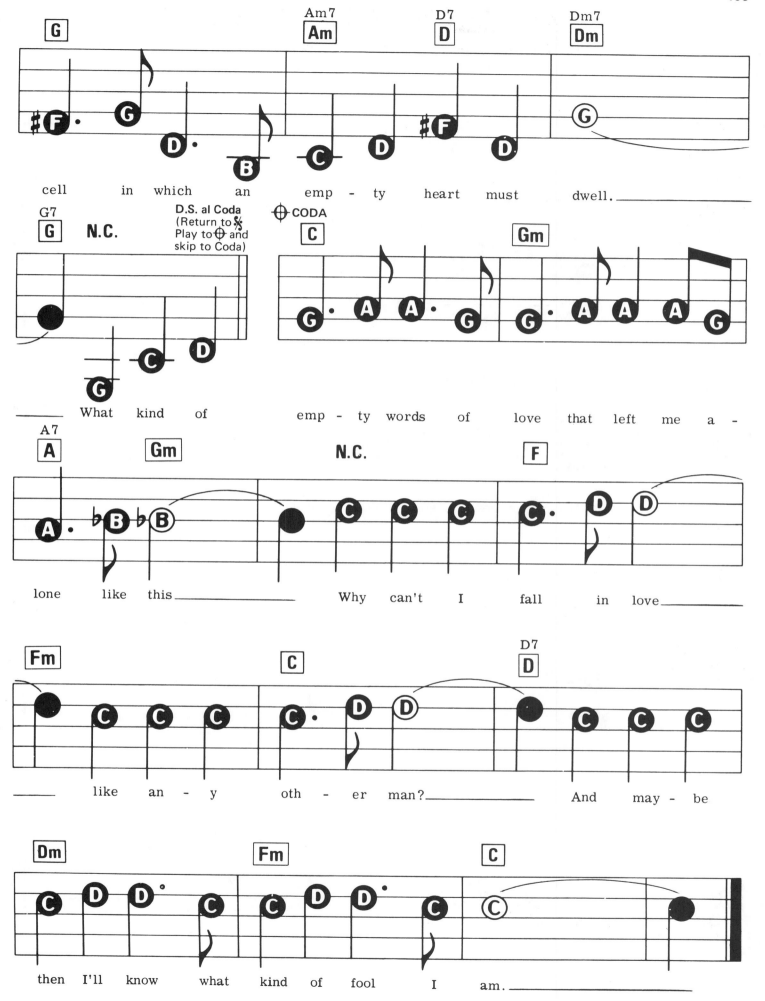

Where Is Love?

(From the Columbia Pictures - Romulus film "OLIVER!")

Registration 2
Rhythm: Ballad or Fox Trot

Words and Music by
Lionel Bart

Where _____ is love? Does it fall from skies a -

bove? Is it un - der - neath the wil - low tree that

I've been dream - ing of? Where _____ is

she who I close my eyes to see?

Where Or When

(From "BABES IN ARMS")

Registration 9
Rhythm: Ballad

Words by Lorenz Hart
Music by Richard Rodgers

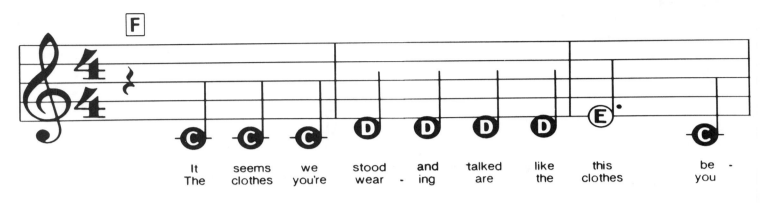

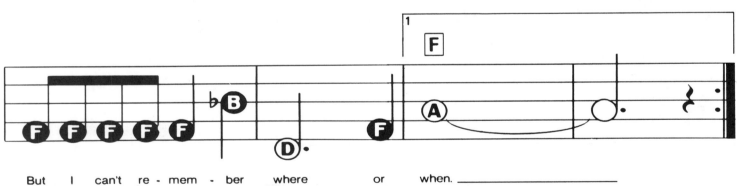

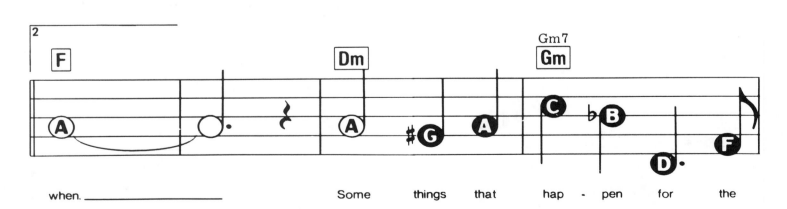

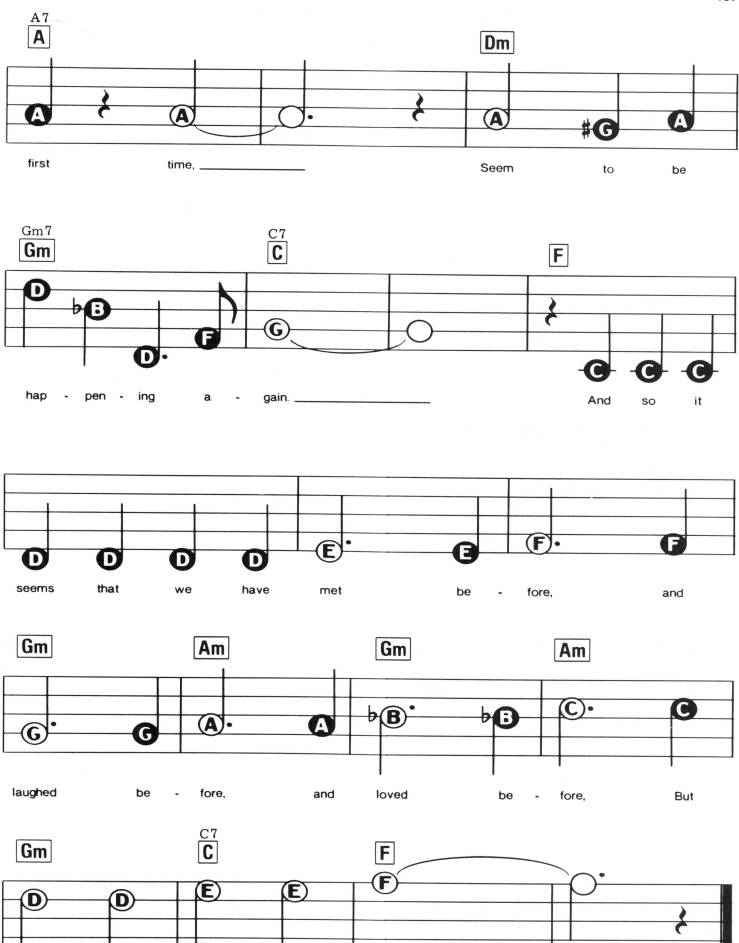

Who Can I Turn To
(When Nobody Needs Me)

(From the Musical Production "THE ROAR OF THE GREASEPAINT — THE SMELL OF THE CROWD")

Words and Music by
Leslie Bricusse and Anthony Newley

Registration 10

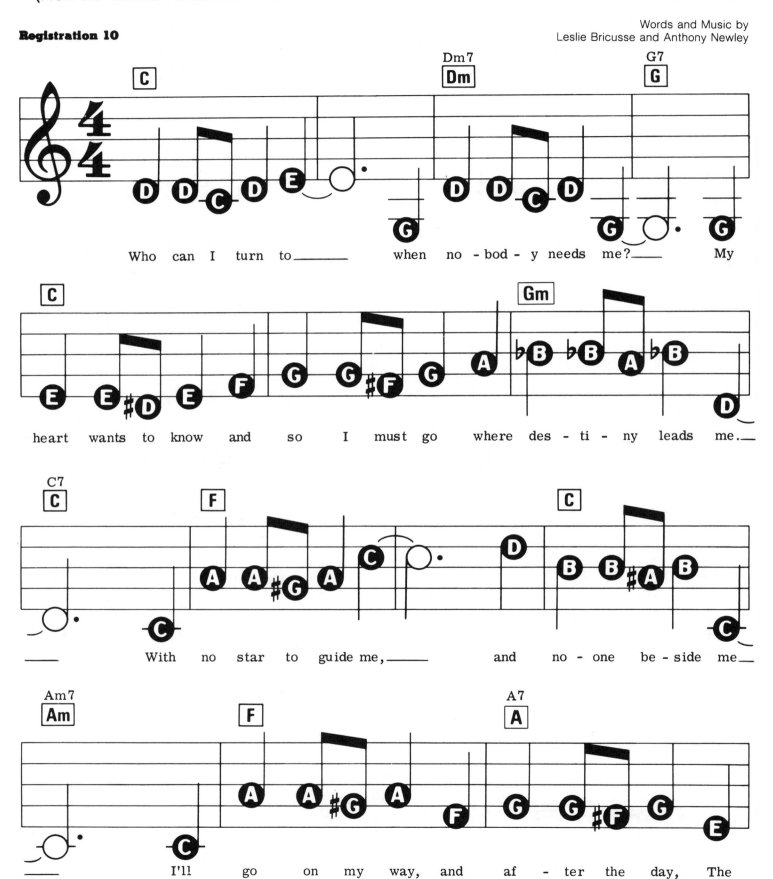

Who can I turn to ____ when no-bod-y needs me? ____ My
heart wants to know and so I must go where des-ti-ny leads me. ____
With no star to guide me, ____ and no-one be-side me ____
I'll go on my way, and af-ter the day, The

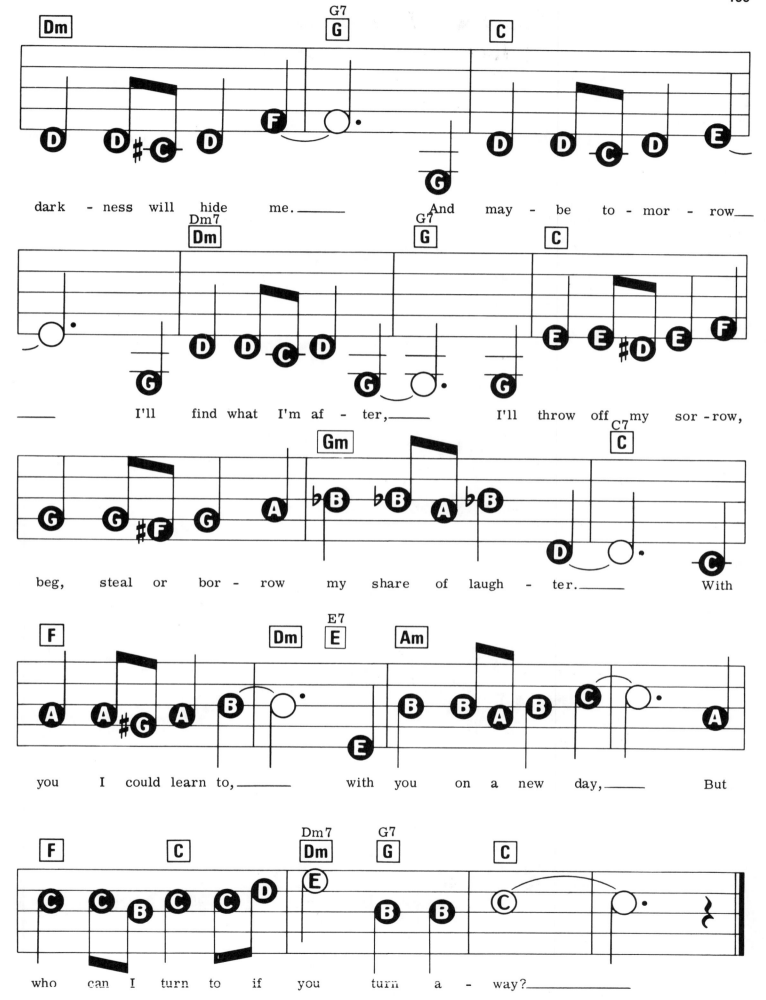

Wouldn't It Be Loverly

(From "MY FAIR LADY")

Registration 5
Rhythm: Fox Trot

Words by Alan Jay Lerner
Music by Frederick Loewe

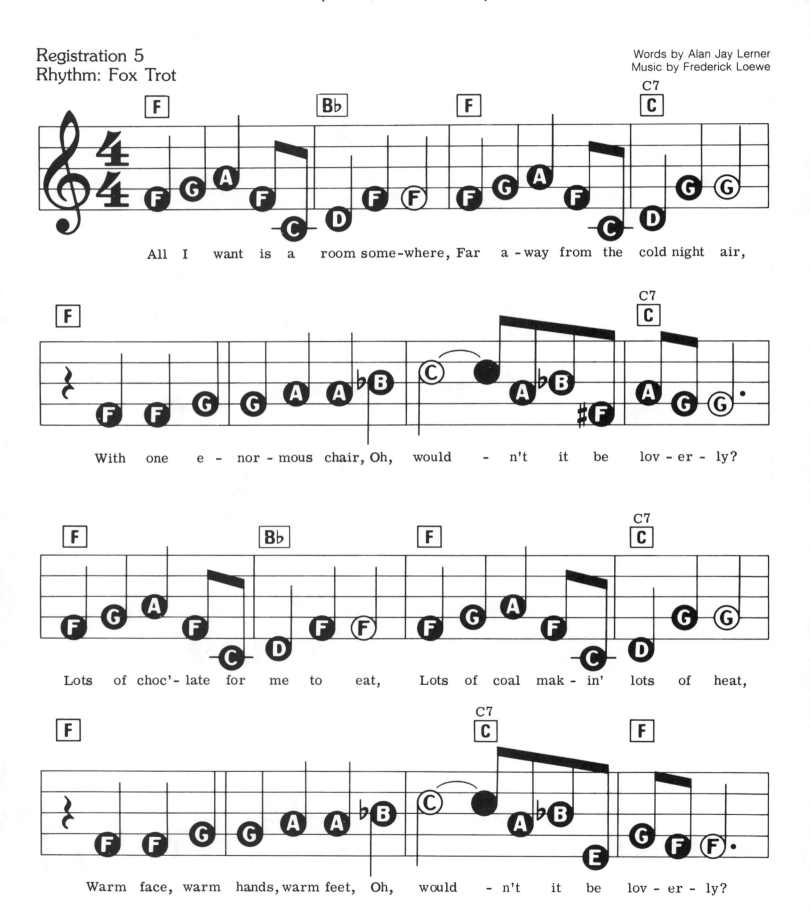

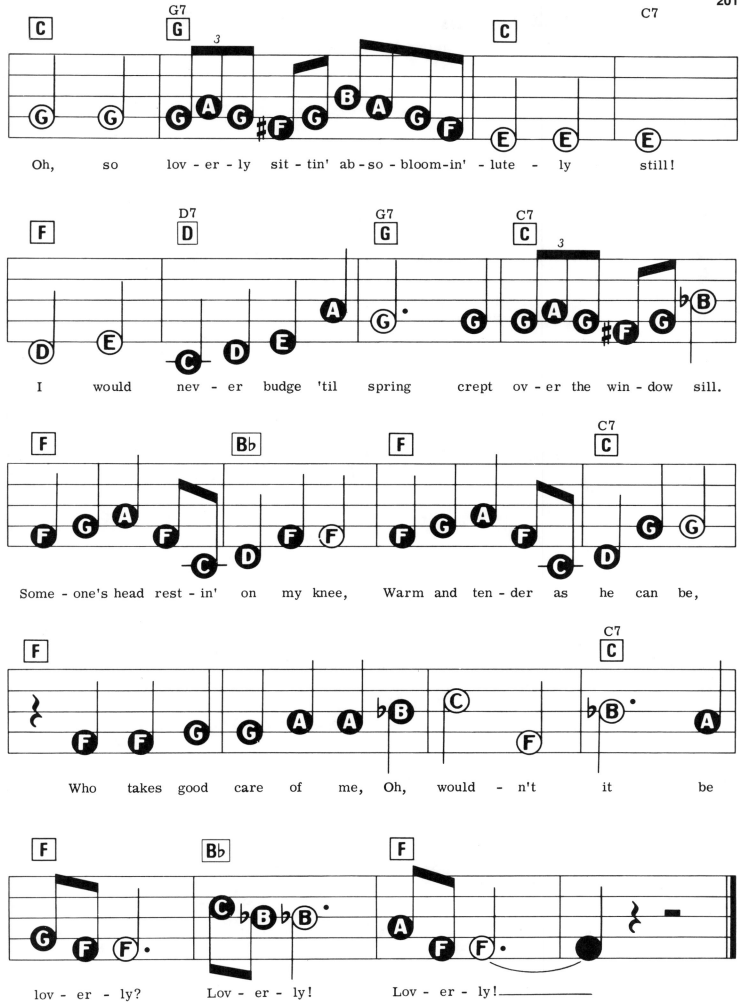

Oh, so lov-er-ly sit-tin' ab-so-bloom-in'-lute-ly still!

I would nev-er budge 'til spring crept ov-er the win-dow sill.

Some-one's head rest-in' on my knee, Warm and ten-der as he can be,

Who takes good care of me, Oh, would-n't it be

lov-er-ly? Lov-er-ly! Lov-er-ly!_____

You'll Never Walk Alone

(From "CAROUSEL")

Registration 5
Rhythm: Ballad

Lyrics by Oscar Hammerstein II
Music by Richard Rodgers

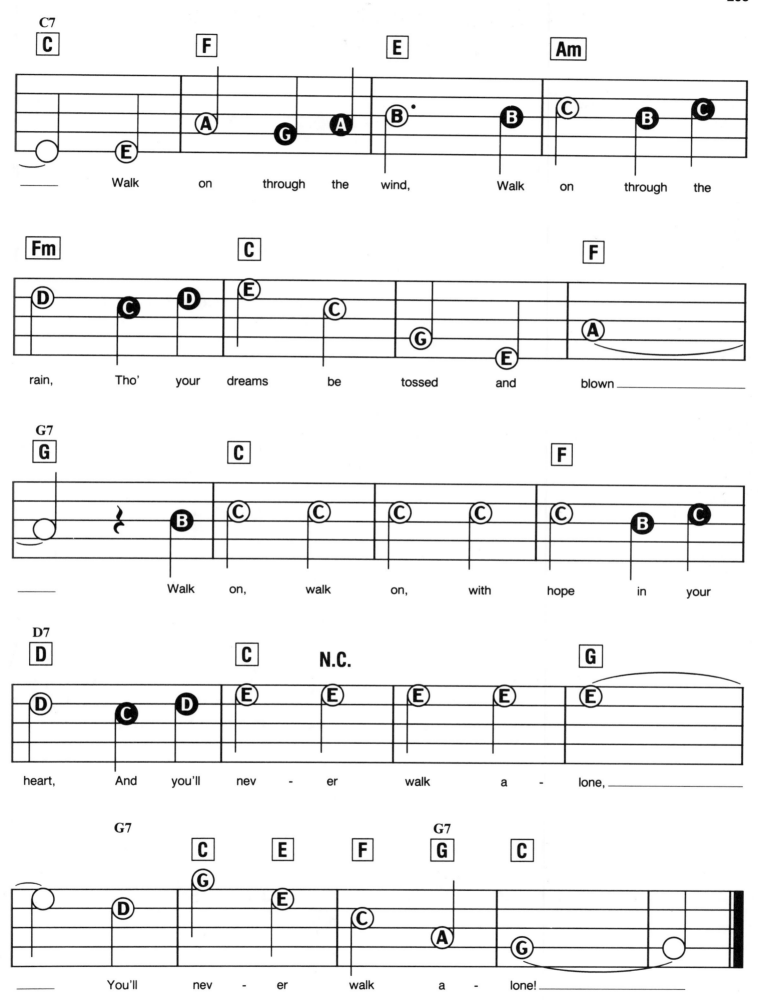

Younger Than Springtime

(From "SOUTH PACIFIC")

Registration 4
Rhythm: Fox Trot or Swing

Lyrics by Oscar Hammerstein II
Music by Richard Rodgers

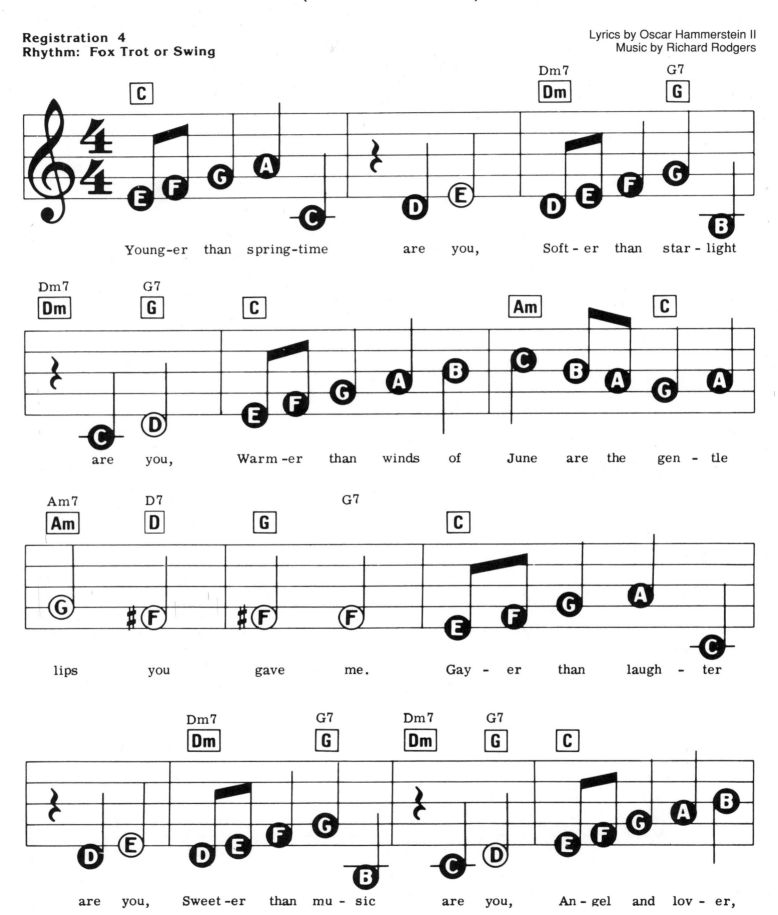